Alterhumanism

Critical Green Engagements

Investigating the Green Economy and Its Alternatives

James Igoe, Molly Doane, Tracey Heatherington, Melissa Checker,
José Martínez-Reyes, and Mary Mostafanezhad
SERIES EDITORS

Alterhumanism

Becoming Human on a
Conservation Frontier

Piergiorgio Di Giminiani

THE UNIVERSITY OF
ARIZONA PRESS
TUCSON

The University of Arizona Press
www.uapress.arizona.edu

We respectfully acknowledge the University of Arizona is on the land and territories of Indigenous peoples. Today, Arizona is home to twenty-two federally recognized tribes, with Tucson being home to the O'odham and the Yaqui. The University strives to build sustainable relationships with sovereign Native Nations and Indigenous communities through education offerings, partnerships, and community service.

ISBN-13: 978-0-8165-5571-0 (hardcover)
ISBN-13: 978-0-8165-5570-3 (paperback)
ISBN-13: 978-0-8165-5572-7 (ebook)

Cover design by Leigh McDonald
Cover photo: *Paso Manuil Malal* by Luis Araya @larayav
Typeset by Sara Thaxton in 10.5/14 Warnock Pro with Trade Gothic Next LT Pro, Helvetica Neue LT Std, and Baskerville URW

Publication of this book was made possible in part by support from the Center for Intercultural and Indigenous Research at the Pontificia Universidad Católica de Chile.

Library of Congress Control Number: 2025007325

Printed in the United States of America
♾ This paper meets the requirements of ANSI/NISO Z39.48-1992 (Permanence of Paper).

To Lorenzo

I would go into the forest—I could wander around it endlessly. Here things were quieter; the forest was like a vast, deep, welcoming refuge in which one could hide. It lulled my mind. Here I didn't have to conceal the most troublesome of my Ailments—the fact that I weep. Here my tears could flow, bathing my eyes and improving my sight. Maybe that's why I could see more than people with dry eyes.

Olga Tokarczuk

Contents

List of Illustrations   *xi*

Introduction: Alterhumanism   3

PART I. FOUR WAYS OF BECOMING HUMAN

1. *Hacer Patria*: Settlers' Intimate Nationhood and the
    Domestication of Frontier Forests   31

2. Indigenous Settlers? Histories of Resettlement and Care
    in Mapuche Frontier Life   59

3. The Experience of Ecocentrism: Enchantment and Human
    Authenticity in Environmentalism   91

4. The Birds' Forest: Conservation Science and Avian Life
    in the Shadow of Human Disturbance   121

PART II. REMAKING THE HUMAN IN CONSERVATION

Interlude: Saving Nature, Remaking the Human   153

5. Becoming Environmentalists: Enclosures and Mediations
    in Nongovernmental Conservation   163

6.   Becoming Ecological Citizens: State Commons and Indigenous
     Sovereignties in Participatory Conservation   191

     Epilogue: Crisis and Rewilding in the World to Come   223

     Acknowledgments   *237*
     Notes   *241*
     References   *255*
     Index   *279*

Illustrations

1. Bus ride leaving Pucón   9
2. Map of protected areas and towns depicted in this book   28
3. Family of settlers in southern Chile, circa 1940   41
4. Sawmill   52
5. A school in Maite   69
6. Hiking through an araucaria forest   95
7. Pucón with the Villarrica volcano in the background   111
8. Preparing the piper to inspect a nesting cavity   125
9. Welcoming hikers   177
10. "Close the Door"   189
11. Entering the Hualalafquén National Reserve   195
12. Flower of quila (*Chusquea culeou*) from southern Argentina   222

Alterhumanism

Introduction

Alterhumanism

Imagine you are riding a bus or perhaps driving down a fast, single-lane road. Trees line both sides, standing in neat rows as you pass. Expansive fields of lush green grass stretch out around you where large herds of cows placidly graze. In the distance, mountains rise, their slopes blanketed by dense forests that reach all the way to their tops. Along the roadside, various signs catch your eye: advertisements for a small grocery store, directions to a nearby lake, or pointers to a small hotel. The houses you pass are charming, single-story wooden buildings, each surrounded by a fence that encloses a small garden where carefully tended roses bloom in vibrant colors. If it is a summer day, the weather is likely hot and dry. If it is winter, it is cold, possibly foggy, with snow visible on the mountaintops.

After a while, you turn onto a gravel road, and the ride becomes bumpy. The valley here is much narrower than the one you were in before, now surrounded by dense forests. Amid the thick trees, a small but fast-flowing river winds. Soon, you cross it via a wooden bridge, and the road begins to climb steeply, twisting as it goes. A couple of pickup trucks roll by in opposite directions, announced by a dust cloud. You see a couple of people along the road; one is waiting to hop on the bus, while the other is herding a cow. At some point you hear the sound of a motor. You realize the sound is coming from a modest building with a small zinc roof and no walls. Around the building lie large piles of wood and piles of debris. It is likely a small sawmill.

As you continue along the road through the forest, small patches of grassland enclosed by barbed wire begin to appear. Here and there, old tree trunks bleached by time lie scattered across the ground. Wooden, single-story houses are tucked away, blending into the landscape so well that they're frequently hidden from view. Often, a simple wooden gate is the only clue to their presence. Signs occasionally hang beside these gates, marked with words like "Bread" or "Eggs," suggesting you might find these items for sale at the nearby houses. One sign reads, "Let's protect life. No to the hydroelectric plant," while another features a beautifully painted tree alongside the words "Lodging" and "Indigenous Tourism."

At some point, you run into a larger building, a one-floor wooden structure with a flagpole and a sign at the entrance saying "School." You see more signs; many of them simply say "For Sale." As you go up the valley, you realize many houses are surrounded by understory. Everything points to the fact that they were abandoned years earlier. Finally, the road stops at a gate; you've reached the last house. There are trails that you can take to walk farther up the hills and into the dense forest, or perhaps, after taking in the surroundings, you decide to turn around and head back toward the main valley. The gentle slope eases up, the open landscape comes back into view, and soon the familiar sights of the larger valley unfold before you once more.

This brief trip might feel familiar to anyone who lives near or has ventured into one of the world's many temperate forests. What at first might appear to be untouched nature reveals itself as a complex palimpsest of past and present human labor (Mathews 2022, 54). Scattered around these landscapes lie many signs (in some cases, literal ones) that give clues to the many stories of the people who have made these forests their homes. These signs point to interdependent stories of the growth and retreat of forests as well of the human collectivities dwelling around them (see Rival 1993). Images of land abandonment and rewilding are recurrent, but so are hints of the relentless expansion of residential and transportational infrastructures. The enduring effects of deforestation materialize in the irregular patchwork of grassland and forests.

This journey feels especially familiar to those acquainted with the landscapes of the southern Chilean Andes. Here, the landscape reveals stories marked by conflicting experiences: violence, resistance, grief, hope. . . . All of them stem from the transition of a settler frontier into a global hotspot for forest conservation and a booming tourism industry since the 1990s, when Chile began welcoming an unprecedented influx of international visitors following the end of Augusto Pinochet's brutal seventeen-year military dictatorship. The inhabitants of the southern Andean valleys are largely descendants of settlers who established homes here in the early twentieth century or of Mapuche families displaced by the Chilean army's invasion of Wallmapu, the sovereign Mapuche territory. This invasion, officially termed the "Pacification of Araucanía" (1863–1884), was, in reality, a violent campaign that led to widespread displacement and acts of genocide.

Fast forward to the late twentieth century and the beginning of the current conservation boom, and new neighbors have settled around these valleys: environmental activists and entrepreneurs, most of them urbanites attracted to a lifestyle that makes close contact with nature possible. The many protected areas found around these valleys—some of them run by private foundations and NGOs, others corresponding to older national parks established in the early twentieth century—have become the privileged site for conservation scientists to launch their message about the fragile future of frontier forests and their nonhuman dwellers.

It is no coincidence that the historical Mapuche homeland in this region came to be known as "the Frontier," *la Frontera* (see Klubock 2014). The particular spatial articulation of Andean valleys in southern Chile originates in the historical transition from a settler to a conservation frontier. Such a transition is one of continuity as well as disruption. Inequalities in land access and labor conditions continue to mark the relations among the region's different dwellers, in particular those involving wealthy landowners, Mapuche landholders whose historical properties were drastically reduced, and lifestyle migrants with professional jobs. Conservation frontiers, however, have also led to the radical transformation of the forests, which have materially and discursively transitioned from resources to be extracted to wilderness to be experienced, protected, and commodified.

A frontier "is not space itself. It is something that happens in and to space" (Rasmussen and Lund 2018, 338). Conservation frontiers (see Buchadas et al. 2022; Og and Elliott 2023) shape spaces where wilderness is depicted and envisioned as a delicate tapestry of life forms—a powerful entity that can influence and transform humans while serving as a sanctuary against the encroaching threat of agro-industrial civilization (Abram and Lien 2011). At the same time, these areas are rendered accessible through infrastructural developments, including park design and transportation routes (Dicenta and

Gerard 2023). On conservation frontiers, wonder and loss (see Ogden 2021) are powerful affects that furnish desires of authenticity and self-discovery. In this context, the masculinized trope of adventure, deeply rooted in the settler frontier imagination of the world's ends and extremes (Nouzeilles 1999), converges with a desire to engage with the enlightening forces of nature, embodied by the affect of the *sublime* (Mendoza 2018). This interplay gives rise to emerging ethics of care (see Araos et al. 2023; Trentini 2023) toward forests, where responsibility for both their destruction and their nourishment lies with humans. Conservation frontiers also reshuffle what was previously assumed to be natural and evident. They are "analytic bordering zones" (Gago 2017, 31) where a radical mutation of concepts and binaries—such as *human* and *nature*—unfold. In the current Anthropocene crisis, where humanity is increasingly understood as a geological force, conservation frontiers epitomize the urge to rethink the human question while we come to terms with the uncertainties of the future habitability of the planet.

This book is set on a conservation frontier. The reader will hear stories of the settlers at the margins of the colonial project who are invested in forest domestication, Indigenous Mapuche landholders struggling for survival away from their ancestral territories, environmental activists and entrepreneurs spearheading the conservation boom since the 1990s, and conservation scientists crafting a message about the fragility of nonhuman communities. The people who live and work around these forests interact with landscapes that are not entirely distinct; there are no independent forests existing in isolation, and forests cannot be seen simply as objects that exist independently, each signified differently by various cultural groups. Instead, the forest we will explore is more than just a singular entity, yet less than a multitude: in other words, more than one but less than many (see Strathern [1991] 2004). Another way to say this is that, while there may be many interpretations or perspectives on what a forest is, the forests themselves are not entirely separate or disconnected. This multiplicity of forests arises from distinct yet potentially overlapping projects that ontologically frame our understanding of the world around us. In this ongoing and always surprising process, the articulation of distinctions and relationships among different entities stems from embodiments and conceptualizations unfolding simultaneously as a form of world disclosure that is individual and yet collectively structured. As experiential spaces "where the logic of distinction goes astray" (Harrison 1992, x), forests are opaque epistemic objects whose knowledge never unfolds as a unilateral process of signification, because forests are also capable of directing our perception and even our comprehension of the world (see Kohn 2013).

In this book, I will consistently argue that the oneness and manyness of forests, like other spatial constructs, originate in the various interpretations of humanity that are formed through productive interactions with both nonhuman and human others. These interactions not only influence our understanding of forests but also inform our perceptions of all entities that are collectively defined and interconnected. What it means to be human is neither an existential nor a normative question. Rather, it is fundamentally both an ontological and an ethical question. Although it may not yield definitive answers, the human question encourages us to reflect on the boundaries and potentials of agency—both human and nonhuman—and the responsibilities that arise from our unique capacity to nurture or diminish the lives of others. Nonhuman alterity matters not as an insurmountable border separating us from what stands beyond us, but as a productive space for the ongoing formation of human subjectivity. In such a configuration of humanity, the human is a salient category but is never a given, static, or universal condition. In places marked by environmental destruction and care, ontological questions about humanity and its alterity intersect with ethical inquiries concerning the sustainability of more-than-human coexistence in an uncertain future for human habitability on the planet.

Becoming human through and with nonhuman others is the shared and yet plural human experience through which the world emerges under different socially arranged forms and meanings. This is the argument that I present in this book. It is also the central idea of *alterhumanism*, an empirical model that I propose to attend to the emergence and transformation of different models of humanity from stories of environmental engagement. Alterhumanism is an invitation to pay attention to the enduring legacy of the human question in making sense of the world around us without reasserting the exclusionary and exceptionalist principles of Western humanism. Universalist claims about humanity have effectively fostered consensus around a shared understanding of human dignity and the recognition of humanity as a geological force intrinsic to the concept of the Anthropocene. However, this approach comes at the expense of overlooking the diverse ways in which we can become human (Phillips 2015). The "alter" of alterhumanism concerns both the plurality of humanity as a concept and also the significance that the "other" holds in the paradigmatic definition of who we are as humans.

At the heart of the alterhumanism proposal lies a paradigmatic definition of humanity based on four principles: First, our relationships with nonhuman others are fundamental to our sense of belonging as humans; second, the experience of being human is our primary means of engaging with the world; third, as relations of alterity evolve over time, the process of becoming human takes precedence over a static notion of being; and fourth, humanity serves as the framework from which we organize our relationships with others and derive meaning, thereby contributing to a more ontologically stable understanding of the world. In the proposed model of alterhumanism, one needs to ask how people "create distinctions and bifurcations if the world in which they live constantly drifts toward entanglement, blurring stark oppositions" (Ballestero 2019, 3). As Agamben reminds us, "Everything happens as if . . . life were what cannot be defined, yet, precisely for this reason, must be ceaselessly articulated and divided" (2004, 13). Definition, articulation, and division of the world begins with the question of what it is to be human. The answer to this question is not to be found in the form of a claim or a moral principle. It rather originates in individual embodiments that are socially organized and signified, capable of both reinforcing and reshuffling categories of humanity and its alterity.

Even when it reproduces the idea of human paternalism toward nonhuman others, conservation has historically provided one of the most compelling critiques to human exceptionalism. For this reason, it constitutes a fertile ground for the examination of the emergence of existing alterhumanisms. On conservation frontiers, alterhumanisms rise in conflict-ridden yet entangled histories of environmental destruction and care. By depicting the memories and experiences of settlers, Indigenous Mapuche landholders, environmental activists, and conservation scientists, my goal is to present a model of alterhumanism for each of these groups. I also explore the types of transformation that alterhumanisms are subject to by paying attention to the institutional power of conservation, in particular its effects in directing engagements with nonhuman others and ethical queries about more-than-human coexistence. The idea of alterhumanism, as I hope to show, can be an empirical model illustrative of the centrality of the human question for thinking about ontological pluralism as well as the place of humanity in the current environmental crisis. Rethinking the human question can help in the

FIGURE 1 Bus ride leaving Pucón (Photograph by the author)

development of an ecologically sound ethic, one capable of recognizing the entangled nature of humanity as well as its exceptional role in the present crisis.

What Is Alterhumanism?

Understanding humanity as a substantialist condition implies acknowledging that human attributes are universal and exist independently of any interaction with nonhuman others. A decisionist interpretation of humanity presupposes that being human depends on volition and in turn leaves the characterization of specific ways of being human to political deliberation. To these two powerful thought traditions about the human, we can add an alternative: a paradigmatic model of humanity, whereby humanity is a given ontological condition, but its forms are unstable and are only partially framed by shifting relations of alterity. In advancing the idea of alterhumanism, I follow a paradigmatic approach to the human question. In such an approach,

alterity is the starting point in examining the emergence of multiple humanities rather than the a posteriori denominator of negatively defined non-
humanity. In alterhumanism, "alter" refers to the existence of three modes
of being other: representational, ontological, and ethical. In other words, it
pertains to the representational existence of diverse accounts of humanity,
the role of alterity between humans and other life forms as a fundamental
aspect of these accounts, and the characterization of this alterity with nonhumans as an ethical consideration.

The first meaning of "alter" in alterhumanism addresses the potential to
articulate and represent all those views of humanity that may be seen as alternatives to dominant Western humanism. Alter-politics refers to political
actions focused on exploring alternatives to prevailing models of democracy
and development, rather than opposing or directly confronting them (Hage
2015). Alterhumanism, then, presupposes the plurality of the human category as a contested political field in which the justification of dominant models entails the delegitimization of others. The definition of humanity as a universal condition may have helped consolidate global discourses on human
dignity, but it has also led us to disregard differences among ourselves. As
Phillips warns us, "To think of oneself primarily as a human being is to dis-
count, in some way, the significance of the divisions we otherwise maintain
between people" (2015, 1). The reductionist effect of mainstream humanism,
as revealed in feminist (see Soper 1990) and decolonial critiques, consists in
the reassertion of a version of proper humanity that corresponds mostly to
that of a Western male (Braidotti 2013, 24). Imagining other humanities is
possible, but this requires recognizing that these alternative visions do not
emerge solely from distinct discourses on humanity and the environment.
Instead, they are rooted in collective experiences of interacting with human
and nonhuman others—experiences that are often subject to both material
and symbolic erasure.

The delegitimization of other humanities is a central problem in traditions of decolonial critique, which sees the diffusion of Western humanistic
values as functional to the colonial civilizing project. The drive for mastery
over nature was often regarded as a universal trait of "civilized" humanity.
Colonizers, however, perceived colonized groups as inherently lacking the
inclination to such values unless their culture, society, and environments
were transformed. European humanism, as proposed by Kumar, can serve
"as a rhetorical device to transform the 'raw man' (native) into a 'real man,' a

paradoxical transformation given that the colonized had always been human, but disfigured as not-yet-human by colonialism itself" (2011, 1560). Within the decolonial debate, the term *alterhumanism* has been mobilized as a general commentary on the work of Frantz Fanon, in particular the question of how the colonial gaze with its dehumanizing effect can be overcome as part of the search for a new type of humanism (see Ciccariello-Maher 2006; Kumar 2011; Mbembe 2019). In Fanon's proposal, humanism among the colonized can only rise after a subjective and material rupture from the colonial gaze. Mutual recognition of humanity between colonizers and colonized is insufficient for the rise of new humanisms, since the other's recognition has imprisoned the colonized subjects in an externally determined and devalued conception of themselves (Coulthard 2007, 444). Instead, political struggles for liberation can bring "oxygen which creates and shapes a new humanity" (Fanon 1965, 181). Fanon's humanism appears as "self-consciously (and self-critically) open and undefined; an empty space to be filled by radical thought and politics" (Ciccariello-Maher 2006, 162). Reclaiming the humanity of the colonized is therefore possible only as a process of social and political restoration. As Mbembe reminds us, "The critique of Western humanism also took the form of attempts to reassemble some form of the social and of community and, as such, the form of attending to matters of care and matters of repair" (2019, 159).

The second configuration of alterity concerns the ontological constitution of the human through relationships with nonhuman others—in other words, *becoming human through nonhuman others*. The recognition of the irreparably entangled nature of humanity is the first step for the rearticulation of the human question beyond anthropocentrism. In Connolly's proposal, an entangled humanism consists of a still-problematic "priority to the human species in its interdependencies and imbrications with other beings and forces it neither masters nor owns" (2017, 171). In experiencing the uncertainties of a world inhabited and moved by indeterminate nonhuman agencies, humans engage in reflexive understandings of the *anthropos* (Harvey et al. 2019, 3) and become aware of the particularities of their agency (Kipnis 2015, 56). In Kohn's words, "We can develop a more robust and fruitful way of thinking about 'the human' in terms of how our relation to that which stands beyond us also makes us who we are" (2012, 136).

The idea of alterhumanism I present in this book is animated by a similar call for the reimagination of the human category. In explicitly approaching humanity as a paradigmatic condition, I argue that in every social context, different understandings of humanity are drawn from collectively organized engagements with human and nonhuman others. The ontological characterization of the human goes beyond being an analytical issue; it serves as a practical approach to understanding oneself and others. This perspective emerges at the intersection of embodied interactions—through which knowledge of others is gained—and the cosmological frameworks that shape perceptions of the agencies composing one's social world. Focusing on the productive tension between political discourses on humanity and the lived experience of being human reminds us that the relationship between a humanistic emphasis on representation and a posthumanistic attention to embodiment is not irreconcilable; rather, it generates a dynamic and constructive interplay (Cherstich et al. 2020, 93).

My reference to the paradigmatic role of nonhumans is not without flaws. This approach inherently negates and establishes a dependence on the category of the human, which remains the default point of comparison. Speaking of nonhumans also reiterates the naturalistic effect of dismissing the singularity of different entities and merging them into a generalized category. Despite this, the category of the nonhuman remains salutary as a compelling articulator of humanity. Recognizing the importance of categorizing the nonhuman requires us to avoid relegating nonhuman subjects to mere negative symbols. Instead, we should focus on their capacity to shape human perspectives and inform our sense of self.

Of all those environmental engagements through which ideas about humanity and its alterities take form, labor is perhaps the most compelling, given its central role in bolstering or diminishing nonhuman vitality. Unlike traditional vitalism, which assumes vitality as an ontologically given condition of specific entities, the vitality I have in mind appears as a potentiality that cannot be contained within any specific entity but is rather activated by relationships, including those enabled by human labor (see Duarte 2021; Greco 2005). As suggested by Course, experiencing the limits and possibilities of human abilities to confer but also to lessen the vitality of others encourages us "to reflect upon and reconsider, and ultimately recenter the relational parameters of what it means to be human" (2021, 49). The stories of forest destruction, domestication, and care presented in this book exemplify how embodiments and representations of human labor and its exceptionality coemerge in a reflexive consideration of the human condition. This condition is shaped by the particularities of life on conservation frontiers, where human and nonhuman vitalities are inextricably linked in unstable processes of rewilding and domestication.

The third aspect of alterity within alterhumanism addresses the ethical dimensions of humanity's unique capacity to both deplete and nurture the vitality of other beings, along with the responsibilities that these entail for more-than-human coexistence. In other words, *becoming human through nonhuman others*. My emphasis on engagement with others—especially nonhumans—as a core aspect of ethical self-formation stems from existing references to the term *alterhumanism* in moral philosophy, particularly in discussions surrounding Emmanuel Levinas's ethics and the significance of alterity within his framework (see Llewelyn 2012, 281). For Levinas, alterity is the experience through which the world and the self are provided with meanings. Such an experience is not an abstract contemplation on distant otherness, but rather a pre-reflexive encounter with the concrete presence of others, an idea that Levinas has captured through an emphasis on the effects of face-to-face encounters in questioning and destabilizing the solidity of the perceiver's self. Levinas sees ethics as the "calling into question of my spontaneity by the Other" (1979, 43). With its emphasis on the phenomenology of human intersubjectivity, Levinas's ethics posits that the will to be human is not in itself sufficient to become a moral subject and that the embodied experience of being human is inseparable from ethical projections. The ethics of encountering otherness thus remains irreducible to any expression of totalizing politics or morality (Critchley 2014, 221).

Despite an evident absence of questions concerning environmental and animal rights in Levinas's works, some commentators have proposed that the significance of face-to-face encounters might extend to the realm of nonhuman life. This extension necessitates that nonhuman others be recognized as subjects engaged in affective relationships, rather than merely as objects of an anthropomorphic empathy that is typically reserved for nonhumans like companion species, with whom we can more readily identify. Under this premise, encounters with nonhuman alterity are key to the articulation of multiple and conflictive definitions of being ethically human (see Atterton and Wright 2019; Bunch 2014).

In alterhumanism, ethics is experienced as part of the larger project of *becoming human with others*, both humans and nonhumans. As for environmental ethics in general, central to the ethical dimension of alterhumanism are reflections on the unique depletive and regenerative effects of human labor on world-making. Reflections on the normative limits and possibilities of engagement with nonhumans originate in affective contexts, where nonhumans are not symbolic objects associated with social sentiments such as empathy or disdain, but rather subjects capable of affecting our perception and sense of self through their presence. In alterhumanism, ethics thus can only be understood as ordinary. As Das defines it, ordinary ethics unfold in a "dimension of everyday life in which we are not aspiring to escape the ordinary but rather to descend into it as a way of becoming moral subjects" (2012, 134). Becoming moral subjects is a process inseparable from our attempts to stabilize and categorize the life forms with which we engage.

The Lessons of Posthumanism

The idea of alterhumanism I present in this book stems from a revisitation of posthuman theory. It emphasizes the ongoing relevance of the human question, particularly in the context of conservation and the Anthropocene. Far from a rejection of the human question as a meaningful framework for exploring human differences, this era compels us to reconsider the notion of human exceptionalism, prompting a deeper examination of our role within the wider ecological context.

The very definition of humanity and its perceived exceptionalism has long been central to Western humanism, shaping a worldview grounded in anthropocentrism—an outlook that posthuman critiques have specifically sought to dismantle. In Agamben's definition, humanism has historically worked as an "anthropological machine" in charge of defining humanity by separating it from the specific animalities of humans (2004). This categorical articulation makes possible the demarcation of proper human life (*bíos*) from bare animal life (*zoē*), the latter being a category assigned to animals as well as other humans as victims of political projects of dehumanization (Lorimer 2015, 37–38; Rossello 2017, 752).[1] By relegating the animality of humans to a latent condition that has to be overcome if human dignity is to be respected, substantialist and normative accounts of human nature have helped consolidate a vision of humanity as an autonomous and universal condition (Phillips 2015, 23). As Descola proposes, central to Western humanism is naturalism, an ontological model built upon belief in the existence of a thing called *na-*

ture and its opposition to *humanity*. In naturalism, humans share an animal exteriority with other beings, but their interiority, whether we call it a soul, subjectivity, or thought, is discontinuous and thus unique in relationship to other beings (2013). In humanism, the human question had clearer answers than those in other traditions, among which posthuman theory has been the latest and perhaps most vocal manifestation.

Dissenting traditions of thinking about humanity have always existed, even in the West. For example, across Catholic Europe, practices like preaching to animals treated both humans and nonhumans as divine or godly beings. This continued long after the Renaissance, which is often seen as the peak of humanistic culture's celebration of human exceptionalism (Fernández-Armesto 2005, 53).[2] In the twentieth century, critiques of traditional humanism became more and more common. Shaped by various historical forces—such as decolonial struggles, the existential and psychoanalytic critiques of human rationality, and the rise of cybernetics—diverse theoretical projects emerged with the explicit goal of exposing the underlying logics and discourses that shape and govern different forms of human life, often beyond the intentions of institutions and individuals. This new approach to the human question came to be known as anti-humanism, a heterogenous field of reflection in which humanist representations of humans as agents with full epistemic control of themselves and their surroundings (Phillips 2015, 16) were abandoned in favor of the structural features that mold human behaviors.[3]

Another inspiration in thinking beyond anthropocentrism comes from environmental philosophy and ethics, particularly from those proposals contributing to a general agenda of ecocentrism, a broadly defined ideology built around the recognition of the intrinsic value of all forms of life and their interconnectedness. I will discuss the principles of ecocentrism later in this book when I review the main political and theoretical orientations of environmental activism in Chile. A similar aspiration to reconsider the place of humanity within larger agential networks can be found in ecologically oriented approaches to human cognition, usually gathered under the label of *system theory*, and in transhumanism, which consists in a reflexive focus on the implications of technological hybridity and the transformation of the human body for human life (see Badmington 2000; Wolfe 2010).[4] The most complex ontological and ethical alternatives to anthropocentrism come from all those historical ontologies built around more relational principles that contrast with the human-nature dualism of Western humanism.

Ontologies often categorized under the umbrella of animism are grounded in more relational understandings of what it means to be human. This is exemplified by Amerindian theories of humanity and animality, where distinctions among beings are based on their behaviors and bodily predispositions, rather than on pre-established hierarchies such as the assumed absence of sociability and communication among nonhumans (Kopenawa and Albert 2019, 387). In animist ontologies, the cosmos is inhabited by beings with disparate outward appearances but who are nonetheless essentially human in their subjectivities and behaviors (Descola 2013, 131). Humanity, therefore, is a transient and relative condition determined by one's perspective and exchanges, as highlighted by Viveiros de Castro's characterization of Amerindian ontologies as perspectival insofar as the subjectivities of all beings are shaped by the perspectives that others project onto them. For example, an animal may be perceived as a human by another being while simultaneously being seen as an animal by a human observer (see 1998).[5]

Inspired by critiques and alternatives to anthropocentrism, posthuman theory emerged in the late twentieth century as a diverse field of inquiry focused on the empirical analysis of the agencies, intentions, and responsibilities intertwined within political, economic, and religious phenomena involving both human and nonhuman actors. In posthumanism, human agency is redefined as part of a broader network of human and nonhuman relations, moving beyond an exclusively human domain of design, intentionality, and political decision-making (see Bennett 2010, 32). The empirical focus is not only on the agential qualities of all forms of life but also on the constitutive effects of the connections in which they are enmeshed. In posthumanism, the collective unit of analysis is no longer society or culture, but a broader assemblage of more-than-human interactions endowed with constitutive potentials and thus capable of directing human intentions and actions, as in the evocative image of the rhizome introduced by Deleuze and Guattari (1987).[6] Actor-network theory (ANT), mostly associated with the work of Latour (2005), and new materialism are the two analytical proposals that best exemplify posthumanist approaches to politics, particularly those concerning environmental controversies and conflicts. In new materialism, political affairs unfold in a world "whose material forces themselves manifest certain agentic capacities and in which the domain of unintended or unanticipated effects is considerably broadened" (Coole and Frost 2010, 9).

There are many lessons of posthumanism that inspire this book. Post-human analytics is concerned with situating human practices and ideas in a world where humans inevitably fail to live up to their self-assigned role of being the measure of all things, and thus they require the measures of others, *pace* Protagoras. This lesson is particularly relevant in thinking about the human condition as it is reconfigured by the current climate crisis and the idea of the Anthropocene, itself responsible for reshuffling human and natural history. Indeed, the current value of posthuman theory for Braidotti lies in its role as a "generative tool to help us re-think the basic unit of reference for the human in the bio-genetic age known as 'anthropocene'" (2013, 5). Just as posthumanism offers many valuable insights, it also presents cautionary tales about the potential risk of disregarding human perspectives on the world and its representational aspects (see Chernilo 2017). When posthumanism involves an irreversible decentering of the human, it may inadvertently signal a new form of exceptionalism—this time, self-assigned to observers and analysts who claim the ability to transcend their embodied, and thus inherently human, conditions of knowledge. These individuals position themselves as capable of representing a transparent world where more-than-human relationships can be objectively ordered and understood. Paradoxically, posthumanism could end up returning to the humanistic assumption that human minds have the ability to detach from the world in order to represent it.

A more balanced view of posthuman embodiment is needed. As Wolfe reminds us, "Posthumanism . . . isn't posthuman at all—in the sense of being 'after' our embodiment has been transcended—but is only posthumanist, in the sense that it opposes the fantasies of disembodiment and autonomy, inherited from humanism itself" (2010, xv). I will add that embodiment is carried out from an inexorably human perspective, even when the content of the human is indeterminate and dependent on relationships with others to frame the specific humanity we assign to ourselves. Another implication of a posthuman disregard for reflections about the human condition is the potential lack of attention paid to the involvement of nonhuman agencies in the specific process of self-making as a human. With the following words, Haraway has expressed her discomfort with any version of posthumanism that shies away from asking how humans become who they are with others: "I am not a posthumanist; I am who I become with companion species, who and which make a mess out of categories in the making of kin and kind" (2008, 19).

If we follow the basic lesson of posthumanism—that human actions and intentions are shaped by interactions with other agencies—then posthumanism should not be interpreted as an ecocentric reversal of anthropocentrism. Instead, it should be understood as a reconsideration of how humans engage with and represent the world, acknowledging that such engagements are also guided by forces beyond ourselves. In this less radical interpretation of posthumanism, therefore, the human question does not simply go away. Without anthropocentric certainties, the answers to the human question are to be found in reflections on constantly shifting relations of alterity and subjectivity built upon the still-relevant but uncertain divide between human and nonhuman life (Herbrechter 2013, 149). Alterhumanism recontextualizes the tenets of posthumanism by placing the human question as the articulator of ontological pluralism, a general reconsideration of social differences as profoundly ontological rather than symbolic or semiotic. The human question thus remains significant as a reflexive operation that helps organize fundamental ontological and ethical categories of subjectivity and alterity in an epistemically complex and unruly world. With posthumanism, we have come to the recognition that the ontological status of the human is unstable and always in the process of becoming something else. With alterhumanism, we are reminded that humanity is also a salient and plural category of belonging that is socially organized in the attempt to order the world around us, ontologically and ethically. A challenge that this book must face is to provide a methodology for the demarcation of multiple versions of humanity responsible for the ontological plurality of a common world without falling prey to essentialist and reductionist risks of representing human collectivities as self-contained cultures or societies.

Actually Existing Alterhumanisms: Boundaries and Transformations

How many alterhumanisms can be said to exist? Are there boundaries among them? And how do they change over time? These questions might remind the reader of a broader debate about human differences within social sciences. We can replace *alterhumanism* with *culture* or *society*, and we might go back to established methodological discussions. Accounting for human differences has often entailed excessive emphasis on symbolic elements or traditional features of cultures, which in turn become easily identifiable—at the cost of losing their internal complexity and dynamicity. The distinction between alterhumanisms and other categories of collective human life, such as culture or society, lies in the fact that experiences of becoming human are shaped both by ontological distinctions and by ethical predispositions shared within a social group, simultaneously affecting and being affected by these factors. So, to answer the three questions: There are many alterhumanisms that one could depict, and their boundaries will inevitably depend on the shared conditions in which the process of becoming human unfolds, as well as on the specific distinctions through which different groups define their life and work. Finally, their transformation is continuous, as the experience of becoming human occurs within highly dynamic affective contexts, allowing individuals to engage with multiple human collectivities simultaneously.

Alterhumanisms do not exist as easily distinguishable cultural contexts. They become visible when one acknowledges the existence of multiple configurations of the ontological category of *the human*, which exist simultaneously as both universal and particular phenomena. *The human* is a universal category indicating a species and a particular condition for its members, but how one becomes human and the very meanings of *humanity* are irreducible to a singular definition. The oneness and manyness of the human, like any entity, arise from its internal proliferation. By adopting different perspectives, any entity or concept gains new ontological qualities, thereby becoming multiple.

For Strathern, "awareness of different voices" (Strathern [1991] 2004, 36) entails the recognition that any entity is always "more than one, less than many" (see also de la Cadena 2015; Haraway 1991). The multiplication of categories is enabled by practices that constitute it, and yet this multitude can be coordinated into a singularity (Mol 2002, 81). The multiplication of humanity is never a mere rhetorical expression of different ethical accounts of being humane. It is the very articulator of ontological pluralism. This idea stands as a critical reminder of the exclusionary premises of liberal modernity, whereby categories such as *the human* are ontologically singular and universal, and their difference lies only in the existence of "matters of belief" (Law 2015, 127) or cultural interpretations that do not conform to such categories' universal premises (see Escobar 2017; Goldman 2013). Despite

the promises of liberal multiculturalism, the modernist divide between nature and culture, rationality and belief, continues to enforce the demotion of
non-dominant ontological principles into "weak matters of political concern
when confronted to the facts offered by science, the economy, and nature"
(de la Cadena 2015, 275). Different experiences of becoming human prompt
not only different cultural narratives about humanity but also perspectives
guiding conflicting and overlapping projects responsible for the constitution
of a "world of many worlds" (de la Cadena and Blaser 2018).

The debate around ontological pluralism, mostly associated with proposals advocating for an "ontological turn" since the early 2000s, has resulted
in a shift of analytical attention from social, cultural, political, or other con-
structions to ontological presuppositions, defined by Holbraad and Pedersen
as all those "basic commitments and assumptions about what things are,
and what they could be (including things like society, culture, politics and
power)" (2017, 5). Recent attention to ontological pluralism in the social
sciences has converged into two tendencies. The first, mostly associated with
studies in science and technology, emphasizes the open-ended multiplication of worlds enacted in practice. The second highlights the self-contained
nature of ontological theories drawn from practices and principles guiding
social life in specific geographical and historical contexts. So, "whereas the
first [tendency] sees ontological politics as an emergent effect of heterogeneous interactions, the latter emphasizes peoples' deliberate efforts to
endow things with new properties" (Jensen and Morita 2015, 84). The two
tendencies are not mutually exclusive. Practices enact worlds, but practices
are guided by assumptions drawn from ontological agreements, such as the
idea, common in Western history, that something like "nature" exists.

In this book, I assume the existence of different alterhumanisms within
the same space: frontier forests. I represent these alterhumanisms by ab-
stracting the diverse ways in which beings engage with one another and how
these engagements contribute to the consolidation of ontological categorizations, such as those that distinguish humans from other beings. Categorization unfolds as a collective process of relating, an action that I understand as
both embodied and conceptual at once. *Relating* is the action of constituting
categories that are exposed to each other and thus become comparable and
distinguishable. The idea of relating that I have in mind draws on Strathern's
contribution to the development of a relational heuristics in the social sciences (see 1988, 2004, 2020). Rather than self-evident connections between

entities immediately accessible to the observer's perception, relationships are transformative actions, whether intentional or not, through which entities are endowed with multiple perspectives and genitive qualities. An example is the case of forests being something specific to someone—wilderness under threat to an eco-activist or a source of timber to a forester. In Strathern's definition of relation, the "conception of an entity's self-referential 'identity' becomes modified when that entity is thought of 'in respect to' another" (Strathern 2020, 7). In accordance with its Latin etymological origin, *relatio*, meaning "to bring back," relating can be understood as the act of reporting something, generally an essence, to an observer rather than a self-evident connection between two entities unaffected by their relationship (Strathern 2020, 4). Relationships therefore work as morphological actions (see Holbraad 2020) capable of providing new and changing conceptual shapes to entities by adding new perspectives onto them. In this light, any observation pointing to the lack of relationships among apparently unrelatable entities is still a productive action of relating, as new relationships are articulated through the denial of others (Holbraad and Pedersen 2017, 264; Strathern 2020, 110). An illustrative example of non-relating comes from the legal concept of property, which serves to legitimize relationships between owners and their properties and deny others, as is the case for foresters claiming use rights over forests that they do not own.

Relating is at once an embodied experience and a conceptual operation. This is because it unfolds not within a purely conceptual field, but in concrete "affective atmospheres" (Berlant 2011, 15), where notions and concepts are elaborated and communicated through our bodily, often pre-reflexive responses to constantly changing stimuli. The term *affect* refers to an understanding of human life in which relationships do not unfold between univocally recognized subjects and objects, but by entities with porous bodies capable of affecting and being affected by others (Massumi 2002, 35; Seigworth and Gregg 2010, 1). In Deleuze's definition of *affect*, "the distinction between power and act . . . disappears in favor of two equally actual powers, that of acting, and that of suffering action, which vary inversely one to the other, but whose sum is both constant and constantly effective" (1990, 93). The idea of affect reminds us that human representations do not consist of the mere arrangements of passive objects whose knowledge is simply transmitted or made to circulate. The subjects that one relates to while pursuing daily actions like caring, exploiting, loving, or hating have the potential power of affecting us and in turn directing our conceptual relations and categorizations. For this reason, the objectivation of the world around us can never be complete and will always be subject to transformations over which no full epistemic control is possible.

Let us take the example of forests. Their categorization and distinction as well as that of their dwellers is complicated by their indeterminacy as a consensually defined entity and the perceptive conditions they engender. As suggested by Kohn, the semiotic potential of forests consists in their morphological abilities to articulate the different shapes that humans utilize in crafting their own representations of forests and the environment at large (2013, 182). A forest, in other words, "exhibits some of the properties of thinking—such as end-directedness and generalization—that we tend to associate exclusively with humans" (Kohn 2022, 404). While forests partake in their objectivation, this process is necessarily informed by linguistic schemes, interests (such as the desire or refusal to see something as a forest), and legal definitions (such as those at work in state programs of natural resource management) (see Di Giminiani and Haines 2020).

Actually existing alterhumanisms can be drawn from different collective experiences of *becoming human through and with nonhuman others*. These unfold as part of different and hierarchically organized histories of humans' transformation of their surroundings, such as those at work in the constitution of settler and conservation frontiers. In this book, I depict accounts of humanity and its alterity, along with the experiences that inform and sustain them, among four collectivities from the conservation frontier in Chile: settlers, Indigenous Mapuche people, environmental activists, and conservation scientists. I use the term *collectivity* instead of *cultures* or *social groups* because it brings together a practically oriented form of grouping—such as the idea of communities of practice being defined by shared professional backgrounds—with a more abstract and historically deep social arrangement of the world, captured by the idea of ontology. The demarcation of the four alterhumanisms depicted in this book will be aided by anthropological comparison, an analytical tool shared by the social scientist and the people actively defining themselves and others, which, in Candea's proposal, consists of the assessment "of similarities and differences, continuities and breaks, between three or more entities, at least one of which includes the perspective from which the comparison is taking place" (Candea 2019, 323). This includes, of course, that of the observer.

Part I, "Four Ways of Becoming Human," is dedicated to the depiction of these four models of alterhumanism. In chapter 1, I illustrate the domestication of frontier forests and nation-building as drawn from experiences and memories among settlers at the margins of the colonization project. These experiences are central to the emergence of an understanding of humanity and its alterity, which only partially reflects the settler fantasies of mastery over nature. In chapter 2, I present a model of Mapuche alterhumanism drawn from both Indigenous ontological and cosmological principles for the explanation of human and forest agencies and from memories and experiences of displacement and resettlement. These originated in the invasion of the Mapuche homeland, Wallmapu, by the Chilean army in the second half of the nineteenth century. In chapters 3 and 4, I present two forms of alterhumanism stemming directly from the conservation boom that began in Chile in the 1990s. Chapter 3 illustrates how enchantment is thought of among environmental activists and entrepreneurs and how it is carried as a perceptive predisposition designed to foster experiences of ecocentrism. Inexorably, ecocentrism can only be experienced as a desire rather than a sustained form of engagement in a world still framed by anthropocentric principles. Chapter 4 focuses on practices and knowledge produced by conservation scientists. Through the development of attentiveness to birds' perspectives on the forest world, conservation scientists craft a message in which humans figure as both an external disturbance of natural ecosystems and as beings emotionally and practically entangled with nonhumans.

Alterhumanisms are sturdy because they are grounded in shared and recurrent experiences of engagement with nonhuman others. Yet alterhumanisms are also highly transformative in two ways. First, affective engagements with others are unstable, as the environmental conditions under which they unfold are subject to multiple material and representational changes. An example central to this book is the role of protected areas in fostering the experience of forests as wilderness. Second, alterhumanisms are inserted into historical contexts, where powerful discourses on humanity circulate across multiple social fields. By affecting the comprehension of human and nonhuman agencies and responsibilities, a discourse can prompt concrete changes in our behaviors. Today, the power of conservation lies not only in providing material means for very diverse projects, from capital accumulation through green investments to biodiversity protection from agro-industrial expansion. It also consists in the reproduction and circulation of ideas about human-environmental relations capable of molding behaviors and attitudes toward nature without the necessity for strict policing or coercion of populations living around conservation hotspots. Among its diverse manifestations, conservation also appears as an institutional project of remaking humanity through discursive means, highlighting the dangers posed by humans to nonhumans and the responsibilities that these dangers entail. Images of humanity made available by conservation institutions inevitably encounter, entangle, and enter into conflict with other narratives of humanity, such as those present in the models of alterhumanism depicted in this book.

In part II, "Remaking the Human in Conservation," I characterize the power of conservation as an institutional project designed to foster changes in collective behaviors inspired by environmental discourses, particularly those reproduced by institutions in charge of enforcing conservation initiatives. Through a heuristic loosely inspired by Foucault's attention to subjectivization, I examine the process of self-transformation that individuals undergo in specific historical contexts, where they are compelled to embody the ideal subjects envisioned by various institutions (see 1982). I analyze the consequences of both the adoption and rejection of conservation values and practices among the inhabitants of the conservation frontier (see Agrawal 2005; Cepek 2011; West 2006).

In conservation, the remaking of the human is not the irreversible and linear process of transformation into an ideal environmental subject, as might be overly attributed to the potential of institutional action. Rather, it materializes as an unfinished project capable of molding understandings and experiences of human-environmental relations without necessarily erasing existing configurations of humanity as those associated with the models of alterhumanism. The recalcitrance of alterhumanism is a reminder that humanity is not the epistemic object of dominant discourses capable of replacing others, but the result of paradigmatic arrangements of humanity and its alterity stemming from shared embodied experiences and ontological arrangements. To say that the subjectivization is unfinished is not equivalent to saying that it is ineffective or that it is interrupted by a contrary reaction or resistance. Rather, it means recognizing that subjectivization is a latent and ongoing process of reproduction of knowledge and value that targeted populations need to adapt to while they navigate the normative and legal possibilities and limitations that come along with institutional intervention. The reader will learn about two specific projects of subjectivization that farming populations living in the conservation frontier of southern Chile have experienced: In chapter 5, I examine the experience of becoming environmentalists, a term that in this case corresponds to an ideal ethical subject envisioned in environmental grassroots activism. Collaborations, conflicts, and mediations involving local foresters, cattle ranchers, and local landholders on one side and conservation actors—in particular private protected area managers—on the other reveal the significance of landscape experiences in shaping the acceptance or rejection of conservation discourses. Chapter 6 continues my depiction of participatory conservation, this time with a focus on the articulation of contrasting forms of ecological citizenship emerging from relationships between Mapuche landholders and forest officers in the context of Indigenous reclamation of state-owned protected areas.

While my focus on conservation as a powerful articulator of new, contested ideas of humanity and the environment might resonate with readers familiar with different social contexts across the globe, it is undoubtedly molded by the historical contingencies of a particular, loosely demarcated territory that I became familiar with in my position as an anthropologist. The stories and locations depicted in this book are mountain valleys, protected areas (both public and private), and towns located within the adjacent municipal areas of Villarrica, Pucón, and Currarehue.[7] To most people in Chile, the names of these three southern towns will likely ring a bell. Pucón and Villarrica are well-known international lake resorts and commercial hubs for the local area. And once a border outpost on the way to Argentina, Currarehue has experienced a more recent tourism boom due to its proximity to national parks and hot springs. These three areas, all of them located within the region of Araucanía, are part of a broader territory that, in this book, I refer to as a conservation frontier.[8] Loosely defined, the conservation frontier in southern Chile coincides with mountainous areas close to the border with Argentina and home to a high concentration of protected areas, which were established in the twentieth century as part of the Chilean government's strategy to enforce state presence and reassert sovereignty over frontier territories.

The setting of this book has an inevitable degree of arbitrariness. My research was scattered across multiple fieldwork experiences from 2012 to 2018. Throughout those years, I was able to follow different stories that I felt would represent the major processes responsible for the emergence and constitution of settler and conservation frontiers. Conveniently, the university where I still work had a campus in the town of Villarrica, which is also the location of several local offices of state institutions, such as the forest service CONAF (Corporación Nacional Forestal). In Pucón, I was exposed to perhaps the oldest and most successful ecotourism boom in the country. Not far from there, the private protected area of *Santuario el Cañi* ("Cañi Sanctuary") stands as one of the earliest cases of community-based conservation in Chile, while further away, a few kilometers from the town of Currarehue, the Hualalafquén national reserve is the setting of mobilizations and collaborations involving the forest service and Indigenous Mapuche residents. Valleys such as Liucura, Maichín, and Coilaco are home to heirs of early twentieth-century settlers (*colonos*).[9] These valleys are also punctuated by a few Indigenous Communities (*Comunidades Indígenas*), an official unit with limited political representation corresponding to a conglomeration of privately owned plots of land where Mapuche families live.[10]

The four alterhumanisms and their transformations that I present to the reader reflect not only the unique characteristics of the specific localities where the research was conducted, but also the particular relationships and collaborations that made this research possible in the first place. My research was never a lonely pursuit of self-discovery, as idealized in the tradition of Malinowskian anthropology since the early twentieth century. The interviews and ethnographic observations that I present are drawn from my participation in and coordination of multiple research teams, whose members changed over the years. The most enriching collaborations were with Julián Moraga, Martín Fonck, Daniela Jacob, and Paolo Perasso, all recent graduates in the social science at the time, with whom I had the privilege of thinking and writing.

Collaboration was also the main form of engagement with many of the people appearing in this book. This is the case of the avian ecologists whose ideas and work are described in chapter 4, some of whom I collaborated with on different research projects. My work with the farming communities portrayed in this book also followed a collaborative logic. In Chile, as in the rest of Latin America, fieldwork in social science is shaped by an overt call—and a very welcome one—from students, academics (or at least some of them), civil society organizations, and state institutions to design research strategies that are of interest and potential benefit to local populations affected by field activities. Collaboration in this case materialized in the elaboration of ethnographic reports designed to guide the actions of local neighborhood associations, as well as in the publication of a history book authored by members of a local organization, intended as an accessible testimony of their past and present.[11]

Collaboration should not be naively taken as a viable recipe to create equal relationships between the writer—in this case one with job security at a private university—and some of the protagonists of the stories I tell in this book, especially when the structural conditions in which our lives are embroiled make evident the differences in our social and economic capital.[12] Instead, collaboration reminds us that the stories we tell belong to others, and of course we make mistakes in recounting them, as I am sure I have in writing these pages.[13] In reproducing the stories of others, my aspiration is to convey, with some inevitable omittances, the complexities and overlaps of different human collectivities in a context marked by racial and other inequalities. I also hope that this book will be a reminder that even when we fail to establish a more symmetrical relationship, it is only by learning from others that we can envision the many types of human life we wish to cherish and see endure amid the Anthropocene crisis.

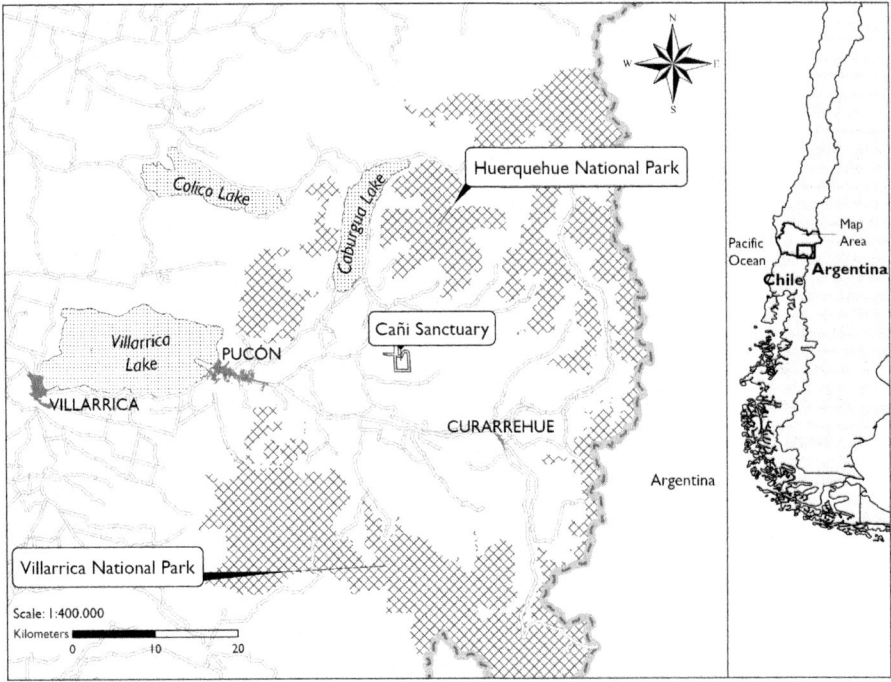

FIGURE 2 Map of protected areas and towns depicted in this book (Credit to Felipe Elgueta)

PART I

Four Ways of Becoming Human

Chapter 1

Hacer Patria

Settlers' Intimate Nationhood and the Domestication of Frontier Forests

Once a small rural town, Pucón acquired its fame as an exclusive lake resort in the 1940s. While maintaining some of its elite status, the town has enjoyed a surge in its popularity since the 1970s, when it became the main ecotourist hub of southern Chile, attracting foreign visitors in search of eco-friendly experiences. Today, it is the undisputed showcase of all southern Chile can offer to a tourist: serene views of Villarrica Lake surrounded by imposing snowcapped volcanoes, safe beaches for swimming in the summer, lush forests with long trekking paths, and tumultuous rivers ideal for rafting. The town also offers shops and street markets selling Indigenous Mapuche craftworks, a cosmopolitan party vibe with cocktail bars and sushi restaurants, and an idyllic countryside with yoga retreats and hot springs offering breaks from the crowds. English is widely spoken (something rare in the rest of southern Chile). For many Chileans, Pucón is a such a desired vacation destination that visitors are willing to deal with traffic volumes around Lake Villarrica in summer that can be worse than in the capital, Santiago.

Beyond its tourist attractions and gated communities, however, the countryside around Pucón is not that different from other areas in southern Chile. Here, one can find one-story wooden houses, food kiosks selling bread and other produce, and small enclosures fenced with barbed wire for sheep and cattle. While the countryside around Pucón has over the years become home to middle- and upper-class professionals often commuting to the regional capital, Temuco, most rural dwellers self-identify as *campesinos*, a category that encompasses both Mapuche and non-Indigenous smallholders and refers to anyone working in agriculture as a laborer or independent producer. For farmers, the tourism boom of the past decades is marked by deep contradictions. While it has certainly brought prosperity in the shape of temporary jobs, this boom has done little for the endemic crisis of small-scale agriculture; it has even worsened it because of the rise in living costs that has come with the growth of the real estate market. For many small landholders, selling their property to middle- and upper-class buyers from Santiago is a desired prospect, and yet this is often untenable since land sales concentrate around a few areas with existing road and electricity infrastructure. Over the last few decades, an aging population and declining profits for small-scale farmers have left many rural residents with few options if they want to avoid migration to towns and cities, where younger members of their families are studying and working.

For many rural residents around Pucón, the impasse between the promise of tourism and the distressing prospect of abandonment is reminiscent of the longer and ongoing struggle to turn the remote mountain valleys of the area into their homes. Many landowners here are heirs of settlers, *colonos*, who reached these valleys at the beginning of the twentieth century as squatters hoping to succeed in establishing their homesteads and having their land rights recognized by the authorities of the time. Unlike European migrants, who were simply labeled as *colonos* and endowed with attractive properties through the mechanisms of colonization law, the forerunners of today's settler community residents were mestizo (mixed race) squatters, officially labelled as *colonos nacionales* (national settlers) once they could secure ownership rights. To this day, for some locals they are still *colonos*.

I have become familiar with the past and present struggles and aspirations of small landholding colonos in one valley, Coilaco. Today, unlike for much of the twentieth century when transport was much more precarious, Coilaco is easily reachable from Pucón thanks to an almost daily bus service. As the bus takes more than an hour, if residents are in a bigger hurry when they need to run errands, it is a shorter trip in a pickup. The valley begins at a junction located a 20-minute drive from Pucón, heading toward the Andes—or simply *la cordillera*, as it is commonly called throughout Chile. A dirt road surrounded by forest runs side by side with the small homonymous river for more than fourteen kilometers, where the last houses of the valley are located. As one moves toward higher parts of the valley, some of these grazing areas become punctuated by the white stumps of chopped trees or fallen trunks left behind, probably because their wood was of little use. Next to a couple of small patches of former woods, one can find open storehouses with a few pieces of heavy machinery and piles of wood planks. Anyone familiar with the southern Chilean countryside would recognize that these are family-owned *aseraderos*, or sawmills. These facilities stand as reminders of the past glories of forestry in the area, an activity that now survives only in higher stretches of Andean valleys, among landowners with slightly more land.

In places like Coilaco, the process of settlement did not result in irreversible changes in the landscape, with dense native forests being replaced by the vast open fields that characterize agricultural estates (*fundos*) in most of southern Chile, or timber plantations owned by transnational companies. For smallholding colonos, settlement is not a historical event but a precarious, ongoing achievement. Their stories diverge sharply from the triumphalist narratives of settler colonialism often portrayed in traditional historiography and fiction. Dunlap's powerful statement that "settlers were less interested in understanding the land than remaking it" (1993, 28) holds true in the characterization of the colonial ideology of emptiness, whereby land constitutes a tabula rasa from which a new environment can be molded (Nouzeilles 1999). But while this trope sheds light on the ideals driving settler expansion, it does not fully account for the ways settlers embody and represent forest landscapes, as seen among the residents of Coilaco Valley.[1] Literature on settler colonialism has recently begun taking a larger interest in the phenomenology of settlers' environmental engagements as part of the broader processes of settlement and property-making (see Blair 2017; Campbell 2015; Dominy 2001; Freddi 2022; Gressier 2015; McIntosh 2016; Rasmussen 2021; Suzuki 2017). Settler indigeneity—in other words, the ways in which settlers feel native to particular localities (Blair 2017, 580)—does not stem from identification with something resembling a shared settler culture or society but is rather articulated through experiences and memories of settlement, here understood as a process of transformation and adaptation to the environment that does not exhaust itself in a foundational event.

In this chapter, I begin my exploration of alterhumanism as an empirical model that reveals the situated configurations of humanity and its alterity. I do so by identifying and defining one of its specific manifestations, particu-

larly central to the formation of the settler frontier. Drawing on the memories and experiences of domestication and settlement among smallholding
settlers in southern Chile, I outline a model of settlers' alterhumanism focused on ontological and ethical questions regarding the possibilities and
limits of human labor within an unruly forest world. I refer to it as *settlers'*
alterhumanism rather than *settler* alterhumanism to highlight the impact of
settlers' embodied experiences of settlement and on the formation of situated notions of humanity. This distinction also serves to differentiate it from
broader discourses on human nature linked to settler colonialism, while still
acknowledging its role in driving the settlement process itself.

Settlers' alterhumanism is a form of *becoming human through others* that
emphasizes the ontological status of humans as domesticators. It is also a
form of *becoming human with others*, animated by the ethical recognition
of human labor as capable of bestowing vitality on nonhuman life as well
as causing its demise. Memories and experiences of settlement reveal that
domestication can be only a momentary ontological achievement, though
necessary to ensure the continuity of settlement as an intrinsically precarious and reversible project. At the margins of the settler colonial project,
settlement is a project animated by, on the one hand, a frustrated desire
for permanent transformation and, on the other hand, an understanding
of domestication as the articulation of affects between people and forests
informing a two-way relationship in which forests are responsive to human
labor in unpredictable ways. Domestication involves transforming otherwise
indeterminate assemblages of nonhuman agencies into a domestic space
where trees are recognized as entities with use-value. This shift is reflected
in the categorization of forests, distinguishing them as either domesticated
or wild. The history of settlement is the history of the growth and retreat of
forests, remembered by colonos through visual signs scattered around the
forest landscape.

Settlers' histories tell us of intimate struggles in finding one's place in the
world and making sense of this intergenerational experience. While settlers
cannot be reduced to mechanical gears within the political-economic structure of settler colonialism, there are no settlers outside the history of settler
colonialism. Individual and collective trajectories of settlement are part of
a broader history of capital accumulation, Indigenous dispossession, and
nation-building. In Chile, settlement unfolds as a process of place-making,
carried out both through state mechanisms and against them. For many

smallholder settlers, nation-building, commonly known as *hacer patria*, literally "making homeland," was meant to spearhead and anticipate the development of state infrastructure in frontier areas, even though they were frequently treated as squatters posing a threat to a supposedly centralized and regulated colonial process of land distribution (see Harambour 2019; Klubock 2014; Núñez et al. 2014). Among colonos, belonging is ultimately experienced through their ambivalent participation in the project of *hacer patria*, which, to this day, continues to animate enthusiastic identification with the nation as much as a feeling of neglect from the state. As configurations of humanity and alterity are inseparable from the experience of domestication, they are also inextricably shaped by involvement in the contested project of nation building.

Settler Colonialism in Chile: A Brief History

What does *settler colonialism* mean in southern Chile? The answer to this question is not straightforward. In Latin America, the term *settler colonialism* holds relatively little weight in historiographic discussions about European conquest and native genocide. The equivalent term in Spanish, *colonización por poblamiento*, figures as a secondary phenomenon in historiographic and political debates, especially when compared to other aspects of colonialism in the region, such as ideological subalternity to European ideals, or *colonialidad* ("coloniality") as Quijano (2000) among others has referred to it. A possible explanation for this apparent absence is that the expression *settler colonialism* has historically served to distinguish a specific mode of conquest in British colonialism based on settlers' land occupation and native replacement from indirect rule, which entails the exploitation of native labor and resources from a distance (see Elkins and Pedersen, 2005). The other key reason for the "absence" of settler colonialism in Latin American historical and social debates concerns the definition of *settler* as a national subject living apart from native populations. Such a definition finds little resonance with *mestizaje*, the framework under which nation-building and racialized identity have been customarily understood in the region (see Gott 2007). *Mestizaje* is a deeply cemented discourse and ideology whereby national identity is built on the dialectical merging of white Europeans and Indigenous people.[2] While the discourse of *mestizaje* has arguably promoted actual racial mixing more than in British colonial contexts inspired by segregational models of governance, it has also served to promote a problematic image of racial and national unity, with the consequent demotion of Indigenous status to a condition of the precolonial past. By celebrating European and native miscegenation, *mestizaje* has obfuscated how profoundly white settlers have shaped environments and societies in Latin America.

In Chile, the term *mestizo* is used less frequently than in other Latin American countries, but the more general term *chileno* or the more customary *criollo* expresses the same idea. If we take settler colonialism as a historical process based on economic, spatial, and biological replacement of the native population by settlers (Wolfe 1999, 163), then this phenomenon clearly applies to regions of Latin America, such as southern Chile, that were subject to a deliberate governmental plan of selective migration. Similar to other whitening projects, these plans were designed to encourage large waves of European immigrants to settle on newly available public lands (see Goebel 2017).[3] As Wolfe has eloquently warned, the rejection of binarism in settler-native relations in favor of a strong focus on such relations' intricacies might work as a potential instrument in downplaying the ongoing colonial condition suffered by native society and persisting inequalities with colonizing actors (2013, 259).

The intersections of the settler, mestizo or Chileno, and Indigenous categories are deeply rooted in the history of the settler frontier in Chile. It was common for Chilenos and even Mapuche squatters to claim land access by adopting the status of colonos at the turn of the nineteenth century, and some even identified as settlers, as we will explore in the next chapter. The challenge in this case is how to recognize the power that settler-native dichotomies hold in the governance of Indigenous lands and people, while acknowledging the entanglements and intimacies of settler and native lives across frontier territories.

The origins of settler expansion in the twentieth century can be traced back to over three centuries of Mapuche resistance against colonial encroachment by the Spanish crown, beginning in the 1600s. After its failed attempts to conquer Mapuche land, the Spanish crown recognized the sovereignty of the territory south of the Biobío River, known as Wallmapu in Mapuche contexts, through a series of negotiations called *parlamentos*, literally "parliaments" (Marimán 2002; Zavala 2005). These negotiations primarily resulted in the ratification of treaties, the most well-known of which was signed in the locality of Quilín in 1641 (Bengoa 2007). In the aftermath of the independence war against the Spanish in 1810, Chilean authorities partially recognized existing Spanish treaties, recognizing de facto Mapuche sovereignty (Mariman 2002).

However, over the following decades, economic elites and policymakers openly voiced their concern over the presence of a large Indigenous region, not under the control of the Chilean state, separating southern Chilean territories from central parts of the country. By the mid-nineteenth century, *la Frontera*, "the Frontier," as Mapuche territories were known to many Chileans at time, was increasingly depicted in public discourses as lawless country with frequent clashes between the Mapuche population and Chilean squatters venturing south of the Biobío (see Herr 2019; Klubock 2014). Pro-invasion arguments, emphasizing the need for economic development, quickly became dominant in the public discourse, with only a small minority of policymakers and clergy members raising concern about the potential for a significant death toll among the Indigenous people (Pairican 2020; Pinto 2003). In 1866, a legal bill (*Ley del 4 Diciembre 1866*), based on the same theoretical principles of the *terra nullius* logic, whereby Indigenous territories were considered nobody's land since they lacked formal ownership, declared the Mapuche region to be state-owned land (*terrenos fiscales*). Soon after, General Cornelio Saavedra was appointed as leader of a military campaign, euphemistically presented to the public as *la Pacificación de la Araucanía*, "the Pacification of Araucanía." In reality, the "pacification" was a series of military actions from 1866 to 1884 aimed at a heterogeneous resistance movement, resulting in a death toll among the Mapuche population that clearly fits within standard definitions of genocide (see Bengoa 2000, 11).[4]

The end of the war marked the zenith of two parallel and yet entangled histories, that of settler expansion and that of Mapuche confinement. The annexation of Indigenous lands to national territories was soon followed by the displacement of the Mapuche population into small, collectively held plots of land, known as *reducciones*, whose dimensions corresponded to roughly 5% of the entire region (Mariman 2006). The rest of the former Mapuche territories was redistributed to settlers, mostly through state auctions. Much of the rationale behind settlers' land redistribution in southern Chile rested on the racist idea that white European settlers, possibly Catholic, were better equipped to lead the future development of *la Frontera*. This ideal animated legislation like the 1845 "Law of Colonization" (*Ley de*

Colonización y Terrenos Baldíos), which granted land concessions to private companies, known as *concesiones de colonización*, in charge of overseeing the settlement of migrants from Europe (see Correa et al. 2005, 37). As part of the agreement with colonization companies, migrants were endowed not only with legal titles over land properties, but also with the logistical support needed for the development of agricultural fields (see Quiroz 1985). Albeit imagined and designed as a centrally planned process, land redistribution proved to be a highly deregulated process, resulting in land concentration being capitalized by a few individuals and families, as well as illegal occupations, evictions, and property disputes between settlers and local Mapuche populations and among settlers themselves. The most visible effect of deregulated land accumulation was the emergence of large agrarian estates known as *fundos*, where landless non-Indigenous peasants and Mapuche residents of *reducciones* were working under a debt peonage system until the 1960s (see Di Giminiani 2018, 42). Land concentration, lack of diversification in agricultural production, and reliance on the exploitation of a precarious labor force explain low productivity at these southern estates and the consequent chronic economic stagnation of Araucanía (Klubock 2014, 56), still visible today in macroeconomic indicators placing this region among the poorest of the country.

In a few decades, a two-tier social system separating landowners from the rest of society came to characterize southern Chile, as pointed out by José Bengoa: "In those years, a totally fractioned society was being built. The world of the colonos, recorded in the newspaper of the time, was settling in the region above everything else that existed before it" (2014, 111). To this day, especially in more central sections of southern Chile where the largest *fundos* are located, wealthy landowners, known colloquially as *patrones* ("patrons") or *gringos*, for their European looks, are key players in regional politics, in most cases spearheading conservative parties and organizations opposing Indigenous Mapuche mobilizations for land restitution (see Richards 2013).[5]

In remote Andean valleys, a slightly different scenario for Indigenous-settler relations has unfolded. Here, state-owned land became subject to occupation by both displaced Mapuche and poor Chilean squatters (see Klubock 2014), who were later categorized as *colonos nacionales*. The life histories of the heirs of these *colonos nacionales* are hardly comparable with those of powerful non-Indigenous landowners, whose companies often represent the only source of available employment to Mapuche rural residents.

"National settlers" are generally considered small to medium-sized land-holders, as their properties rarely exceed one hundred hectares. Among *colonos nacionales*, social relations are not restricted to a settler circle separated from other farmers through clear-cut markers of class distinction. Many smallholding settlers living around Andean valleys have Indigenous relatives and claim their mixed status through affirmations such as having Mapuche blood (*sangre Mapuche*).

The history of colonization around the town of Pucón reflects the two scenarios distinctive of settler colonialism in southern Chile: that of a regional elite of white settlers and that of a more intermingled sociality involving national settlers, landless farmers, and Mapuche landholders. Founded as a Chilean military outpost in 1883 at the end of the invasion of Araucanía, Pucón soon became a magnet for European settlers who reached the area through a few colonization companies. Concesión Lanin, the first large land concession in the area, benefited a large number of German immigrants endowed with roughly 150 hectares for each household (Marimán 2006, 119). The image of a bountiful land through which colonization companies attracted European settlers did not, of course, always coincide with the reality of settlement. The testimony of an elder resident of Pucón, María Valencia, shows settlers' difficulties very vividly: "Many of these Germans didn't know anything about Chile. They just saw the advertisement about all these free gifts in the newspaper. When they reached Quilaco [a local valley] they found only bushes and trees" (Gray 2015, 68). As in many other frontier regions, the history of southern Chile is narrated through the trope of settlers' resilience and adaptation to a novel environment. In reality, European immigrants adapted only partially or momentarily to the challenges of settlement, often looking for opportunities outside the agricultural sector. In Pucón, many of them eventually moved to town, where they became successful traders and entrepreneurs thanks to professional qualifications, capital obtained from the land, and connections to the emerging local elite.

While early European settlers were not immune from precariousness in agricultural activities, this prospect was much more severe for the *national settlers*, who were to compete for less attractive land. Coilaco was subject to a land redistribution process only in the 1930s, years later than the less rugged areas around Pucón. A first attempt at settlement had occurred in the 1920s, but as recounted by an elder local resident, "In two years [these settlers] hadn't even managed to build a single post to protect themselves from sun and rain. This is how they lost their land rights."[6] Eventually, they abandoned the valley. Farmers arriving in the 1930s had a different ending to this story, even though they faced the same struggles as the first settlers of the valley. As once told by a local resident, Gisela, their settlement was marked by great uncertainties: "My grandfather came here with nothing, not even documents. For many years, he and his family lived in a tent. Eventually, crops such as potatoes began to come out. That's how they could stay there." Achievements in farming, however, did not always guarantee property rights. Non-Indigenous and Mapuche squatters were constantly under threat of eviction, known as a *lanzamientos*, typically at the hands of investors who would acquire rights over state-owned land from distance, even when farmers had already settled there. Evictions were typically carried out by local police, but it was not unusual for a landowner to take matters in their own hands, often in the form of arson. The evictions were a dramatic depiction of the deep contradictions of governmental attitudes toward settlers' occupation of frontier land. On the one hand, settlement by squatters was celebrated as a poignant instance of *chilenización*, the process of nationalizing frontier areas (see Bengoa 2014; Harambour 2019); settlers moving to remote areas saw themselves as courageous embodiments of nationalistic values at the time of nation-building. On the other, uncontrolled land occupations were a time bomb for property disputes, which were typically tackled through repressive state action. As indicated by Klubock, "The nationalist sentiment that the frontier had to be made Chilean by distributing land to Chilean laborers [made] its mark on colonization law, encoding both a series of property rights claimed by landless laborers and a central contradiction with other colonization policies based on land auctions and colonization concessions" (2014, 52).[7]

Nationalist feelings animating the occupation of frontier areas have traditionally coalesced around the expression of *hacer patria*, "making homeland." This expression might seem synonymous with *chilenización*, a term commonly employed in Chilean historiography in reference to the official project of integrating frontier areas into the national territory. This initiative aimed to regularize land access for farmers, who at the time were a transient population moving between Argentina and Chile.[8] The use of the expression "making homeland" is widespread across Chile. It refers to any action aimed at securing a position within a contested space, such as a political organization entering a negotiation involving state and private actors. In the

FIGURE 3 A family of settlers in southern Chile, circa 1940 (Photograph by Einar Altschwager, Copyright© Colección Museo Histórico Nacional)

case of settlers, *hacer patria* refers to the intentional action of continuing to live and leave their mark around frontier territories vis-à-vis the prospect of abandonment. One of the occasions when I heard this concept publicly mentioned was during a mayor's speech at the inauguration of a farming festival: "I would like to thank all the campesinos living in this beautiful valley. Every single day, with big efforts, they are making homeland, *estan haciendo patria*." For past settlers and their heirs, making homeland entails both an intimate desire for inclusion in the nation and enrolls an emotional connection with the land they settled in. In their case, settlement is not only an event of the past, but an ongoing project indistinguishable from the precarious domestication of frontier forests.

From "Woods" to "Forests" and Back

The fire, which ignited in different parts of the forest, grew with such an unforeseeable speed that the poor *indio*, the tireless Pichi Juan, could save himself only thanks to the refuge he found in a rotten *coihue* [southern cone beech], under which, in its humid and wasted roots, he could save himself. The hideous fire, whose flames could not have been stopped, not even by the torrential rain falling almost every day, lasted for over three months, leading to great devastation; and the smoke that rose up from the flames, pushed by southern winds, made the sun darken to the point that it could be stared at with naked eyes in Valdivia.

This anecdote (Otero 2006, 77) is drawn from the diary of explorer and politician Vicente Pérez Rosales, who led the settlement of German immigrants in the southern province of Llanquihue in the 1850s, a time when the Chilean army had yet to defeat Mapuche resistance. The central Mapuche character in the story, Pichi Juan, is no longer depicted in heroic terms, unlike the way Mapuche figures from the Spanish colonial period are typically portrayed in official historiography (Crow 2013, 23). Now he is depicted with racist, condescending tones, simply labelled with a diminutive name such as Pichi ("small" in the Mapuche language Mapudungun) and described by Pérez Rosales as a "drunk Indian" in other excerpts of his travelogue. The transformation of the Mapuche people from independent fighters to humiliated servants was parallel to the more triumphant transformation of the southern forests through the raging force of fire.

Settlers found an ideal partner in fire in their struggle to "obtain beautiful fields with an uncommon suitability for agricultural works," in Pérez Rosales's words (Camus and Solari 2008, 20). While the Indigenous people of south-central Chile had applied fire for underbrush clearing before the European conquest, it was not until settler expansion that fire took a more predominant role, becoming the primary cause and means of deforestation (Lara et al. 2003). In settlers' chronicles, deforestation was described as the act of "cleaning the fields," or *limpiar los campos*, an achievement that fire, more than any other means, made possible. Given the ability of fires to rewrite land tenure and thus speed up settlement (Escalona and Barton 2024, 27), political authorities were tolerant of this unregulated practice. Only in the early twentieth century, once the social and environmental dangers of fire, capable of destroying entire towns, became clear, were restrictions on clearing by fires introduced (Otero 2006, 87–97). The relationship between fire and settler colonialism is well known. As Pyne eloquently states, "Colonization expanded fire by transferring European fire practices to receptive landscapes or by breaking down old biotas and adapting native burning, reconstituting those lands with Euroasian surrogates" (1997, 19–20). Forest clearing by fire is perhaps the most dramatic strategy employed by colonizers to transform wilderness into a Europe-like landscape, as noted by Crosby (2004) in his formulation of Neo-Europes (Blair 2017, 597). Even though settler fantasies of complete environmental transformation were not always fully realized, fire has remained a crucial tool in settler colonial rule, effectively marking and making visible new land property arrangements (Ogden 2011, 55).

While forest clearing has been the main strategy behind the domestication of frontier territories in Chile, colonization never consisted of a purely foundational and irreversible event. The eventfulness of settler colonialism, which often serves to obscure the ongoing dispossession of colonized peoples (see Povinelli 2002; Simpson 2014), contrasts with the reality of forest domestication on the frontier in Chile, a far more precarious and unstable endeavor. The foundational idea of settler landscapes is further challenged by the fact that, for many settlers at the margins of the colonial project, the ability to adapt to the environment may be more important than their supposed capacities to transform it. As Campbell describes in his ethnographic account of contemporary colonization in northern Brazil, "the road, the rain, the presence of contradictory colonial visions, and the materialities of property-making are elements in an unpredictable landscape, in which migrants find themselves disenthralled as colonial masters and more concerned with learning how to survive and thrive in Amazonia" (2014, 250). Learning to adapt to frontier forests seems an appropriate descriptor of the past and present of many settlers living around remote areas of southern Chile. In this scenario, domestication appears as a human potentiality necessary for the vitality of forests and other natural resources, and yet one inextricably linked to forests' agential abilities to affect human life.

Among present-day settlers in southern Chile, the centrality of domestication in their engagements with the forest is exemplified by the articulation of two local categories. These are *bosque*, literally "wood," and *selva*, "forest," a term that can be replaced by its synonym *monte*, literally "mountain," as forests typically concentrate on hill slopes in southern Andean valleys. A *forest* refers to any forested area that is rarely accessed by farmers, with certain exceptions like cattle ranchers who practice forest grazing. Forests are rich in undergrowth and difficult to navigate. Cautionary tales about the dangers of forests abound. Many of them illustrate how easy it is for unprepared tourists to lose their way; in extreme cases hikers have even simply disappeared. Forests also pose a threat to farmers' crops and livestock, as they are inhabited by animals like wild boars (*Sus scrofa*) and mountain lions (*Puma concolor puma*) which, although rarely attacking humans, can cause significant economic damage.

While logging activities may occur within them, forests are never fully transformed into stable, predictable reservoirs of natural resources that can be accumulated and extracted by loggers. In contrast to *woods*, which are deemed as more apt space for commercial forestry, *forests* show some of the qualities that Latour has associated with an ontological formation defined as *plasma*, "namely that which is not yet formatted, not yet measured, not yet socialized, not yet engaged in metrological chains, and not yet covered, surveyed, mobilized, or subjectified" (2005, 244). Another key feature of forests is their characterization as a primordial feature of the landscape, in contrast with *woods*, which are attained and demarcated through human labor. The origins of forests are sometimes explained as the result of God's action, an idea common among Catholic and evangelical residents living around the countryside of Pucón. Lidia, a resident of the nearby village of Pichares, once recounted her memories of visiting relatives in the closest big city in Argentina, whose surroundings, commonly referred to as *pampa*, immediately looked barren and dry to her when compared to southern Chile: "There, one cannot find any pines to gather *piñones* [araucaria tree nuts]. *Diosito* [God] forgot to sow pines. Well, and in Argentina, he didn't sow much; there are almost no trees there."[9] Although not everyone in the area would explain the origins of native forests in Christian terms, Lidia's analogy remains a powerful reminder of forests as primordial features of the landscape.

Unlike a *forest*, a primordial entity resistant to human domestication, a *wood* is always the result of a particular form of human labor, one ideally intended to ensure their domestication vis-à-vis their constant tendency to turn back into forests if left unattended. A wood can be referred to as a general category, as in sentences such as "the beauty of the wood" (*la belleza del bosque*), which can be overheard in conversations among locals and visitors. Yet, around my fieldwork area, woods are typically described as forested areas produced by human labor. A wood is frequently spoken of in the genitive (someone's wood), thus implying that woods are likely to be acknowledged as objects of property more than forests. A wood is also described according to its potential economic value. Residents recognize differences among woods mostly in terms of their financial worth. Size, of course, is a key economic indicator, but economic value can also be based on the specific types and qualities of trees found within a *bosque*.

In Coilaco Valley, commercial forestry experienced a brief boom in the 1960s, when two companies operated in the area to meet growing demand for the Patagonian oak (*Nothofagus obliqua*), which was considered an ideal wood for manufacturing railroad sleepers (*durmientes*) during a time of network expansion (Otero 2006, 99). Most residents at the time viewed the arrival of these two companies as an opportunity for new income during a period of widespread poverty in rural areas. Those with less land hoped to secure jobs as laborers at the companies' sawmills, working exhausting shifts of over ten hours a day. Others rented out their properties to the two companies, despite being aware that the short-term rental would turn into the future depletion of forest resources. Today, commercial forestry is a main source of income for a handful of local families typically living in a higher section of the valley and owning slightly more land than their neighbors. Even for the owners of the few small sawmills in the area, this activity is typically complemented by other sources of income, either from independent work, as in the case of cattle ranching, or employment in the tourism industry. Yet logging remains a common activity for all residents and is typically carried out in woods rather than forests. These woods are often located farther from households than forests and are more likely within state-owned conservation areas. Not only are woods necessary for the construction or day-to-day repair of houses and storage buildings, but they are also intentionally preserved as safety measures in the face of unexpected economic crises, when wood can be more intensively commercialized to ensure additional cash flow. The sudden onset of an illness of a family member, for instance, would necessitate more timber commercialization, since the support offered by the national public health service (FONASA, Fondo Nacional de Salud) is seldom sufficient to cover costs such as inactivity in agriculture or trips to hospitals.

Preserving a wood for the future is not an easy choice. The prospect of overlogging is a concrete danger exactly because cash flow from wood sales, albeit small, is always readily available. In one circumstance, Francisca, a resident from Coilaco, heard from a distance the sound of a chainsaw and immediately associated it with a younger relative of hers known for his excessive drinking: "He's cutting his trees to buy drinks in town; he's not going to have anything left in the future." Francisca's disapproval of her relative's behavior resonates with a much broader understanding of labor among smallholders in the area, for whom work is necessarily an incessant activity if a family is to remain afloat. Cautionary tales about the need for constant work abound around Coilaco Valley. On more than one occasion, I heard about the case of a local large landholder of British ancestry who was able to expand his properties and establish one of the largest estates in the area. His heir, in only a few years, lost all his family wealth due to a lack of discipline and love of gambling, according to rumors.

The existence of woods depends on a delicate balance between their domestication through logging and the preservation of trees for future use. This balance is precarious, as it requires careful management to ensure that while trees are harvested for immediate economic gain, enough are left standing to maintain the health of the ecosystem and support future logging activities. Woods, which have been created from forests through logging, are always in danger of returning to their previous status. Among residents of Coilaco Valley, the history of their settlement is expressed mainly through memories associated with the transformation of forests into woods through human intervention, as well as the opposite trend. One afternoon, Italo, a man in his fifties, gave me an example of how the forest landscape could reveal local history in ways that I was completely unaware of: "This wood was right where my neighbors used to live," he explained. "It was all clean back then; there were lots of cherry trees, and I used to pick fruit there. The Martínez [family] went away and now it is *monte* [forest] once again."

In Italo's account, woods exemplify the value of farmers' hard work as a temporary achievement, while forests stand for the disturbing prospect of land abandonment and rewilding. Here, I use *rewilding* to refer to the gradual process of wilderness regrowth that occurs when land is left untended by farmers and loggers. In Coilaco, the growth of forests and that of local groups are contiguous and interlinked processes (see Rival 1993, 648). The history of these processes is ingrained in the complex textures that compose what at first sight appears simply as a forest. More than other landscapes, forests are capable of inscribing multiple past activities through traces scattered across the landscape, such as the discreet alternations of the shapes and colors of individual trees and their combinations, whose perception requires refined skills of observation. These traces tell us of histories of anthropogenic forests marked by "biographies of survival in the face of fire, disease, grazing and human cutting, looping and pruning" (Mathews 2022, 54). They also highlight that the domestication of forests and settlement are fragile accomplishments, as the threat of land abandonment always lingers.

Domesticating Forests: What Human Labor Can and Should Do

Domestication is driven not only by a desire for mastery over nature, but also by a belief in the human capacity to ensure the flourishing of nonhuman life in ways the ultimately serve human interests. For smallholding foresters in the southern Andean valleys, forest domestication is a precarious and reversible endeavor, yet it remains crucial for sustaining both the land's productivity and the ongoing continuity of settlements in the face of the persistent threat of rewilding in these frontier territories. Under these conditions, logging is not merely an extractive practice; rather, it plays a vital role in the process of domestication, theoretically preventing certain woods from reverting to their untamed, wild state by maintaining their domesticated status. Italo made this point very clear to me during a conversation we had about the impact of logging on the landscape in and around Coilaco Valley: "Woods [*bosques*] require our intervention to exist. If not, how can we possibly live? This would all be forest [*selva*]."

Without logging, forest regrowth is unstoppable. But logging needs to be carried out in such a way that uncontrolled deforestation does not take place. The carving out of woods from forests is made possible by the habitual practice of selective logging. These practices are intended to create the conditions necessary for an ideal type of wood, typically defined by foresters as *clean*. A clean wood (*un bosque limpio*) is an object of praise by landowners and their neighbors, as it stands for the owner's ability to properly take care of it. It can be easily crossed by humans, as its undergrowth is kept in check and the density of its trees is evenly distributed through the selection of trees to be logged. Selective logging follows a principle said to apply to agricultural work in general: It is performed not through the application of preconceived schemes, but rather thanks to skilled, improvisational responses to a constantly changing environment (see Ingold 2000, 147). Trees that are considered of little use to the landowner, for instance for construction or heating, are left standing. Similarly, young trees struggling to grow due to the intensity of the forest canopy and underbrush are rarely chopped down.

There is no agreed-upon standard for deciding which trees should be logged and which should be spared, but foresters tend to use two informal categories: *good* and *bad*. By conserving the good trees for future commercial use and cutting down the bad ones—those more suited to immediate needs like firewood—loggers aim to extract economic value from the woods while ensuring they are not entirely depleted. At the same, an improvisational practice of selective logging is thought of as limiting competition for resources among trees. The significance of differentiating between young and mature trees for selective logging is evident in the local classification of tree species prized for their timber. In this region, Patagonian oaks are categorized as *hualle* when they are young, while the mature trees are known as *pellín*. The latter is particularly valued as a reliable source of timber for construction.

The activity of keeping a wood clean coincides only partially with the objectives and ideals of forest management. While they are both intended to ensure the future preservation of forest resources through the selective extraction of trees, their logics for the selection of trees often—but not always—diverge. The implementation of forest management plans, overseen by the forest service CONAF, is a prerequisite for obtaining the logging permits necessary for the commercialization of timber. For foresters in southern Chile, forest management plans are primarily viewed as a bureaucratic necessity rather than a clear benefit to their work. While these plans are essential for obtaining the necessary logging permits, they are not without their challenges, often complicating rather than aiding their efforts in sustainable forest use. Management plans are based on the estimation of canopy density, an activity carried out once in the field by a forest officer. The level of canopy density determines the average number of trees to be logged. This estimated level is also used to calculate a minimum distance among trees that should not be logged. For many foresters, the selection of trees cannot simply be based on their distance, a criterion that contrasts sharply with the distinction between good and bad trees to be logged or spared according to specific economic needs. As a forester from Coilaco Valley explained, the selection of trees for logging takes both their qualities and age into account: "If I see two good trees next to each other, I'll leave them. It doesn't make any sense to save a bad tree, which might not grow well and die in a few years, at the expense of a good one" (Di Giminiani 2016).[10]

In Coilaco, aesthetic judgments of forest landscapes, such as those praising the cleanliness of a wood, are deeply intertwined with historical repre-

sentations of successful domestication of frontier forests by the forerunners of today's colonos. As observed in other rural contexts, descriptions
of landscape tend to reveal "a discourse of morality as they emphasize the
role of hard work and the application of knowledge" (Lee 2007, 93) in transforming unproductive land into agricultural fields. In many settler frontiers,
this discourse is closely tied to masculine ideals of mastery over nature (see
Morgensen 2012), as seen in the portrayal of colonos as strong men exerting
force against threatening robbers and wild animals in both fictional and his-
toriographical accounts from Chile (Durán 2013, 18). In the Andean valleys
where this book is situated, forestry remains strongly anchored to images
of male hard work, even when there is not a strictly gendered division of
agricultural labor at play.

Forest domestication, however, is not only a male endeavor. There are
other forms of domestication that stand as achievements in the face of the
latent prospect of rewilding. In one circumstance, Juana recounted with
nostalgia the time when, during her youth, gardens rich in colorful flowers
could be found next to each house: "Where we used to live there were lots
of gardens, but then the *murras* [shrubbery] started to come out, and that
saddened me. Flowers just give you happiness." Historically, gardens have
served as powerful ideological symbols of colonial mastery over nature, as
we see in the growth of botanical gardens paralleling European imperialism
in the eighteenth and nineteenth centuries (see Schiebinger and Swan 2007).
They can also act as productive sites for the articulation of affective relations
between humans and plants (Archambault 2016, 256). Juana's words highlight a profound emotional connection between gardens and memories of
the past, especially those tied to human labor. At the same time, they reveal
a broader history of colonial settlement in frontier territories.

In the memories and experiences of smallholder settlers, human labor
emerges as an effective set of actions contributing to the precarious maintenance of woods as vital and economically productive assemblages of multiple agencies. This image of domestication hardly resonates with common-
place narratives of this same process under settler colonialism. As proposed
by Swanson et al., civilizatory narratives of domestication as an irreversible
process, a project based on mastery and control over nature, fail to capture the complexity of "marginal domestications"—in other words, all those
experiences in which domestication unfolds not as a plannable process of
production but rather as a two-way dynamic, with nonhumans capable of

acting upon human attempts to guide and control their vitalism (2018, 13). While dominant narratives of domestication continue to guide and motivate processes of settler expansion, the experience of domestication is best understood once contextualized "in the gap between what is taken as wild and what is domesticated" (Kirksey 2015, 5). The limits of human labor in concretizing durable forest domestication are largely dependent on the vegetal agency of forests which, as suggested by Bennet, does not respond to a mechanical order of fixed laws. Rather, it unfolds in a scene of not-fully-predictable encounters between multiple kinds of actants (2010, 97).

In a context where domestication is an uncertain process involving entangled agencies with no guaranteed outcomes, there is limited trust in human abilities to transform the environment merely by following initial intentions or without risking depletion. Instead, there is clear awareness of both the objective and normative limits of domestication. In other words, forests are recalcitrant to their transformation into woods and, as such, they cannot be fully domesticated. Furthermore, the practice of forestry itself can lead to environmental depletion rather than sustainable management. For many residents of Coilaco Valley, logging can have catastrophic consequences on the local environment, in particular by causing water loss. Unlike fast-growing cash crop trees, such as *Eucaliptus globulus* and Monterrey pine trees (*Pinus radiata*), commonly known among farmers in southern Chile for their tendency to "suck up water" (*chupar el agua*), "native trees" (*árboles nativos*) that populate frontier forests are believed to be capable of retaining both surface and underground water. Carlos, a resident of Coilaco, illustrates this perspective on the water-forest relationship by referencing a nearby *mallín*, a wetland area with underground water, which has steadily shrunk in size over time: "The *mallín* doesn't carry much water now. As there is little nature left around it, there is little water in it, so that the heat stays high." In this case, deforestation was the main cause of the drainage of this water source, which in turn damaged its ability to attract atmospheric water, leading to higher temperatures. Rain and snow, in this case, are not entirely free of human influence, as higher numbers of native trees would ensure a greater intake of snow and rain in the winter.

A similar perspective on the potential dangers of human interference with forests is reflected in local views on the controlled use of fire. Many residents, especially those with experience in forestry, acknowledge that while the controlled application of fire can be a useful tool for clearing land and managing vegetation, it also carries significant risks. Clearing by fire has almost disappeared over the last decades due to the introduction of environmental restrictions, as well as a growing awareness among farmers that the dangers of the practice outnumber the benefits. Today, small landholders might set fires to clear only small portions of agricultural land and facilitate a fallow period. No landholder in Coilaco Valley would apply fire for forest clearing, as the dangers of wildfire, especially in the drier summer months, are all too evident.[11] The responsibility for wildfires is usually attributed to careless tourists who may have failed to properly extinguish campfires. Less commonly, arson is suspected, with rumors linking it to insurance fraud and land speculation. Wildfires are generally remembered as catastrophic events. Their memory is embedded in the landscape, associated with changes in the color of grass and forest cover, the presence of patches of younger trees next to older ones, and the white skeletons of old trunks. And while fires are generally treated as consequences of human action, their effects and containment lie largely outside of human control. On different occasions, residents explained that fires are often dormant but can be activated at any time, since tree roots might be smoldering underground, ready to ignite in a strong wind. Candea proposes that what fires bring into view "are the tangibly divergent ways in which people and places are assembled and entangled" (2008, 210). The fears and consequences of wildfires around the Andes highlight how the assembly of frontier forests and their human inhabitants is an unstable process. This process is shaped by a form of domestication that is reversible, difficult to control, and unfolds in a world where the responsiveness of nonhumans is highly unpredictable.

While they are mutually responsive and agentive, human labor is the only force able to ensure the productivity and vitality of forests as much as their depletion. I understand *vitality* as a set of forces animating individual life processes but dependent on affective relations over which the individual has limited control. My definition of this term is indebted to some recent manifestations of vitalism in the social sciences and political theory. Unlike classic vitalism, which imagines vitality as a separate force entering and animating a physical body, or as an inherent quality contained within specific forms of life, current approaches to vitalism have drawn attention to the embeddedness of materiality and affects (Bennett 2010, xiii; see also Duarte 2021; Greco 2005). Such an embeddedness refers to the coexistence of two sources of vitality: one given by the agential nature of matter associated with the internal material diversity of each being, as in the case of internal forces that render forests autonomous assemblages, and the other constituted by relationships of mutual influence, or affects, as in the case of the responsive and reciprocal relationship of domestication.

In the experiences of smallholding colonos, the vitality of domesticated forests, or woods, depends on the effects of domestication in limiting and directing forest regrowth. This relation, I claim, is pivotal to a broader understanding of what it is to be human in relation to nonhuman others, specifically those comprising forests as assemblages. *Settlers' alterhumanism* situates labor as a defining feature of humanity and frames it as being at the intersection of two possibilities, neither of them simply reproducing anthropocentric ideas of mastery over nature typical of settler colonial narratives. On the one hand, humanity is associated with an imagined capacity and desire to protect nonhuman life, closely resembling Palsson's notion of paternalism as a "balanced reciprocity, presupposing human responsibility" (2016, 42); on the other, the human prerogative in directing the vitality of nonhumans contrasts with the realization of the precariousness and reversibility of domestication, particularly in the context of settlement. In this case, *becom-*

FIGURE 4 A sawmill (Photograph by the author)

ing human through and with nonhuman others is an ontological and ethical process built around a tension between desires for domestication and the recognition of the unpredictable responsiveness of nonhumans as subjects. A focus on the limits of forest domestication makes evident that settlement, as experienced by smallholder colonos, is a precarious life project that requires the constant application of human labor to curtail any effects of forest growth and abandonment. In this light, belonging among settlers cannot be treated as a mere social condition, but rather as an emotional expression of attachment to land cultivated through memories and experiences of both settlement and abandonment.

"The Small Ones": Settlers' Belonging and the Prospect of Abandonment

Among smallholding settlers in southern Chile, there is no distinct or uniform identification with a community, culture, or particular religious affiliation. Participation in local religious groups, either Catholic or evangelical, is often loose, and there are cases in which identification with either of the two religious groupings is temporary and shifting. Similarly, while conservative sentiments tend to dominate in rural areas of southern Chile, political affiliations among settlers span both right- and left-wing ideologies, making it difficult to discern any clear pattern. Support for political parties and local politicians is, in most cases, contingent on local concerns and personal interests, a scenario that reflects the widespread disaffection with politics in Chile after the initial optimism of the return to democracy in the 1990s (see Luna 2021). Local grassroots associations occasionally emerge and thrive, particularly those formed as part of state and nongovernmental programs for the development of micro-entrepreneurship. Nonetheless, political representation among colonos remains feeble as a consequence of historical rejection of cooperativism in favor of a stronger commitment toward individual and family economic organizations, a tendency amplified by the demise of grassroots rural politics during the military regime in the 1970s and 80s.

But even in the absence of a clear identification with what we might consider a "settler community," feelings of belonging remain strong. Settlers' sense of belonging seldom manifests as a pre-existing social identity tied to a place of origin and reproduced in new settler environments (Dominy

1995, 358). Rather, being a colono is a sense of belonging rooted in both past and present engagement with the ongoing transformation of the local environment. In depicting the life of white settlers in Kenya, McIntosh has shown how belonging is cultivated through lifelong emotional and affective practices of remembering, which include frequent references to childhood memories (2016, 72). Among smallholding colonos of southern Chile, belonging centers similarly on shared histories of attachment to the land, which are transmitted across generations. Identifying as a colono revolves around the challenges smallholder farmers encounter in frontier territories, their participation in the historical process of *hacer patria* (making a homeland), and the sense of comfort and ease that rural life, despite its many hardships, offers in contrast to the alienation and difficulties of city life.

Among small, landholding settlers, the category of *colono* frequently overlaps with the common category of *campesino*, a term indicating both independent farmers and peasants working for bigger agricultural producers. Since the term *campesino* is shared with Indigenous Mapuche neighbors, identification by oneself and others as colonos works as a marker of distinction with Mapuche residents of Andean valleys. Here, Mapuche-settler relations resemble little of the highly hierarchical scenario of more central areas of southern Chile, where heirs of European settlers are today powerful agricultural entrepreneurs employing local mestizo and Mapuche residents. Around Coilaco, colonos and Mapuche residents know each other well from working together in town and attending the same schools and churches. Many families are created by mixed marriages. In the words of many colonos living around Coilaco, relations with *paisanos*—a term colloquially employed to refer to Mapuche people as native—are harmonious, especially when compared to other parts of southern Chile where land disputes are more frequent and tense. Complicity can also emerge as a result of shared political concerns. Around the towns of Pucón and Currarehue, most Indigenous mobilizations target infrastructural projects, such as the growing small-scale hydroelectric plants, known as *centrales de paso*, which often concern settlers just as much over possible waterflow diversion.[12]

Settlers' intimacy with Mapuche neighbors, friends, and relatives, however, does not mean that Indigenous-settler relations are simply free of conflict and racial discrimination. Around Coilaco, animosity between settlers and their Mapuche neighbors might arise in specific legal contentions over property demarcation or land use, but it has rarely turned into claims of land restitution. Racial discrimination, however, is evident in many aspects of daily life, such as the use of demeaning labels like *indios* ("Indians") and *Mapuchitos* ("small Mapuches"), which are occasionally directed at Mapuche people by non-Indigenous residents. These terms are often used casually or even jokingly in everyday interactions, even directly toward Mapuche family members and friends. The persistence of these discriminatory labels can be explained in the intentions of some settlers to reaffirm a higher class and racial status than their Indigenous neighbors, concerned as they are with their derogatory classification as campesinos among townspeople.

Another source of anti-Indigenous sentiment among smallholding colonos is their discomfort with access to affirmative action policies, especially in agriculture. Although they are small, the subsidies endowed to Mapuche rural residents are questioned by many settlers, who feel they share the same needs as Indigenous smallholders, especially in comparison with large landholders. Smallholder colonos in southern Chile often refute the idea that their Mapuche neighbors are unconditionally moved by a spiritual connection with forests, an idea commonly reproduced in environmentalist discourses. As observed in other colonial contexts, settlers' claims to land are built around an image of *hard work* as an authentic form of land attachment, in opposition to representations of Indigenous people that question their role of custodianship (McIntosh 2016, 52). As Indigenous spiritual connections with the forest world are questioned by some settlers, so is hard work elevated as an intrinsic characteristic of settlers in opposition to the Mapuche population, who would supposedly lack such a value. Luisa, a woman living in a nearby hamlet from Coilaco, once recounted her experience of working with Mapuche producers participating in the same technical assistance program: "At first it was hard for them to participate in the producers' group. The Mapuche plan everything day by day, never in the long run. Eventually it all turned out fine." Planning for the future through the economic preservation of resources, such as timber, is one of the most recurrent images through which settlers frame their belonging while articulating alterity with Mapuche farmers, who are denied such value, and powerful market actors, for whom economic growth is made possible by investment practices rather than hard work.

Another key marker of distinction in terms of belonging as frontier residents relates to large agribusiness entrepreneurs and land investors, commonly referred to as the "big ones" (*los grandes*). Many colonos from Andean

valleys self-identify as the "small ones" (*los pequeños*), to highlight the ineq-
uities they face in maintaining a sustainable, family-run enterprise, especially
when compared to the powerful market players. This phenomenon reflects
the asymmetrical nature of land redistribution, a pattern common across
many contexts of colonization (see Campbell 2015, 46–51). Being a small one
means to own an average of around thirty hectares, an amount larger than
residents of Mapuche Indigenous Communities—whose properties rarely
exceed ten hectares—but smaller than large landholders, whose properties
range typically from two hundred to one thousand hectares. While the average land owned by small landholding settlers is often sufficient to maintain
independence as producers and avoid working in the service industry, they
are typically not large enough to make agriculture a viable or attractive source
of income for younger generations. Cash flow is often scarce and inconsistent,
making it difficult to maintain a stable, middle-class status—something that
employment in the service industry could more reliably provide.

A major source of resentment against the big ones is the state itself. Many
colonos in the area see themselves as deeply committed to the historical
process of making homeland. Adherence to nationalist values contrasts with
perceptions of state neglect. The state (*el estado*) is often portrayed as un-
sympathetic to small-scale landholders, who see themselves as outcompeted
by more powerful market actors in attaining public support in the form of
agricultural subsidies. Agricultural and entrepreneurial schemes are capitalized by agribusiness actors, whether through connections to state institutions and politicians or simply because of a positive structural bias toward
large companies for their theoretical ability to generate wealth in a typical
trickle-down fashion. Cynicism about false promises of development on the
part of the state is reflected in a general sense of distrust toward politics.
Relations with local authorities are mostly instrumental, as in the case of
petitions for infrastructural improvement in the area. Elections and participation in political parties might generate interest, but many are aware that
any change is bound to have little impact on their struggle to maintain family
farming and avoid outmigration. On more than one occasion, I heard the
following sentence as a commentary about engagement with politics: "In the
end, one has to keep working anyway."

The status of being small ones that many smallholding colonos assign to
themselves is built around one feeling in particular: that of abandonment

(*abandono*). This motif indicates not only neglect by state institutions, but also the looming prospect of abandonment of fields and agricultural practices caused mainly by migration toward urban areas. As laconically stated by one middle-aged resident, Oscar, "The youth leave, and the old ones die here. They want to sell the land. This will all go back to being forest." Signs of past, present, and future abandonment proliferate in Coilaco Valley. Derelict houses are powerful reminders of recent outmigration to cities. The ubiquity of "For Sale" signs indicate expectations of a real estate boom. Over the past three decades, all around the town of Pucón, urbanites with eco-friendly interests have been purchasing property and, in those cases where they were able to secure jobs in surrounding towns, have moved there. However, expectations often remain unfulfilled, as purchases concentrate in areas with developed infrastructure, leaving many properties for sale, like those in Coilaco, to remain untouched by recent gentrification.

* * *

For small-scale settlers, their engagement with the forest world forms the foundation of both a shared sense of belonging and a broader definition of humanity—one that emphasizes our unique ability to both foster and end the existence of nonhuman life. Such a definition is pivotal to a model of humanity and its alterity that I have called settlers' alterhumanism. In this particular model, shared experiences of *becoming human through nonhuman others* stem from the lived memories and practices of domestication and settlement by settlers themselves, rather than from a broader ideological discourse on humanity and nature typically associated with settler colonialism. Becoming human is an embodied and discursive process through which humans are assigned the ontological role of domesticators, while nonhumans, particularly forests, are recognized as subjects with emotional capacities that respond to human labor and exhibit a tendency toward rewilding. Settlers' alterhumanism emphasizes the ethical impact of domestication, valuing human labor as essential not only for domestication but also for fostering vitality in nonhumans, particularly forests. Domestication is part of a broader struggle against the abandonment of frontier territories, and this struggle is imbued with ethical motives, first and foremost the spontaneous participation within the nation-building process known as *hacer patria.* The ethics also concern the search for a form of domestication that does not translate into depletion, as heirs of early twentieth-century settlers are aware of the cumulative destructive effects of forest clearings carried out in the early historical moments of settlement.

In framing the principles of settlers' alterhumanism, I have emphasized the precariousness of domestication among settlers at the margins of the colonial project within the broader historical process of settler expansion and its transformative and destructive effects. In the next chapter, I explore another model of alterhumanism shaped by the enduring consequences of settler expansion. Among Indigenous Mapuche landholders, cosmological configurations of human and nonhuman agency, alongside memories of dispossession and resettlement, merge into an ontological and ethical view of humanity that emphasizes the mutual constitution of people and place while acknowledging the unique human capacities for care and depletion.

Chapter 2

Indigenous Settlers?

Histories of Resettlement and Care in Mapuche Frontier Life

"The people who founded this place were all Mapuche. They came here as settlers. At that time, around these mountains, there were *winka* [non-Indigenous people], but also Indigenous settlers (*colonos indígenas*)." With these words, Rodrigo, a Mapuche man in his seventies, recounted the history of the small mountain village of Maite, founded by a group of displaced Mapuche people in the aftermath of the Chilean military invasion at the end of the nineteenth century. In the years after Chilean conquest, Indigenous and mestizo squatters flocked to remote areas of this recently annexed part of the country and settled on unclaimed state land (*terrenos fiscales*) or unoccupied private properties, in the hope of having their ownership legally recognized in the future. Squatters' occupations took place at the same time that white European settlers were formally endowed with land in more fertile areas of southern Chile, and Mapuche residential communities, known as *lof* (Millalén 2006, 38), were divided and reassigned, leaving the Indigenous populations with only a fraction of the territory they once occupied.[1] In remote Andean valleys, both displaced Mapuche people and non-Indigenous farmers faced the challenges of settlement as they sought better lives. Today, Maite is a small hamlet located on the narrow and densely forested valley of Río Machín, twenty kilometers from the town of Curarrehue and less than ten kilometers from the border with Argentina. Most houses are concentrated around the two local schools and a medical outpost, with households of both Mapuche and colono families located in its surroundings. To this day, among winkas and Mapuche residents alike, histories about their antecessors' settlement are recounted with pride. As I have learned in Maite over the years, the fact that the category of *settler* is employed as a marker of identity among some Mapuche people constitutes no impediment for fully identifying as Mapuche, an ethnonym that can be literally translated as people (*che*) of the *mapu*, a term meaning land and territory. It is a term that has come to signify the condition of being both native and a victim of colonization.

It was not the first time I had heard about the initially surprising idea that Mapuche people could also be settlers. A few kilometers away from Rodrigo's home, in Coilaco Valley, I met two men in their sixties on different occasions. Alberto used to live in a homestead on the steep side of a small mountain peak, surrounded by trees and overlooking a group of houses corresponding to a local *Comunidad Indígena* ("Indigenous Community").[2] Alberto is well known in the area as a skilled wicker craftsman, selling baskets and furniture to markets in the nearby towns of Pucón and Villarrica. He is also respected as one of the few truly fluent speakers of the Mapudungun language in the area. The other man, Claudio, lives with his wife in a higher section of the Coilaco Valley. From Claudio I had the privilege of learning about the history of local settlers as well as that of the nearby Mapuche community, or "their history," as he phrased it. Only months later did I realize that the two men were brothers. Despite their Mapuche last name, the family of these two men included both non-Indigenous and Mapuche antecessors, mostly from other areas of southern Chile. Alberto identified more as Mapuche than his brother, who saw himself more as a colono. Their family properties, originally located in lots adjacent to a Mapuche community, had been assigned by colonization officials in the early twentieth century at a time when non-Indigenous and Mapuche squatters alike were occupying unclaimed land. Claudio moved away from his household earlier in his life and, after getting married, relocated to an area where most of his neighbors were non-Indigenous settlers. Alberto, instead, maintained close relationships with his elder relatives, learning everything he could about Mapuche culture and language. He also established close links with members of the local Mapuche community, participating actively in ceremonies and meetings.

These two accounts about the entanglement of Indigenous and Mapuche biographies exemplify how social belonging in frontier areas of southern Chile is defined by a colonizer-colonized dichotomy that nonetheless remains unstable in intimate settings. Entanglements of Indigenous and settler statuses, most clearly visible in the apparent oxymoron of *Indigenous settler*, originated in the violent displacement suffered by Mapuche kin groups from their native land, who could secure land access only by relocating to frontier areas and making land claims to state institutions as settlers. In a scenario characterized by unstable cycles of land occupations and evictions under feeble state supervision, "both Mapuches and non-Mapuches staked their claims in terms of the land's status as public and their rights to be considered colonos" (Klubock 2014, 116).

For some Mapuche people, adopting the category of *settler* was often a strategic option with no consequence on their identification with Indigenous practices and values. For others, it turned out to be an irreversible transformation, part of a broader project of assimilation. *Hacer patria*—a process defined in the previous chapter as both an intimate struggle for place-making among settlers and the nationalization of uncharted territories—elicits mixed and often contradictory reactions from Mapuche residents of the Andean valleys. In some cases, it is openly resisted through claims of sovereignty and refusal of national belonging; in others, it is embraced insofar as many Mapuche residents see Indigenous rights over land and aspirations of self-governance as not necessarily discordant with their self-assigned role of citizens, imbricated with the ongoing process of nation-building in frontier areas. In conversations with Mapuche interlocutors from Coilaco and Maite, I frequently heard the view that Indigenous rights need not be justified by a radical separation from the national majority, but rather by emphasizing the unique and integral role of their people within the nation's history. "We were here before anybody else. We are the true Chileans" is a common sentence expressing concomitant feelings of national belonging and desires for Indigenous sovereignty.

The intersections between Indigenous and settler identities highlights a key challenge in understanding settler colonialism: how to emphasize the intersections between Indigenous and settler experiences while also acknowledging the hierarchical and opposing dynamics that shape the unequal distribution of economic and political power between these groups. Any critique of binarism between colonized and colonizers in favor of a perspective emphasizing their hybridity might potentially serve as yet another instrument to suppress the recognition of Indigenous differences (see Wolfe 2013). Dismantling binarism is a necessary step in avoiding the encapsulation of human sub-

jectivities into discursive categories of identity that disregard complex genealogical histories of interethnic relations. Yet the conditions under which social
relations contribute to shifting forms of subjectivities necessarily unfold along
deep structural hierarchies, particularly evident in the enduring significance
of settler-native dichotomies. A central factor in distinguishing Indigenous
and settler identities is the relationship between people and land. For Mapuche communities living on the settler frontier, this connection defines a
unique way of becoming human, reflected in their concepts of personhood
and belonging. In Mapuche thought, the interconnection between land and
people is embodied in the concept of *tuwün*, meaning "place of origin." This
loosely defined locality is an integral part of Mapuche identity, reflected in the
shared traits and dispositions of individuals who are genealogically linked to
the same territory (see Chihuailaf 1999, 51; Course 2011, 46; Ñanculef 2016,
65; Quidel 2020, 111; Quilaqueo and Quintriqueo 2010, 342).

Connections to place are not solely inherited from the past but are also
formed through the active process of engaging with and transforming the
land, which possesses the unique capacity to shape and express one's potential identity (Di Giminiani 2018, 83). Along the settler frontier, attachment
to place among Mapuche landowners is cultivated through histories of forest
transformation guided by both settler and Indigenous environmental values and practices. The emergence of the figure of the "Indigenous settler"
suggests that another form of settlement, one that does not reflect settler
desires of native conquest, mastery over nature, and capital accumulation,
is possible. Indigenous settlement is all about the ongoing transformation
of hostile frontier environments and adaptations to them, which allow the
reconstitution of Mapuche agricultural life. It is also about rearticulating
the enduring relationship with the land (*mapu*), from which a specific way
of becoming human emerges, one desired as part of the precarious struggle
for remaining Mapuche.

In the previous chapter, we learned about the particular configuration of
the human emerging from the history of settler expansion in frontier territories. Now, we turn to another form of alterhumanism, rooted in the violence
of displacement and dispossession, alongside Indigenous ontologies that
shape understandings of nonhuman agency—specifically, the possibility of
the mutual constitution of land and human personhood, which forms the basis of Mapuche senses of belonging. By drawing upon memories of displacement and resettlement and ideas and experiences of human-environmental

relations, I characterize Mapuche alterhumanism as a form of *becoming human through and with nonhuman others*. This perspective acknowledges the importance of domestication and settlement as human actions essential to Indigenous survival, while recognizing that places to be settled and domesticated are animated by diverse nonhuman agencies.

Becoming human in this case is an ongoing work of ontological differentiation from nonhuman others that presupposes emplacement as a primary articulator of humanity. Emplacement in this case is about transforming the place around us to make us who we are. Nonhumans, like forests, can be recalcitrant to human domestication and care. Others, such as crops, are understood as the result of human labor. However, they all share the potential for partaking in the configuration of a landscape capable of molding human behaviors and subjectivities. Mapuche ideas of human personhood emphasize the ability of place of origin, or tuwün, to act as a potentiality of the self for individuals with genealogical connections to the same locality. Rather than a historically continuous condition of consubstantiality, the co-constitution between place and people consists of an open project enabled by settlement and yet also threatened by it when settlement means environmental destruction. A close look at the manifestations of alterhumanism in Mapuche frontier life reveals how the project of becoming human is ultimately built upon relationships with others that are made and unmade in the struggle to find a place in the world. Such a struggle raises multiple ethical questions about human abilities and responsibilities for transforming the world around us, starting from the historical conundrum of having to adopt settler practices and ideas in order to endure displacement and dispossession and ultimately remain Mapuche.

Becoming Settlers, Remaining Mapuche

Settler colonialism centers on dispossession. It is a process facilitated by violent invasions—often genocidal in scale—followed by the settlers' appropriation of land and other resources. However, settler colonialism neither starts nor ends with the act or event of dispossession alone. Defining settler colonialism as a structure of power rather than an event (Wolfe 1999, 163) prompts us to recognize the continuity of dispossession into the present: Once the initial violent phase of appropriation comes to an end, it is replaced by legal frameworks designed to perpetuate the separation of Indigenous people from their land. Characterizing colonial encroachment as a thing of the past, a historical moment (Povinelli 2002, 154), works to delegitimize present-day calls to pay attention to the enduring legacy of colonialism raised by colonized groups (Veracini 2010, 41). This legacy can materialize, for instance, in the ongoing privatization of Indigenous commons. In the continuing disinheritance of colonialism, there is no longer need for overt violence, as consent to commodification can be generated through the mechanisms of multicultural policies of recognition and participation (Coulthard 2014, 13).

The latency and continuity of dispossession means that Indigenous alienation from natural resources is not merely material; it also concerns the erasure of relationships with the nonhumans constitutive of Indigenous belongings. Along many settler frontiers across the globe, dispossession and assimilation are intertwined processes. Across Latin America, assimilatory pressures and lack of alternative economic opportunities have contributed to the incorporation of Indigenous populations into peasantry, *campesinado*. This social transformation led Indigenous connections with land and other resources to become more and more feeble, both materially and affectively.

The history of Mapuche forced confinement into *reducciones* at the turn of the nineteenth century, a process generally known as *radicación* (Marimán 2006, 121), makes a clear case for the mutual articulation of dispossession and assimilation. We know from the previous chapter that violent annexation of Mapuche territories was soon followed by a process of land redistribution designed for the benefit of European settlers. A secondary objective of land distribution was to relocate Mapuche populations by granting collective endowment titles, known as *Títulos de Merced*, coordinated by the Indigenous land agency of the time, the *Comisión Radicadora de Indígenas* (see Calbucura 1996). The establishment of a *reducción* presupposed the designation of a local representative known as a *cacique*, who only occasionally corresponded to the traditional authority of the *lonko*, the headman of a local lineage representing the residential territories known as *lof* (Course 2011, 47; Quidel 2020, 206).[3] While the assignation of collective titles was in theory functional to Indigenous land protection, reservation land often fell into the hands of settlers through opaque transactions (Caniuqueo 2006, 157) or simply by extending fences over adjacent properties, a practice known as *corridas de cerco* (Richards 2013, 52). Caciques occasionally succeeded in contesting illegal transactions in courts overseeing Indigenous land issues, known as *Juzgados de Indios*. But in most cases local authorities turned a blind eye to transgressions by settlers (Correa et al. 2005; Mallon 2005), especially when they were wealthy and influential estate owners.

Land grabbing was one of the main factors behind the spiraling land shortage that affected virtually all *reducciones* a few decades after the imposition of the reservation system. A combination of population growth and limited economic means for acquiring properties outside *reducciones* left the Mapuche population vulnerable to land scarcity and its distressing consequences. This led to a sharp rise in rural poverty, forcing reservation members to either find employment on local agricultural estates (*fundos*)—often under exploitative conditions resembling debt peonage, which persisted until the 1960s—or to migrate to urban areas. With the continued removal of family ties, Mapuche rural residents became more and more accustomed to inhabiting non-Indigenous spaces, particularly workplaces and schools, where anti-Indigenous discrimination was rampant. As shown by Fernando Pairican, this process of forceful transformation was supported by elite imaginaries who saw the Mapuche not as a segregated people, but rather as part of a racialized workforce integrated with mestizo peasants and known in Chilean social history as *bajo pueblo*, "low people" (2020, 276).

During the *radicación* process, one of the few strategies available to Mapuche families to secure land access was to occupy unclaimed land and later legalize its ownership by ascribing to themselves the role of settlers in relations with state authorities overseeing the redistribution process. I became familiar with the history of a group of Mapuche settlers in the early nineteenth century from the mountain outpost of Maite thanks to a collaborative project, which resulted in the publication of a book, *Magti*, whose title is the original Mapudungun name for the locality and which combines oral history accounts with photographs. The book was authored by a group of residents from Maite, in most cases heirs of Mapuche settlers, with the support of a group of researchers, including myself, acting as editors.[4]

In collecting oral history interviews for this book, it soon became evident that the figure of the *Indigenous settler* did not come to symbolize assimilation, but rather a resourceful strategy for survival. Most accounts revolved around the founding cacique Juan Huaiquifil, after whom the local *reducción* was named. While there are many narrative gaps about the early life of this cacique, older residents concur that during his youth Juan Huaiquifil fled his native *reducción*, located roughly seventy kilometers away from Maite, in search of safe and available land near the border with Argentina. Juan Huai-quifil's journey lasted several years, with failed attempts to settle down with his kin in at least two other localities (Curilaf, 2015, 134). For Francisca, a resident of Maite, the settlement of this displaced group of Mapuche was made possible thanks mostly to the cacique's resolution and ingenuity: "He said, 'Enough!' He and his people were being forced to keep running away. The only thing that the state wanted was to push the Mapuche toward the mountains, leaving us with bad land. This is how Juan Huaiquifil settled down. It was here that he made it possible for his family to grow." In 1909, land was officially granted to the Mapuche group led by Juan Huaiquifil through the endowment of the collective property title (*Título de Merced*).

Although flight from colonial violence was the motive behind the foundation of Maite, local accounts of Juan Huaiquifil's journey do not portray him as a passive victim of displacement but rather insist on his leadership and ingenuity. Juan Huaiquifil is remembered as a skillful traveler, a wealthy cattle rancher, and a charismatic diplomat who, throughout his life, established an extensive network of political and commercial alliances across the border with Argentina.[5] He embodied many of the qualities of the traditional authority, the *lonko*, but also that of an *ulmen*, a Mapudungun term that refers to wealthy individuals expected to behave generously toward their neighbors and family members (Boccara 2007, 30). The leadership skills of Juan Huaiquifil proved key to the recruitment of reservation members, a process essential to the occupation of reservation land as a strategy to repel land-grabbing by non-Indigenous colonos.

While the recruitment of displaced Mapuche individuals was undeniably part of caciques' strategy to harvest personal power and prestige, it was also a sign of genuine commitment to Mapuche survival in the aftermath of colonization. As once recounted by Lidia, a resident from Maite, the founding cacique recruited displaced Mapuche families with no kinship ties as a strategy to keep the "race (*raza*) united."[6] The combination of commitment toward people of "his own race," strategic alliances with winkas, and wealth prepared Juan Huaiquifil to act confidently with Chilean authorities, especially in lawsuits over land grabs. The representation of Juan Huaiquifil as a charismatic leader is further reinforced by oral accounts about the consequences of his death in 1942. Upon the cacique's death, no successor garnered recognition as a respected mediator by fellow residents, partly because the authority of caciques in general was declining across Mapuche territories. As José, another resident from Maite, once explained: "This is when the community began to shrink, and people became poor. This is what happens to kings. When the one with strength dies, the weak ones are left with misery." Without a respected leader, tensions over land access quickly escalated among neighbors. His death occurred during a crucial period of Mapuche history, when the extensive commercial networks across both sides of the Andes (see Bello 2011; Huiliñir-Curío 2018) were gradually vanishing as a consequence of impoverishment and increasing border policing.[7]

In a hamlet of roughly three hundred inhabitants like Maite, there are bound to be discordant voices on any topic, let alone the reputation of a historical figure like the founding cacique, Juan Huaiquifil. Unsurprisingly, residents with closer genealogical ties to the caciques have a more idealized representation of his legacy than others. Despite narrative discrepancies, the history of this cacique continues to exemplify that of Mapuche settlers in general, who tend to represent fugitivity from colonial violence and resettlement as a praiseworthy struggle of colonial endurance.[8] Another significant feature of oral accounts about Juan Huaiquifil is the celebration of his status as a successful cacique and colono. His history is an emblematic case of the incorporation of settlers' practices and values as a viable strategy to ensure Mapuche survival. Such a model of incorporation, which figures as a recurrent theme in accounts about local history among Mapuche rural residents (see Di Giminiani 2018), entails the search for an ideal and yet precarious balance between the continuing nourishment of Mapuche practices and participation in the colonizers' society.

In theory, being Mapuche and Chilean are two concomitant forms of belonging. In Mapuche rural areas, full participation in the nation as citizens is not necessarily at odds with the recognition of self-governance rights. Around southern Andean valleys, Chilean flags can be seen waving around houses for Independence Day on September 18 (*Fiestas Patrias*) side by side with the Mapuche flag *wenufoye*.[9] Mapuche rural residents might have no political affiliation but, when they engage in national and local politics, are often divided among right- and left-wing voters, or else they simply support the candidate who has been more receptive to the demands of local organizations. The twofold nature of national and ethnic belonging in Indigenous rural areas explains why Mapuche residents of Andean valleys, just like neighboring winkas, see themselves as protagonists of the ongoing process of *hacer patria* and frame their emotional attachment to a remote locality, such as Maite, not only as a historical contingency but also as a moral commitment to the nation.

While identification with the Chilean nation is in theory compatible with Indigenous belonging, the adoption of settler practices and values rarely turns out to be simply an instrumental act. Among Mapuche people in Chile, assimilation into settler society is typically referred to with the expression *awinkarse*, literally "becoming winka-like." The effects of *awinkarse* are evident in the decline of practices and skills essential to Mapuche identity, including the loss of fluency in the native language, Mapudungun (see Course 2013), which is central to Mapuche knowledge and ethics. Historically, discrimination in the workplace and schools compelled many Mapuche parents to encourage their children to abandon customary practices, adopt Chilean lifestyles, and finally even deny their Indigenous status.

Conversion to Christianity, of course, has been another major force behind assimilation. While many Mapuche members of evangelical churches, colloquially referred to as *evangélicos*, assert their Indigenous identity with pride, others from more fervent congregations consider Mapuche religious practices as antithetical to their Christian faith. To many Mapuche activists on the forefront of cultural revitalization, the spread of evangelical churches in rural Chile, most of them organized as groups of local devotees meeting in small church buildings, is a contributing factor to ongoing assimilation more than Catholicism. The Catholic Church in Chile, as elsewhere in Latin America, has adopted a tolerant attitude toward religious syncretism and double belonging. Mapuche residents committed to cultural revitalization and decolonial education are often critical of neighbors who willingly deny their Mapuche belonging to present themselves as more Chilean, labeling them sometimes as "social climbers" (*arribistas*) for aspiring to be recognized as more integrated with mainstream urban culture. Accusations of hypocrisy are also common, as residents denying their Mapuche status may still apply for state subsidies and scholarships endowed as part of affirmative action policies, whose main requirement is to hold a genealogical certificate known as a *Certificado de Calidad Indígena*.

Claims of Indigenous belonging and its refusal are significant factors in explaining the roots of colonial assimilation. Yet being Mapuche is never a simple question of ethnic identification. It consists of a form of subjectivity dependent not only on genealogical conditions but also affirmed through actions that can make someone more or less Mapuche, according to oneself and others. This is why, for example, ethnically mixed individuals—often referred to as *champurreados* and now constituting a significant portion of the Mapuche population—are not inherently more likely to become *winkas* than their neighbors and family members who are considered more genealogically Mapuche (González Gálvez 2016, 92). Far from being only an instrumental process, the adoption of settler values and practices can lead to a condition of irreversible cultural loss captured by the expression *awinkarse*. Historically, Mapuche engagement with settler alterity does not appear to be the open-ended process of incorporation and resignification that has come to define many anthropological representations of Indigenous groups in South America, inspired by Levi-Strauss's principle of openness to the other present in Amerindian cosmologies (1995; see also Gow 1991). Any representation that emphasizes the openness of engagement with colonial alterity in Mapuche society inevitably downplays the possibility for the "failure to balance the engagement with difference" (Course 2013, 794). Remaining Mapuche is a struggle carried out through both intentional actions, such as involvement in revitalization politics, and everyday experiences, in which Indigenous values and practices associated

FIGURE 5 A school in Maite (Photograph by the author)

with ritual, sociability, and linguistic fluency may often inform relationships with more-than-human others.

As I show next, for Mapuche residents of Andean valleys, forest engagements are among the most profound experiences for reflecting on both human and nonhuman vitality. These engagements offer insights from Indigenous cosmology into how humans have the unique capacity to either extinguish or nurture the lives of others.

Respecting Forests and the Question of Nonhuman Autonomy

Members of Mapuche communities in Coilaco and Maite, most of whom speak Spanish as their first language, typically refer to forests with the Spanish terms *bosque* and *selva*, literally "wood" and "forest," much like their settler neighbors. At the same, they are familiar with the Mapudungun term for "forest," *mawida*, which also applies to "hills," as most forests in the area are located on mountain slopes.[10] Unlike other areas in southern Chile characterized by the presence of vast timber plantations, in these Andean valleys, forests are not the site of large lucrative activities. Yet, they are essential to household economies, being for instance sources of firewood for heating and timber used for house construction. Forests also provide access to non-timber products such as the araucaria pine nut, *piñón*. Little difference exists in forest use between Mapuches and colonos in this area, perhaps with the exception of those landholders with slightly more land than average who have converted timber extraction into a commercial activity. For Mapuches and winkas alike, forests rich in endogenous species hold a central role in the preservation of water sources, especially in comparison with commercial timber plantations, which are made of species with high water consumption. Deforestation is a shared apprehension, even though settlers were the ones responsible for massive deforestation in the past. Yet, to a lesser degree, Mapuche landholders also see themselves as part of the problem, as pressing needs for firewood and timber have left them with little option but to clear sections of their properties.

Shared practices and attitudes toward forestry among settlers and Mapuche landholders remind us of the overall scenario depicted in the previous chapter, in which friendship and kinship relationships between the two groups are just as common as feelings of animosity originating from property disputes and experiences of racial discrimination. In Mapuche rural areas, any representation of Indigenous-forest relations focusing uniquely on customary local environmental values is destined to reiterate the false, romanticized image of Indigenous people so common in global environmentalism (see Nadasdy 2005). Even when the daily and utilitarian performance of forestry seems to have little correspondence to what is generally understood as Mapuche culture or religion, it still allows Mapuche residents of Andean valleys to be exposed to particular and, at times, unsettling manifestations of nonhuman agency and autonomy that find their ontological explanation in Indigenous cosmology.

Mapuche landowners in Maite and Coilaco Valley enter the forested slopes of surrounding mountains for different reasons: to log; to take cattle grazing, especially for summer cattle transhumance (*veranada*); to gather non-timber forest goods such as the *piñón*; and for recreational purposes, especially when hosting visitors from urban centers or, more rarely, taking tourists on mountain tours. Although residents praise and admire the beauty of the forests, they prefer to enter these areas only when necessary, acknowledging the many dangers they may hold. As for other visitors, I was often dissuaded from visiting nearby mountains, especially without a local guide. Such fears are not exaggerated—particularly the danger of getting lost in swiftly changing weather conditions. Tragic stories about tourists' disappearances are remembered vividly in the area.

The idea of forests as dangerous places is common among both the winkas and the Mapuches in this region. However, for many Mapuches, the perception of this danger carries an additional layer of meaning not shared by their non-Indigenous neighbors: Forests are home to a high concentration of powerful nonhuman entities that are responsible for the forest's vitality. Of these, the most important is *newen*. Generally translated in Spanish as *fuerza* ("force"), *newen* is an ethereal and highly mobile force that is both inherent to specific entities and external to them, as it mediates relationships among different entities, both human and nonhuman, capable of giving and receiving it (Course, 2011, 48; Ñanculef 2016, 47; Skewes et al. 2020, 393). Land, for instance, is thought of as capable of infusing *newen* onto human and nonhuman dwellers. Humans can direct *newen* only partially, as in the case of healing and ritual practices aimed at exchanging this vital force among humans and powerful nonhumans. An ideal setting for the exchange of *newen* among humans is the *ngillatun*, a two-to-three-day event encompassing several ritual and celebrative activities carried out to express gratitude and raise petitions to the main deity Chao Ngenchen (see Alonqueo 1979; Ñanculef 2016, 91–123).[11]

The presence of *newen* is generally associated with an unusual perception of awe and rejuvenation. Renata, a Mapuche educator working at the local school in Maite, explained her feelings whenever she visited higher forested sections of the valley: "The beauty of the place makes you want to stay there forever, because it is there that you can connect with the power of the mountain (*cordillera*). It feels like your head is changed by a whole different air, a force." The perception of *newen* as a spiritually enriching experience, such as that described by Renata, resonates with that of environmental activists living in the area, who sometimes express their connection to the mountains with references to Mapuche cosmology, as we will see in the next chapter. Yet, unlike environmentalists' depictions of forests, Mapuche residents acknowledge that this same force can pose a threat to human visitors. The unpredictable nature of *newen* makes this force either benevolent or malignant depending on the particular intentions of those humans and nonhumans involved in its exchange. As described by Ñanculef, *weza* ("bad") *newen* can generally emanate from evil beings known as *wekufü* or *wefuke* (2016, 60).

Newen is not distributed equally across the landscape. Certain topographic features, such as mountains and forests, have more pronounced agential capacities than others. They stand out among other entities because they are both containers of *newen* and other powerful nonhumans, as well as entities in their own right, demonstrating behaviors that reveal a high degree of autonomy in their relations with humans. Given their tendency to respond to human actions in unpredictable ways, mountains and forests need to be approached with deep respect. They can have vengeful responses to humans' disrespectful behaviors, and as a result mountains are often referred to as resentful, *celosos*.[12] One of the biggest dangers associated with mountains is the ease with which humans can lose their way and eventually disappear in a sudden thick mist, known as *kolüm* (see Course 2010). This event is typically attributed to the mountains' retaliation against disrespectful humans, even though the actions of mountains described as "resentful" are unpredictable and often unrelated to such specific causes. Ways to be respectful on entering a forest or a mountain include avoiding screaming and making unnecessary fires. As explained by one resident in her forties, Marcela, there are no clear reasons for mountains to be hostile or rancorous, except perhaps that they resent human presence around them: "Hills are resentful [celosos], even though I'm not sure exactly why. I believe that they do not want to be disturbed. There are people who think of themselves as owners and lords of everything." Resentment, in this case, would be a consequence of being importuned without due respect.

Topographic features animated by *newen* are frequently also home to *ngen*, the other main kind of nonhumans responsible for the unpredictability and vitality of forests. The term *ngen* has been customarily translated as "master spirits," *espíritus dueños*, in Spanish (Grebe 1986), although this translation does not align well with Western concepts of ownership (Di Giminiani and González Gálvez 2018, 6), as it more accurately reflects ideas of custodianship (Quidel 2016, 717).[13] Ngen are both hypostases for general environmental features, such as water, and entities corresponding to features of a landscape, such as specific rocks and watercourses. The only exception is the main deity, Chao Ngenchen, often described by rural Mapuche residents as equivalent to the Christian God and roughly translatable as "master spirit (ngen) of people (*che*)" (Alonqueo, 1979, 223).

The presence of ngen is usually perceived by humans through different manifestations, as in the case of the floating skin of a black bull (*kürü kullin*), associated with the most ubiquitous master spirit, that of water, *ngenko* (Di Giminiani 2018, 100). Around Coilaco, lagoons in higher sections of the valley have also been described by some Mapuche residents in the area as resentful. As explained by Elvira, a Mapuche elder respected by many in the area for her knowledge of Mapuche culture, loud screams coming from lagoons typically signal an imminent danger. Animals such as horses may be manifestations of the *ngenko*, sent to attract visitors, make them lose their way, and finally cause their disappearance. Another powerful ngen known in the area is *el dueño de la cordillera*, "the master of the *cordillera*," as it was referred to by some residents in the process of editing the history book of Maite. One of the most common manifestations of ngen associated with mountains is the *pukuka kushe*, described as an elderly woman living in the middle of the mountains, where she takes care of araucaria trees.

Perceiving and being affected by powerful nonhumans is not a simple matter of adherence to a culture or a belief system. The widespread and lamented condition of being winka-like, *awinkado*, associated with the forceful adoption of settler culture, is the main reason behind the fact that in any

Comunidad, some residents would typically dismiss sightings of ngen as traditional beliefs or even superstitions (*supersticiones*) (Di Giminiani 2018, 71). Yet, for many, the possible presence of these entities is a cause for worry: The sight of a ngen sparks the expectation of misfortune, such as the eruption of an illness affecting the witness or a close relative. In line with a general valorization of individual autonomy in Mapuche society (see Course 2011; Murray et al. 2015), individual truth claims, such as the sighting of a ngen, are unlikely to be discarded a priori (González Gálvez 2015).[14] The presence of ngen thus appears more as an indeterminate possibility determined by predispositions to its perception or simply by chance than a disputable fact.

Attentiveness to nonhuman agency and cosmological relations cannot be reduced to a simple matter of belief. As proposed by Eduardo Viveiros de Castro (2011, 133), to characterize cosmological possibilities as beliefs entails belittling them as symbolic elements of a worldview, rather than allowing that "worlds of vision" can be perceived by senses other than vision. Attentiveness to nonhuman agencies and their cosmological context is actively cultivated through a particular form of education that teaches humans how to properly approach mountains and forests. As suggested by Ingold (2001), perceptions of events and relations that are typically labeled as extraordinary, as in the case of cosmological expressions of nonhuman agencies, depend on practical experiences—both those shared among present-day people and those inherited from past generations—that help perceivers to attune their attention toward different actions and events, including those apparently invisible. This point explains why winkas, even though they are not exactly prevented from perceiving, are less likely to perceive the actions of powerful nonhumans associated with Mapuche cosmology. The particular education in attentiveness that informs the perception of powerful nonhumans, along with the appropriate behaviors for engaging with them, aligns with the broader understanding of customary knowledge in Mapuche society. *Kimün,* commonly translated in Spanish as "knowledge" (*conocimiento*) or "wisdom" (*sabiduría*), indicates a way of learning, knowing, and perceiving the world based on both transmitted knowledge of the deep interconnectedness of the Mapuche cosmos and on observation of ecological and cosmological relations in their making (see Millalén 2006; Quilaqueo and Quintriqueo 2010).

Although in many Andean valleys no clear boundaries can be established between forests and agricultural fields, entering the forest world is experienced as an escalating exposure to intricate visual patterns and auditory stimuli. In depicting forest life, landholders' images and anecdotes insist on the transformative potential of forests on human senses and subjectivities. A threshold, albeit one that is hard to delimit, seems to exist upon entering a forest from other, more comfortable, spaces. For Manning and Massumi, when an experience "passes the threshold toward change, it poses the existential question of what germinal form of life and future qualities of experience lie beyond the threshold" (2014, 126). Forests represent a threshold that can separate familiar, anthropocentric subject-object relationships from a more profound realization of the decentered nature of human perspective. In these agential networks, nonhumans emerge as more autonomous and powerful than typically recognized.

An example of the affective shift of forest engagements and its consequent decentering of human perspective comes from a phenomenon described earlier on in this chapter—the appearance of sudden and dangerous fogs, known as *kolüm*. Their appearances are sometimes attributed to humans labeled as *kalku*, "witch," or to evil spirits known as *wefuke*, but mostly to mischievous ngen. Victims of *kolüm* typically lose their ability to see and hear, leaving them overwhelmed by the anxiety of being watched by an unseen presence, most likely a ngen, invisible to their eyes (Course 2010, 252). The experience of human decentering prompted by forests evokes the phenomenological idea of *bracketing*, or *epoche*, a Greek term proposed by Edmund Husserl in the early twentieth century to indicate the attempted suspension of assumptions about the world existing prior to embodiment. Bracketing does not unfold in a world free of existing assumptions, but rather intervenes and problematizes ontological assumptions on the nature of beings. As suggested by Pedersen, an "ontological epoche" takes place when unexamined assumptions are swept away, opening new possibilities in thinking about the ontological status of humans and nonhuman others (2020, 31). The sentiment that arises from forest engagements and their decentering effects on human perspective resembles fear, but perhaps *reverence* might be a more appropriate descriptor.

Knowledge about powerful nonhuman forces and entities such as *newen* and ngen has powerful ethical implications. By emphasizing the unpredictable responsiveness of nonhumans, it reinforces the idea that human involvement in social, ecological, and cosmological relationships should follow the value of "respect," *respeto* in Spanish, *yewen* in Mapudungun. Respect is based on recognition of the other person's will and autonomy (Course 2011, 56) and the consequent refusal of any action entailing the denial of the individuality and existence of the other being imbricated in the relationship. One way in which respect is put into practice in human sociability is through mutual exchanges of greetings and gifts, which help to consolidate mutual trust and a symmetrical relationship with the other.[15] In Mapuche etiquette, respect also informs relationships with elders, who should be approached with deference by younger family members and neighbors. One of the most noticeable manifestations of the value of respect is the act of requesting permission (*permiso*) to ngen spirits before performing agricultural tasks (Ñanculef 2016, 52). In the past it was common for loggers to seek permission from a ngen before chopping down a tree or entering a forest, through ritualized enchantments known as *llellipun*.[16]

Today, ritualized permissions are rarely sought, with the noticeable exception of *veranadas*, community-based summer transhumances, in which cattle owners ask for permission for the journey through the forest and for the protection of their animals in higher sections of the mountain. Summer transhumance is increasingly performed as part of land reclamation (a point I return to in greater depth in chapter 6). In the context of human engagements with forests, the two most important ways humans can show respect are avoiding loud screams and not making unnecessary fires. As mentioned earlier, disrespectful transgressions are expected to provoke mischievous responses from ngen. Disrespect doesn't always involve a material act; it can manifest as a skeptical attitude toward the existence of powerful nonhumans or as excessive confidence when entering spaces like forests. On one occasion I heard the story of a local member of an evangelical church who lost his way in one of the forests near Coilaco. For some of my interlocutors, this brief but frightening misadventure was caused by the man's incredulous feelings toward "Mapuche culture." The decline of practices of respect is part of the general process I described earlier as *awinkarse*. Among Mapuche landowners, respect is frequently mentioned as a quintessential feature of social life among "the ancient ones," *los antiguos*, which has sadly declined over the years.

The ethical significance of respect is to be found not only in its role in guiding relationships of mutuality with others, but also in its ability to highlight the subjectivity of others as a necessary condition for the establishment of diplomatic more-than-human coexistence. Respect, under this light, appears aligned with the idea of reverence proposed by Chakrabarty as the ideal ethical predisposition for life in the Anthropocene: "Reverence is not simply about curiosity, wonderment, or biophilia. Reverence suggests a relationship of respect mixed in with fear and awe, with proto-Italic roots that mean 'to be wary'" (2021, 198). Among Mapuche frontier dwellers, respect toward forests brings together sentiments as diverse as fear and wonder because it shows how forest life can shape and determine human perceptions of oneself and others. The key question here is not what we perceive in forests but how forests allow us to know. As suggested by Kohn in his depiction of forest engagements among the Runa people in the Amazon, the power of forests resides in their ability to articulate multiple and ever-changing forms that shape human perception. In a context where nonhumans act less as objects of thought and more as subjects imbricated in human epistemic processes, "humans do not just impose form on tropical forest: the forest proliferates it" (2013, 182).

In the Mapuche lived world, engagements with nonhumans are not exempt from the possibility of objectification (see Di Giminiani and González Gálvez 2018). Human labor invested in the transformation of forests cannot be reduced to an anthropocentric phenomenon based on the exceptionalism of the human capacity to transform a natural background into a cultural foreground, nor to an ecocentric process whereby human agency is equal to other agencies (see Kipnis 2015). Yet humans are rarely in full epistemic control of the conditions under which signification unfolds. Forests are loosely demarcated by a phenomenological threshold which, upon being crossed, exposes the human subject to a particular type of decentering capable of revealing nonhuman responsiveness as well as human vulnerability and relatedness to otherwise hardly perceptible agencies. Forests, in other words, think and make us think about what it means to be human. The revelatory power of forests is central to the characterization of ideas about humanity at the core of Mapuche alterhumanism.

The experience of *becoming human with and through others* around Mapuche frontier forests is grounded in the simultaneous recognition that nonhumans, especially those contributing to the vitality of the forests, are autonomous subjects who demand respect and can influence human behaviors and dispositions. At the same time, humans can bear responsibility for the well-being of nonhuman life around the frontier forests. To better illustrate the mutual constitution of people and environment in Mapuche frontier life and the forms of care that this relationship enables, I provide a summary, inevitably too synthetic, of a general theory of place originating in accounts and ideas about Indigenous land connections. My goal in the following pages is to provide a tentative answer to how the local environment shapes human subjectivities and, in doing so, to point toward the key principles of Mapuche alterhumanism.

Being from Somewhere, or What Makes Us the Humans We Are

When we talk about *place*, several things quickly come to mind: emotional attachment, memory—whether comforting or distressing—and political commitment, among others. For this reason, in philosophy and the social sciences, place has come to be understood as an essentially phenomenological category—in other words, a geographical construction known and experienced first and foremost through embodiments, emotions, and affects (see Casey 1996; Feld and Basso 1996). Place matters because it holds a power over us, over which we do not seem to have full control. As suggested by Casey, the self is necessarily geographical because "the relationship between self and place is not just one of reciprocal influence (that much any ecologically sensitive account would maintain) but also, more radically, of constitutive coingredience: each is essential to the being of the other" (2001, 684). The constitutive power of place entails that primary access to the world, and thus its comprehension, is in place rather than space (see Casey 1996). Thus, place is not the object of an existential process through which individuals can attach meanings to space, understood as a tabula rasa. Rather, it is the lived world from which traces from the past and emerging meanings in the present can be gathered and reformulated through acts of embodiment. Place is built, materially and ideologically, as the outcome of relations imbued with power inequalities (Cresswell 2004, 26–27). This includes those that have forced Mapuche groups in Andean valleys to relocate to previously unknown territories, later to develop emotional attachments and commitments to them.

In any social context, place evokes different feelings and actions. In Mapuche society, *emplacement*—in other words, the condition of being attached to particular places—is a central dimension of personhood. The ethnonym

Mapuche, literally "people of the land or territory, *mapu*," emphasizes the status of being autochthonous to a specific land, in contrast with uprooted winka. As suggested by Quidel, *mapu*, a term that is often translated as "land" but that encompasses all the earth and territory, acts as a shaper (*formador*) of *che*, "person" (2020, 89). Of all places, the one that holds a special significance for any individual is *tuwün*, a term usually translated as "place of origin" in the writings of Mapuche authors (see Ñanculef, 2016, 65; Quidel 2020, 111; Quilaqueo and Quintriqueo, 2010, 342). As defined by poet Elicura Chihuailaf (1999, 51), tuwün is "the basic foundation of the family, rooted in the physical space where people were born, have grown up and developed." Around Mapuche rural areas, the notion of tuwün is expressed through deep emotional, affective, and occasionally nostalgic discourses emphasizing a compelling and yet precarious connection with one's place of origin, marked in most cases by a history of a diasporic outmigration to cities (see Alvarado Lincopi 2021). Along with *küpal*, a term roughly translatable as "descent," tuwün is the quintessential element of Mapuche identity, explaining much of their behavioral and even ethical differences with non-Mapuche people, winkas, whose erratic and untrustworthy behavior is often explained in terms of their detachment from a particular place.[17] The difference between Mapuches and winkas—who are also subject to the formative forces of land—thus rests in the absence of the effects that one receives not only from the place in which one dwells, but also those effects associated with past generations, such as the tuwün. The significant historical migration to urban areas and the resulting loss of a recognizable tuwün have contributed to the process of becoming more winka-like (*awinkados*). However, places without genealogical ties, including the urban areas where most of the Mapuche population now resides, can still undergo a process of re-signification, transforming into culturally meaningful and safe Indigenous spaces (Casagrande 2021, 952).

What is really important about genealogical and geographic connections (tuwün and *küpal*) is not the rights they can legitimize, but rather their nature as given features of the self. The power of tuwün consists in its ability to determine shared behavioral features among individuals identifying with the same tuwün (Course 2011, 46). Besides acting as a general marker of difference with tuwün-less winkas, tuwün works to frame sameness and otherness among Mapuche in geographical terms. People with the same origins would potentially resemble each other in attitudes and actions as disparate as

being skillful at agricultural work or being too individualistic. But despite its
ability to affect human conduct, tuwün should not be treated as a version of
environmental determinism. Mapuche personhood is at once performative,
geographic, and genealogical. Certain attributes, such as linguistic fluency,
can make individuals more or less Mapuche at the same time that they make
them unique. Accordingly, the influence of tuwün in social life is best understood as a potentiality of the self, whose realization ultimately depends on
individual actions deployed in social relationships and environmental engagement (Di Giminiani 2018, 73). This is consistent with a general emphasis
on the value of individual autonomy in Mapuche society.

   While the notion of tuwün resonates with the phenomenological "prior-
ness" of place over space, there is one key difference. In line with its emphasis on the nature of place as a genealogical construct, the notion of tuwün
emphasizes the role that past human labor continues to hold on land and its
dwellers, and the possibility of place to act as a potentially determining force
on the individual, even in a context of intergenerational removal from native
land. The uniqueness of each tuwün is in fact given by a combination of the
agential abilities of nonhumans unique to a particular space that pre-exists
human transformation of the local environment and those of landscape features that are constituted by the labor of past and present generations. We
are the result of environmental forces, but in some cases, these forces are also
the products of our labor. Such a possibility has been recognized elsewhere,
or at least in all of those contexts where both human exceptionalism and
ecocentrism fail to adequately describe the types of environmental relations
that take place. In speaking of the importance of labor in the constitution of
people and land in Andean rural communities, Sheild Johanson has posited
that "agricultural work is the process through which people gain their full
personhood and land gains its animacy. It is a co-creative practice that sits
at the heart of the Andean ayllu" (2019, 15). A similar idea about land-people
mutuality can be found in rural Mapuche areas. Many of my interlocutors
have portrayed farming as a two-way relationship of giving and receiving.

   The historical process of settlement as "Indigenous settlers" encompasses
two possibilities: on one hand, that land, forests, and other natural resources
can be domesticated and their value objectified; and on the other hand, that
these resources can resist full domestication, leaving their complete objectification as economic resources perpetually incomplete (see Di Giminiani
and González Gálvez 2018). As recounted by residents of Maite, the founders

of this locality in the early twentieth century were largely responsible for the transformation of what used to be a dense forest into a mixed landscape with pastureland suitable for the development of commercial husbandry alternating with forests essential for timber and firewood collection. Forest clearing, however, did not prevent their antecessors from recognizing the power that nonhumans inhabiting this land prior to their settlement held in shaping their life trajectories. Ritualized petitions for permission were common in the early days of Maite. In oral accounts about this epoch, resettled residents used to direct *llellipun* incantations to the main deity, Chao Ngenchen, and the ngen likely to inhabit the area where new activities were to be carried out. This specific act of place-making resembled a ritual described by Quidel as *anülmapun*, literally the "sitting in a place," which was typically performed by a family before relocating to a new portion of land (2016, 718). Settlement requires the transformation and domestication of forests and land, which nonetheless can hardly be reduced exclusively to objectified manifestations of human labor, or in Kolers's words, to the "passive instrument of the human will, essentially worthless until value is inserted into it by mixing labor" (2009, 64).

From memories and experiences of Mapuche dwellers of settler frontiers, there emerges a view of settlement defined not as a process of domestication of wilderness or signification of a space empty of human meanings, as common in historical narratives about settlers' epics, but as an engagement with a place recognized for its potential to shape future social life. Such a configuration also tells us about a more general view of human labor, centered on the limits of human objectification of those nonhuman forces imbricated in the very process of directing life trajectories for local dwellers. Experiences of emplacement among Mapuche dwellers of settler frontiers indicate a particular view of humanity in which humans are uniquely equipped with the abilities to direct life forces and contribute to the vitality of topographic features, such as forests, which nonetheless remain entities independent of human care and capable of shaping collective predispositions and behaviors among their dwellers. Forest engagements constitute the experiential contexts from which Mapuche dwellers of the settler frontier learn to recognize human life as shaped by the responsive actions of unruly nonhuman entities, such as ngen spirits. In Mapuche frontier life, *becoming human through and with nonhuman others* is an ontological process made possible by engagements with nonhuman persons capable of revealing the power of the world in molding specific human potentials. Unlike ecocentric views of humanity that diminish the human perspective in favor of focusing on relationships among beings of equal status, alterhumanism among the Mapuche inhabitants of the frontier is based on the idea that localized life forces—often unfamiliar to the residents and resistant to human objectification—play a crucial role in defining humanity as an inherently geographical category.

Some of the images behind this view of humanity that I draw on from my partial readings of Mapuche experiences in the forest landscape resonate with notions of personhood in Indigenous South America. Across many Indigenous contexts in the region, human personhood reflects the general principles of animism—something which, in Descola's definition, presupposes a potential shared interiority for all beings and a discontinuity in physicalities responsible for alterity among beings (2013, 131). Nonhumans can be persons equipped with subjectivities and capabilities for partaking in social relationships beyond human societies. As suggested by Viveiros de Castro, the many and diverse Indigenous ideas of humanity reveal an "interminable humanism," in which being human is a condition that is constantly being reasserted and diversified in contrast with those finished-and-done humanisms that are responsible for the constitution of humanity into a separate order from nonhumans (2014, 44–45). Mapuche ideas of personhood are, of course, multiple, and therefore hardly reducible to an overall principle. Yet they share an overall depiction of humanity, partly resembling animistic emphasis on paradigmatic differentiation with nonhumans and partly emphasizing domestication as the organizing principle of human engagement with nonhuman life—a view consistent with a long historical adoption of husbandry.

The human person *che* remains an irreducible entity. As suggested by Course, *che* comprises a capability for social relationships and a physical human condition necessary for the performance of social acts (2011, 30): The "interplay of sociality and physical capacity emerges most clearly in the fact that social capacities are necessarily rooted in the physicality of other humans" (Course 2011, 43). Accordingly, the condition of being *che* might not acknowledge those who are unable to socialize, such as infants, as well as those entities with social conduct, such as ngen, but lacking human physicality. Humanity is the necessary condition for personhood, but being a person is an intentional moral achievement that requires constant social engagement with others (Quidel 2020, 188). Social engagement is ultimately a human quality. While the autonomy of others is recognized and valued as implicit in the ideal of "respect" discussed so far, humanity is also endowed with the ability to deeply affect the vitality of others in ways that can be depletive but also nourishing. This point applies to relationships among humans, as in the case of childrearing, but also with nonhumans, as in the case of domestication, depletion, and care of other beings. Humans assign themselves the role of carers for nonhuman life, even if they remain subjects among others in a world hierarchically organized according to shifting and unpredictable qualities of autonomy. If place shapes people, then people, in turn, shape the places toward which they feel a sense of responsibility. In the making of the environment that makes us who we are, care and depletion appear as two sides of the same coin, both inevitable and essential in fostering a deep attachment to the land, especially in agricultural life.

In concluding this chapter, I will highlight some of the challenges facing Mapuche dwellers on the settler frontier in their efforts to sustain the flourishing of nonhuman life. By now, it should be clearer how the frail balance between care and depletion of nonhuman life is a central feature of what I have described as Mapuche alterhumanism.

Taking Responsibility for Nonhuman Life

Around southern Andean forests, agriculture is an essential component of daily life. Even though a large proportion of the Mapuche rural population is employed in the expanding service industry around Pucón and Currarehue, a consequence of the ecotourism boom since the 1990s, in any household, agriculture and forestry provide food and resources that are valued not only out of necessity but also for their positive association with a healthy rural lifestyle. Gardening provides households with homegrown food, such as beans, typically recognized as a fundamental contribution to the health of its consumers in opposition to industrial products (see Bonelli 2015).[18] Livestock ownership is often limited to a few cows and a handful of sheep, so that it rarely consists of the specialized commercial activity it used to be in the past, when Mapuche cattle ranchers were influential economic actors in rural areas. But while husbandry is not a stable economic activity, most members of Indigenous communities would hardly give it up, insofar as it provides meat for domestic consumption, particularly for festivities and, more importantly, works as a form of saving, ensuring cash flow in times of need through the sale of cows or oxen. Forestry is carried out mainly in response to domestic needs, such as firewood.

During my time in Maite and Coilaco, I observed that descriptions of agricultural labor often highlight two key points: the inevitable degradation of forests caused by both farming and forestry and the potential to mitigate this degradation through specific techniques and practices. These practices are rooted in both modern eco-friendly approaches to agriculture and in traditional environmental values, such as the principle of respect. Yet one term stands out as the most commonly used to define an ideal engagement with nonhuman life: care, *cuidado*. Across Chile, this popular term applies to any act meant to sustain and nourish the life of another being, who could be another human or a domesticated animal or species. Caregivers (*cuidadores*) are driven by necessity, as with domesticated plants that rely on human care to grow and eventually provide economic benefits. However, their actions are also shaped by an ethical sense of responsibility, often linked to emotions like empathy or solidarity.

The trope of care through which many Mapuche landholders frame their ethical responsibility toward nonhuman life reflects the generally ambivalent nature of this action. The emergence of the notion of care in public debates on sociality and crisis over the last few decades in Chile, as elsewhere, has led to a growing critical appraisal of this notion. As defined by Fisher and Tronto, care is "everything that we do to maintain, continue, and repair our world so that we can live in it as well as possible" (1990, 19). Yet the ways in which care manifests itself can be so disparate that this work of maintenance and repair permeates not only relationships of solidarity but also those of domination (see Krøijer and Rubow 2022; Mol et al. 2010; Puig de la Bellacasa 2017). As Puig de la Bellacasa reminds us, care "involves material engagement in labours to sustain interdependent worlds, labours that are often associated with exploitation and domination" (2012, 198). Care is ambivalent because it guides practical actions through which relations of coexistence are sustained from different views and interests. In a world that is increasingly understood as animated by nonhuman agencies responsive to human actions, often in unpredictable ways, care never unfolds as univocal engagement with others imagined as passive objects. It is rather pursued in affective contexts where the responsiveness of the subjects of human care, including the refusal of care, as in the case of native forests of southern Chile, remains elusive and unpredictable.

In the Andean valleys where this book is set, as in many other agricultural contexts, taking care of plants requires attention to growth and to the particular environmental conditions in which such growth can occur. Forms of domesticated plant life such as potatoes, beans, and other garden produce, recognized as lacking autonomy, need human care to flourish. In this case, *taking care* requires actions such as directing water flows and tilling soil to create the ideal conditions for the crops to grow (Di Giminiani 2018, 105). As for other social contexts marked by shifting expressions of the wild/domestic binary (see Descola 2013, 40), varying forms of care for forests and cultivated crops highlight a stronger sense of autonomy in the former, compared to domesticated life forms that depend on human intervention. In other words, the less autonomous a being is, the more human care it will require. Forests thus can be taken care of, but with strategies that require more detachment than constant attention. One way in which humans can take care of forests is by clearing the fast-growing underbrush commonly referred to as *maleza*, a term alluding to bad plants, which hinders human access.

During one of my stays in Maite, my colleague Martín and I decided to visit a nearby lagoon with Marcelo, a local resident who had recently begun offering guided tours of the area. As we were walking along the steep forest path, Marcelo warned us against the dangers of uncontrolled understory growth for cattle ranchers: "*Maleza* grows quickly around here. We need to keep an eye open if we don't want to lose this path." Keeping a clear path is an action necessary for the healthy coexistence of forests, cattle, and humans. Through this action, the dangers of wildfire can be reduced, cattle ranchers have an easier time moving across forests with their animals, and tourists can be guided to avoid getting lost. Taking care of forests thus entails a balance between the intention of keeping a respectful distance and taking up the more active engagement necessary for human activities to thrive therein. Care in this case brings together a concern over deforestation (caring for forests), a sense of caution (being careful around forests) in relationships with powerful and autonomous nonhumans, and a more active engagement (taking care of forests) needed to ensure human cohabitation of forest environments. More generally, in relation to domesticated and wild nonhumans, care works to draw an ideal delimitation for extraction, as in the avoidance of over-logging as well as encouraging a type of agricultural labor necessary to ensure the proper growth of plants and animals, such as in clearing underbrush from forests and agricultural fields. While care can help nonhumans to acquire more animacy, an excess of care can put them at risk of losing their vitality.

For Mapuche landholders in the southern Andean valleys, the concept of care is inseparable from the recognition of nonhuman vitality and the human responsibility to sustain it. Care ultimately consists of a set of intentions and actions aimed at favoring the vitality of others. This happens through the demarcation of limits for human labor, given its potential contribution to depletion. Therefore, care frequently appears as more of an aspiration than an actual practice. Intergenerational loss of attentiveness to cosmological relationships and agential principles, as well as the material erasure of powerful nonhumans, are deeply embedded in the experiences of colonization among many Indigenous societies (see Glaskin 2018). For many Mapuche rural residents, reaction against environmental degradation associated with soil and water depletion requires not only legal and political efforts to curtail the effects of agribusiness and megadevelopment projects around their properties, but also a conscious transformation of everyday agricultural practices they recognize as invasive. Adoption of less invasive new and past agricultural practices is unthinkable in separation from the reclamation of an environmental ethic capable of prompting a renewed sensitivity toward cosmological relatedness and the affective potentials of different nonhumans.

Reclaiming a Mapuche environmental ethic is a struggle enabled by multiple educational practices and discourses. It can be part of a highly emotive personal journey to reconnect with Mapuche practices and values, especially among urban residents. It can also unfold as a more overt form of collectivity. Since the 1990s, coinciding with the return to democratic rule and cultural revitalization, the Mapuche social movement has risen and taken on various agendas. It has become a central part of the broader decolonization (*descolonización*) effort led by activists seeking to break cycles of dependence on state aid and promote self-governance. At the same time, it aligns with the state's recently introduced multicultural policies, which focus primarily on linguistic and heritage preservation. While some Mapuche activists view these policies as opportunities, others see them as potential instances of cooptation and clientelism (see Radcliffe and Webb 2015). The most common example of cultural revitalization comes from the work of traditional educators (*educadores tradicionales*) employed in local schools to teach about

Mapuche culture and language as part of intercultural education policies run by the state (see Quintriqueo and Torres 2013). In educational activities led by traditional educators, emphasis is placed on Mapuche cosmology, in particular relations with powerful entities, Indigenous ethical values such as respect, and knowledge of local history and the environment. In Maite, for several years the local school has offered workshops (*talleres*) in which pupils were invited to learn in the open air about the ecological and cultural values of specific places, such as lagoons, known by local elders as the locations of powerful ngen, as well as the settings for historical events.

The reclamation of Indigenous environmental ethics does not mean a romantic return to past agricultural practices, which are considered by many Mapuche landholders to be simply unviable. Rather, projects of reclamation unfold as experimental and improvisational assessments of present and past environmental practices and notions, some of them treated as quintessentially Mapuche, others understood as more foreign. Neither is cultural revitalization a politically innocuous implementation of cultural policies, an opinion held by many in the public arena, either critically or positively. Such a work of reclamation can facilitate and drive more disruptive political processes, such as claims for the restitution of dispossessed ancestral territories, which require the reactivation of historical geographic knowledge to prove connections with claimed territories. As Offen reminds us, "Meanings and spatial organizations are not ontological givens but are bound up with the lived experiences that give them sustenance. . . . Place meanings and the social networks woven through them can never be separated from the political process seeking their territorialization" (2003, 48). As I will show in greater detail in chapter 6, knowledge about forests, their cosmological relevance, and the local history of forestry is essential to the forging of claims over protected forests and their consequences as state commons. Ethical aspirations of care and respect depicted in this chapter are not only part of a broader struggle for identity endangered by a violent history of assimilation; they are also embedded within a narrative of humanity that recognizes the abilities of nonhumans, especially those that participate in the constitution of certain places, to make us who we are, and human predispositions to care for and erase other lives. The alterhumanism that emerges from the story of displacement and resettlement of Mapuche frontier populations tells us how the project of becoming human rests on relationships with others that are made and unmade in the attempt to find a place in the world.

* * *

I opened this chapter by exploring resettlement and the adoption of settler status as an examination of human-environment relations among Mapuche landholders and, in turn, the related notions and representations of human agency and responsibility. Along the settler frontier, place-making among displaced Mapuche populations has been enabled by a particular practice of domestication that does not necessarily reiterate settler ideals of environmental transformation. In this case, the conjoined projects of settlement and domestication are guided by attentiveness to nonhuman agency and autonomy, particularly powerful entities affected by acts as diverse as care and depletion. Yet the adoption of settler practices and values has come with costs. In the face of land shortage and displacement, Mapuche dwellers have been left with little option but to replicate the ecologically damaging practices that contributed to settler expansion. Forces and entities responsible for the vitality and autonomous character of forests have become increasingly elusive, as is the case for many ngen spirits that have been displaced or even disappeared in response to detrimental human actions, such as overlogging, or to deteriorating environmental conditions including the drying up of bodies of water (see Bonelli 2017). Among Mapuche frontier populations, *becoming human through and with nonhuman others* is an experience marked by an inevitable ambivalence between the need for domestication and the aspiration of engaging with land features through values, often unfeasible, such as respect.

The alterhumanism I have presented in these pages should not be treated as a culturally stable normative model for human-environmental relations. Certain ethical and ontological principles are prominent in infusing affects such as fear and respect toward nonhumans that reveal the possibilities for nonhumans not only to act responsively to human practices but also to partake in the constitution of plenary places capable of guiding and molding human subjectivities. Yet among Mapuche frontier populations, these principles coexist and even clash with the widespread celebration of domestication and settlement that allowed early Mapuche settlers to build their homes in hostile mountain valleys. The adoption of settler practices and ideas are embedded with a form of alterhumanism that has emerged historically, not from a context of continuity between past and present Mapuche generations, but rather from the trauma of displacement and the struggle for resettlement.

Along the conservation frontier in southern Chile, Mapuche alterhumanism consists of a configuration of humanity animated by a sense of loss and hope for the restoration of a type of environmental ethics that could speak to today's concerns over colonial assimilation and ecological crisis. The articulation of emerging environmental ethics rests on the adoption and transformation of conservation values that have circulated widely among frontier populations in the last three decades. For Mapuche residents of the Andean valleys where this book is set, conservation has generally been experienced as a set of hierarchical encounters with institutions, civil society organizations, and economic actors leading the ecotourism boom of the last decades. However, relationships with environmentalist actors have also been fruitful in providing new ideas and means to encourage forest protection. Environmentalist ideas, practices, and sentiments have significantly influenced the reflections of Mapuche landholders regarding the meanings of humanity and our responsibility toward nonhuman life. This perspective often stands in stark contrast to experiences of domestication and settlement. Additionally, it clashes with Indigenous cosmological principles, which are based on hierarchical configurations of autonomy and agency among various types of nonhumans. Such principles are difficult to reconcile with paternalistic attitudes toward ecological protection. But environmentalism is not a monolithic set of ethical guidelines. The experiences and affects that it guides can converge into creative entanglements of Indigenous and environmentalist ethics.

After learning about two alterhumanisms among settlers and the Mapuche population that have emerged from the violent constitution of the settler frontier in Chile, I now turn to the depiction of practices and ideas about humanity that have followed the constitution of the conservation frontier that we know today. The human, imagined and enacted in environmentalism, is the outcome of manifold and often contradictory practices through which activists and ecotourist entrepreneurs alike articulate ways of valuing nonhuman life. In the next chapter, I explore the specific form of alterhumanism that emerges from environmentalism through a focus on the experiences and ideas of a new collectivity, generally labeled as *the environmentalists* throughout southern Chile, which have reshaped demographic, economic, and political social life around frontier forests. This collectivity might be difficult to demarcate but has played a central role in the making of conservation frontiers since the 1990s.

Chapter 3

The Experience of Ecocentrism

*Enchantment and Human Authenticity
in Environmentalism*

"One realizes that walking in the forest is like entering the infinity and the mystery of the world, because here, the world touches you on every level, from the most basic, the most physical to the most subtle and spiritual." These words, spoken calmly in Spanish, come from a voiceover as we witness a man walking slowly through a forest. In the next shot, he is bathing his feet in a small creek. The mist and the color of the leaves suggest it is a cold day in the fall. The soothing voiceover and the sound of water streaming down a creek contribute to a sense of calm and curiosity for the viewer. The scene is drawn from *Cañi*, a short documentary directed by filmmaker Josefina Buschmann (2018). Through interviews accompanied by images of forests and the countryside across the four seasons, the documentary introduces the viewer to the lives of different dwellers living around the five hundred hectares of the Cañi nature reserve. Among them, environmental activists, farmers, and scientists voice their personal relationships with forests and what they have learned from them. Explaining the sensory power of forests is John, a renowned environmental educator and activist for forest protection originally from the United Kingdom. Some years ago, during the late 1980s, a decade when forest protection in Chile was still a minor political concern in comparison with pressing demands for the restoration of democracy, John was among the founders of some of the earliest environmental nongovernmental organizations (ENGOs) devoted to forest protection in southern Chile. He was also offering courses in ecotourist training to the point that, for many of his farming neighbors, he was the one who taught them that forests are valuable for more than their timber. In this documentary, his words tell us of the forests' abilities to surprise us and constantly reveal something new, not only about themselves, but also about ourselves and our perception of the world. While forest activism often takes the form of detached and informed scientific authority, in the experience of many environmentalists like John, forests can be properly protected only once we establish long-term affective relationships with them, through which one can experience their power to transform our consciousnesses and, in turn, uncover a truer, more relational form of humanity than that offered by the illusions of urban civilization.

Since the 1990s, a vibrant and diverse community of environmental activists, educators, and entrepreneurs has spearheaded profound changes around the towns of Pucón and Currarehue, including the establishment of new protected areas—some of them privately owned—the development of a booming ecotourism industry, and the deterrence of many development projects led by the agro-industrial and hydroelectric industries. In the new green economy they have helped build, the experience of wilderness has become the primary commodity. In this chapter, we will explore how environmentalism has profoundly shaped the creation of conservation frontiers as new spaces of experiential consumption and political activism. We will also examine how environmentalism has influenced the emergence of new understandings of humanity and the diverse ways we relate to others.

The definition of environmentalism that guides this discussion is rooted in the understanding that economic and political practices are deeply intertwined and cannot be easily separated. Environmentalism is typically defined as a form of activism geared toward the protection of the environment (Schlosberg and Bomberg 2013, 1). The means by which to achieve the protection of the environment remain very much an open question. While environmentalism can materialize in grassroots actions against the agro-industry and advocacy for climate justice (see Gatt 2018; Krøijer 2020; Pike 2017), it can also reiterate privilege and class distinctions (see Dauvergne 2016) and, in doing so, prompt new processes of land accumulation and gentrification associated with lifestyle migration (see Janoschka and Haas 2013). In the experiences of many environmentalists, effective environmental protection can be achieved by embarking on very different projects, including participation in the ecotourism industry through which new commercial and ethical values can be bestowed on forests as alternatives to resource extraction. Environmentalism might materialize in collective actions geared toward the protection of specific biodiversity hotspots, but in its daily manifestation it consists of individual life projects built on persistent and always surprising experiences of learning about nature and one's sense of selfhood. As John's words remind us, touching, smelling, and feeling the forests are just some of the ways in which one can learn about oneself and others. Learning from forests about ourselves and others is an essential step for those who wish to not only to protect nature, but also to advance and foster a new way of being human—one that emphasizes attentiveness to a world whose vitality largely depends on humans stepping back from wilderness. This approach calls for a deeper understanding of our place within the natural world, prioritizing respect and restraint over control and exploitation.

This chapter is dedicated to the depiction of the third form of alterhumanism discussed in this book. The previous two chapters explored contrasting perspectives—the experiences of colonos and Mapuche populations who have suffered violence and dispossession. These chapters illustrated different understandings of humanity that emerged historically, with the establishment of a settler frontier in southern Chile at the turn of the twentieth century. In this chapter, I examine a more recent form of alterhumanism that has emerged alongside the transformation of this territory from a resource extraction zone to a conservation frontier. While timber and water extraction continue, it would be misleading to view conservation frontiers solely as areas dedicated to conservation and ecotourism. Since the 1990s, environmental activists and entrepreneurs—mainly from other regions of Chile and abroad—have played a significant role in shaping a new political economy. As a result, environmentalist practices and ideas about the human-environment relationship have become widespread among large segments of the population living in and around the southern forests.

In the following pages, I focus on the multiple manifestations of *environmentalist alterhumanism* as it unfolds through the practices, discourses, and experiences of environmentalists within the conservation frontier in southern Chile. It is important to remember that the concept of alterhumanism assumes the existence of multiple ways of *becoming human through and with nonhuman others*. As a dialogical category, humanity is defined through transformative relationships with nonhuman entities. While being human is an inherent ontological condition, it is always diverse and continuously evolving. Environmentalist alterhumanism conceptualizes humanity by recognizing that anthropocentrism is a perceptual and ethical stance that can be transcended through the experience of ecocentrism, even if this shift is inherently precarious and imperfect. Indeed, the human is still often perceived as a separate entity from nature, capable of being an external force behind both ecological destruction and protection.

The radical potential of *environmentalist alterhumanism* largely stems from the tradition of ecocentrism, defined here as a broad ethical and philosophical approach that recognizes the fundamental equality of all beings and the importance of every ecological relationship in the broader process of world-making (see Woodhouse 2018). Although ecocentrism holds potentially disruptive implications for more-than-human coexistence, it also reflects some of the broader principles of naturalism—an ontological framework that distinguishes humanity from nature based on the exceptional nature of human subjectivity (see Descola 2013). In environmentalism, nonhumans are intentionally approached as others, subsumed under the general category of nature. Instead of deconstructing the paradox of environmentalism trapped between the ideal of ecocentrism and the recognition of human exceptionalism (see Argyrou 2005), my main aspiration in discussing environmentalism in southern Chile is to show the emergence of a particular version of humanity in which nature is dissolved and yet persistently reappears. Such a configuration of humanity begins with a desire for self-transformation, which, in Pike's terms, leads to the biosocial becomings (2017, 6) experienced by environmentalists. The transformative experience of environmentalism is sustained by the intentional cultivation of emotional connections with nonhumans (Milton 2002) through which environmentalists learn to be affected by nonhumans (Lorimer 2015, 15), effectively becoming the subjects of their transformative potentials.

In characterizing practices and ideas of environmentalism capable of spurring the experience of ecocentrism, I draw upon the idea of *enchantment*. As defined by Jane Bennett, enchantment is an action-oriented form of attentiveness toward others that prompts feelings of surprise and awe but which is also capable of fostering durable relationships with ethical responsibilities. Enchantment is "something that we encounter, that hits us, but is also a comportment that can be fostered through deliberate strategies" (2001, 13). Enchantment is never a fleeting moment, but a relationship ca-

pable of uncovering the world around us in limitlessly new ways. In environmentalism, enchantment is a predisposition intentionally cultivated as part
of a broader aspiration to experience ecocentrism and, in doing so, restore a
more authentic version of humanity—one situated within the realm of wilderness even when humanity remains a disruptive and external condition to
nature. In the following pages, we will explore the contentious role of science
and spirituality within the environmental movement.

Environmentalists offer varying persepctives on how one can become
enchanted with nature, which is often seen as a necessary step toward a
strong ethical commitment to its protection. In the biographies of environmentalists living around frontier forests, eco-activism and entrepreneurship emerge as intertwined yet distinct endeavors. This observation does
not downplay the problematic aspects of commodifying the wilderness
experience, such as the gentrification of rural areas or the homogenizing
effects of the tourist gaze on nature (see Fletcher 2014; Mendoza 2018;
West and Carrier 2004). When environmentalist enchantments are commodified, they can be reduced to easily accessible consumer experiencies
offered by the ecotourism industry, often with minimal lasting impact on

FIGURE 6 Hiking through an araucaria forest (Photograph by author)

personal transformation and self-growth. However, enchantments always hold a significance beyond their commodified forms (Bennet 2001, 115). In theory, there is nothing preventing the experience of wilderness through ecotourism from inspiring the same environmentalist enchantments that animate a deep, radical commitment to protecting nature. In conservation frontiers, our feelings and perceptions of the world develop within what I call the political economy of enchantment—an assemblage of production relationships where nonhumans are transformed into subjects with enchanting potentials and are imbued with political, economic, and ethical values that are inherently contradictory. These contradictions give rise to changing understandings of humanity.

Environmentalism in Chile: A Brief History

Across the globe, the early 1970s saw a growing intersection between political liberation movements and conservation (Fletcher 2014, 93). Demands for social and political change merged with environmental philosophies such as deep ecology, an ethical philosophy inspired by the writings of Arne Næss (1989), which built upon the recognition of an essential equality of value for all forms of life (de Steiguer 2006, 200). Both deep ecology and countercultural politics have played crucial roles in the ideological formation of environmental activism in Chile in the last decades. However, there are two other historical conjunctures, both older and more specific to Latin America (see Gudynas 1992), that have significantly influenced contemporary environmentalism in Chile. Research in the natural sciences in the early twentieth century stood as the first effective action in introducing a politics of forest protection. A later wave of critiques against natural and human exploitation associated with the latifundia system and the agro-industrial complex came with peasant movements in the 1960s. Although nature protection was not their main motivation, agrarian movements in Latin America exemplify many features of the "environmentalism of the poor," an expression coined by Martínez-Alier (2002) to indicate experiences of eco-activism, mainly from the Global South, which contrast with versions of this phenomenon where commitment to nature protection appears a marker of upper- and middle-class distinction, *sensu* Bourdieu (Mendoza 2018, 44).[1]

The earliest and most overt instance of advocacy for conservation in Chile took place in the first decade of the twentieth century when a few renowned foresters and biologists, among them the German-born Federico Albert, lobbied for legal reforms geared toward the introduction of forestry regulations and the establishment of national parks in areas of southern Chile affected by swift deforestation at the hands of settlers (Camus 2006; Wakild 2017). For much of the twentieth century, environmentalism was restricted to scientists' advocacy for national parks. Environmental organizations began to adopt a more critical approach toward industrial and agri-business development in Chile in the 1960s (see Aldunate 2001), at a time when the activist scene was dominated by class-based and Marxist politics, which saw political claims other than wealth redistribution, such as environmental conservation, as secondary concerns (Rojas 1994, 97). Yet environmentalism began to make its way gradually into national debates, mostly thanks to the work of scientific organizations advocating for biodiversity protection. Unlike the Global North, for much of the twentieth century, scientists in Latin America have actively participated in political debates, mostly in response to social movements and left-wing parties who feel that science should first and foremost provide solutions to pressing social issues (Barandiarán 2018, 34–35). One of the most enduring environmental organizations established by scientists in the 1960s is CODEFF (*Comité de Defensa de la Flora y Fauna de Chile* or "Committee for the Defense of the Flora and Fauna of Chile"), whose mission was to bring public attention to environmental hazards, such as illegal logging or industrial pollution (Ulianova and Estenssoro 2012, 187).[2]

For much of Pinochet's dictatorship (1973–1990), environmental organizations were compelled to abandon critical stances toward economic development, focusing on supposedly less politically engaged aspects of wildlife education. Yet, under the guise of scientific authorities, environmental organizations organized successful campaigns for the protection of specific biodiversity spots threatened by illegal logging or industrial activities. One of the most influential scientific organizations of the time was CIPMA (*Centro de Investigation y Planificación del Medio Ambiente* or "Center for Environmental Research and Planning"), founded in 1979 by a group of urban planners who had been previously banned from different university departments for opposing Pinochet's dictatorship (Camus and Hajek 1998, 35). Although repression of grassroots activists by Pinochet's

dictatorship continued until its end in 1990, a combination of economic crisis and a wave of mobilizations in the late 1980s paved the way for the rise of
new ENGOs, which combined conservation concerns with an emphasis on
rural development, participatory planning, and agricultural cooperativism
(Rojas 1994, 101).[3]

The return to democratic rule in 1990, marked by the election of Christian
Democrat president Patricio Aylwin, who was supported by the center-left
coalition *Concertación de Partidos por la Democracia* ("Coalition of Parties
for Democracy"), ushered in a period of heightened environmental activism.
This era led to the implementation of nature protection policies deemed
highly innovative at the time. Despite popular changes in rural development
and environmental protection policies, the post-dictatorship era saw a continuity of neoliberal governance from the previous decade in terms of the
liberalization of the natural resource market and predilection for state support for agro-industry over small-scale production, particularly in forestry
(see Camus 2006; Klubock 2014).

The parallel growth of the agribusiness industry and grassroots politics
in the 1990s resulted in the recurrent eruption of environmental conflicts
(see Barandiarán 2018), mostly involving mining and agricultural companies,
ENGOs, and state actors divided among those concerned with environmental threats and those looking favorably at the opportunity of new investments
and job opportunities in remote and rural areas. For the last three decades,
ENGOs such as the Instituto de Ecología Política, founded in 1987, have
been involved in environmental disputes by offering advisory services to
populations affected by agro-industrial projects in litigation over environmental assessment reviews run by governmental agencies (Rojas 1994, 106–
107). In southern Chile, the most recent and publicly known environmental
conflicts have arisen following the construction of hydroelectric plants (see
Kelly 2019; McAllister 2020; Romero Toledo 2014), whose numbers have
steadily increased since the early 2000s. These are facilitated, among many
factors, by the 1981 water code, which has enshrined a system of water access
based on the transactability of privately owned water rights (Babidge 2016;
Prieto and Bauer 2012).[4]

Within Chile's diverse contemporary environmental movement, historical trends—such as the dominance of an environmentally aware scientific
community—coexist with more recent influence of the Latin American debate on "styles of development" (Martínez-Alier et al. 2016). This dialogue has

inspired not only efforts to protect biodiversity hotspots but also a broader rejection of Chile's economic dependence on infrastructural development, particularly linked to energy projects and the expansion of agrobusiness (Rojas 1994). The adoption of alternative models for rural development, such as agroecology, a paradigm that encourages reliance on ecological processes and knowledge rather than industrial solutions to the shortages of small-scale agriculture (see Altieri 2018), might have had few economic effects on the agricultural sectors in Chile, but it remains a central theme in the environmental movement, particularly in towns at the forefront of the conservation boom like Pucón and Currarehue.

While the concerns of the environmental movement in Chile are broad, from industrial pollution to water protection, forest protection has historically been the most recurrent one and to this day continues to dominate the scene, at least in southern Chile. After the forest protection movement's initial momentum in response to settlers' deforestation in the early twentieth century, forest activism has grown out of a reaction against the expansion of the timber industry, a sector led by a handful of large corporations that have capitalized on Pinochet-era incentives to convert agricultural land into cash crop timber plantations (see Ulianova and Estenssoro 2012).[5] The valorization of native forests and the critique of the industrial forestry model have served as a shared ground for alliances between ENGOs and Mapuche organizations involved in land reclamations from timber companies and moved by a general apprehension of soil degradation (Klubock 2014, 278). But as collaborations are common, so too are tensions between the two groups, particularly when ENGOs adopt a preservationist stance insensitive to Indigenous landholders' customary practices. One consequence of this is the possibility of such groups being alienated from protected areas.

Among the several organizations and foundations that have historically spearheaded forest activism in Chile, three stand out for their enduring influence. The first is the ENGO "Defenders of the Chilean Wood" (*Defensores del Bosque Chileno*), established in 1993 to promote knowledge of and interest in forests to the general public under the leadership of the renowned botanist Adriana Hoffman (Klubock 2014, 273).[6] The milestone of this organization was the publication of a now-legendary book within the forest preservation community, entitled *La tragedia del bosque chileno* (*The Tragedy of the Chilean Wood*), which includes photographs and essays by influential figures in the environmental movement from both Chile and abroad

(Aldunate 2001). The second ENGO is the "Association of Forest Engineers for the Native Wood" (*Agrupación de Ingenieros Forestales por el Bosque Nativo* or AIFBN), founded in 1993. This organization developed a unique approach to forestry in the country, centered on sustainable development and thus distancing itself from preservationist paradigms more common in the forest movement of the time. Its activities include training programs and participatory projects in forest management with small landholders across the country.[7]

The third organization is the Tompkins Conservation Foundation, which continues the legacy of the late entrepreneur and philanthropist Douglas Tompkins, who established the Conservation Land Trust in 1992 with the objective of purchasing large extensions of forested land in northern Patagonia and turning them into conservation areas. In 2018, in what was a keystone of the forest protection movement in Chile, the foundation donated its land properties to the Chilean state for the establishment of two national parks, Parque Nacional Patagonia and Parque Nacional Pumalín Douglas Tompkins. As we will hear more about in chapter 5, philanthropic foundations involved in the management of protected areas are subject to opposite interpretations; they are either treated as exemplary cases of effective forest protection or criticized as responsible for excessive land accumulation, a phenomenon generally known under the label of *green grabbing* (see Holmes 2015). The structural manifestations of the problematic intersection between capital accumulation and conservation are well-known. Less apparent, perhaps, are the combined effects of eco-activism and involvement in the green economy on the more personal and emotional processes of self-formation. These impacts have significant implications for the broader constitution of conservation frontiers as the ideal sites for economic and political experiments in more-than-human coexistence.

Environmentalist Enchantments, or How We Learn to Be Transformed by Wilderness

Around the frontier forests of southern Chile, eco-activists and entrepreneurs usually go by the name of "environmentalists" (*ambientalistas*). It is a diverse group, as this category is loosely applied to anyone with environmental interests or concerns. As observed in other ecotourism hotspots across

the world, environmentalism tends to reflect middle- and upper-class predispositions and tastes. Many environmentalists living in and around the
towns of Pucón and Currarehue are college-educated urbanites who have
moved to mountainous valleys as a lifestyle option. Local landholders, especially those who see environmentalism as incompatible with farmers' needs
and aspirations, label many of these environmentalists as *cuicos*, a derogatory term designating members of the upper class.[8] However, not all activists
are *cuicos*, as some, especially younger ones, come from local smallholding
families. They generally became interested in organic food production or ecotourism as an alternative to farming. Most activists are non-Indigenous, but
Mapuche leaders and representatives are also known for their involvement
in activities and projects run by local ENGOs. While most environmentalists
in Pucón are Chileans, there are a few from North America and Europe who
have moved to southern Chile and pursued personal projects marked by
forest activism and involvement in the ecotourism industry.

The demarcation of environmentalists as a group is hard because collective events are typically intermittent. An environmentalist would typically
participate in the activities of one or more ENGOs, even though in most
cases, participation is sporadic. With the exception of large national and
transnational organizations, ENGOs in Chile tend to be short-lived, given
the enormous difficulties they face in securing stable economic support.
While preparing this book, I heard of only a few cases of local ENGOs that
have successfully turned into durable organizations with a large and loyal
base. One of them is the *Consejo Ambiental Pucón* ("Environmental Council
of Pucón"), which has served as the most influential watchdog organization
in the area, monitoring the activities of potentially harmful businesses, such
as fish farms. A significant achievement for this organization was the attain-
ment of state funding to implement a plan for energy transition in Pucón in
2002. The project, titled Pucón in Transition, encompassed the publication
of an open-access book authored by different activists and experts from the
area, the production of a documentary, and public talks intended to incen-
tivize recycling and sustainable forms of water management.

Another factor contributing to the transient nature of local ENGOs is that
they are often formed in response to specific local and environmental threats
and may dissolve once the immediate issue, such as the rejection of controversial infrastructural projects like small hydroelectric plants (*centrales de
paso*), is resolved. These projects are frequently criticized for subtly disrupt-

ing riverflow in ways that are not always immediately visible. These types of hydroelectric plants have proliferated in southern Chile during the last decade because, for energy companies, their construction is more viable than larger projects that would undergo stricter environmental impact assessments and would have more dramatic social and ecological effects, such as the flooding of agricultural and residential land properties (see Kelly 2019).

While ENGOs may not always provide stable spaces for congregation, there are other ways for communities to socialize through collective events. One of the most well-known and popular in the area is the seed exchange celebration known throughout southern Chile as *trafkintu*, originally a Mapudungun term indicating a ceremonial form of exchange.[9] *Trafkintu* are typically organized by local municipalities or by organizations participating in an international network for local seed protection, such as the *Red de Semilla Libre* ("Network of Free Seeds"). Participants and organizers of *trafkintu* often come from very different backgrounds, as they include Indigenous Mapuche horticulturalists and middle- and upper-class urbanites. Nonetheless, they share a political commitment to the preservation of local crop varieties, such as beans, which have been threatened by the standardization of crop production over the last forty years in Chile as well as by the prospect of the introduction of intellectual property regulations over the genetic composition of local crops. Another significant space for socialization is social media platforms like Facebook and Instagram. These platforms have become essential tools for environmentalists to connect, exchange information, and organize responses to emerging environmental issues.

Environmentalists in southern Chile form a diverse, unstable, and unequal collectivity. However, while getting to know the life trajectories of many environmentalists living around the frontier forests central to this book, I was struck by a common biographical context they share. Being an environmentalist is a lifelong journey of learning about both nature and oneself. This begins with and is continually invigorated by revelatory experiences that highlight the transformative impact of engaging with wilderness and, in particular, forests. Revelatory experiences may happen at any stage of life, even though environmentalists tend to emphasize childhood memories as the formative sites of their new life courses. These memories are frequently narrated with a wistful emphasis on the pleasure of discovering the natural world for the first time, but they may also recollect distressing events, such as the logging of a forest in the proximity of their house (Milton 2002, 64).

Weekend walks with parents around forests and the sounds of specific birds are among the most recurrent childhood memories that triggered an interest in nature among environmentalists from southern Chile. The accounts of such memories help environmentalists to express the value of childhood curiosity as an ideal engagement with the world during their adult life. Such a curiosity is capable of rejuvenating their senses of awe and discovery and, in doing so, animating "alternative ways of knowing and being that become fundamental in activists' worlds" (Pike 2017, 102).

In environmentalist biographies, revelatory experiences might look like events, but often consist of reiterative experiences enabling environmentalists to be exposed to the affective power of nonhumans and their abilities to partake in an open-ended process of self-making. As indicated by Pike, "activist identities emerge from their interactions with many species and landscapes through childhood and young adulthood, as they become human with these others over time, reacting themselves, so to speak, as they relate to trees, nonhuman animals, and landscapes where they find themselves at protests" (2017, 6). Alongside nostalgic childhood memories, encounters with specific places figure as pivotal moments in environmentalists' biographies. Among environmentalists from southern Chile, such encounters, which trigger a relentless attraction to specific biodiversity hotspots and more generally an ethical commitment to conservation, are generally described as an "arrival" (*llegada*) at a specific forest or mountain. While this narrative reflection is more evident among urbanites who have settled around southern Andean valleys attracted by the prospect of being close to wilderness, it is nonetheless present in the biographies of people born and raised around these valleys who might have paid scant attention to forests before, only to later rediscover them in all their affective powers.

John, the environmental educator whom we heard about at the beginning of this chapter, settled in Pucón in the 1980s. A few years earlier, he had moved from Scotland to Chile to work as an English language teacher. His true passion, however, had always been environmental education, something that could combine his love for mountains with his pedagogical experience. He was the first one in the area to offer meditation workshops to tourists and training courses for ecotourist guides. His activities took place in and around his house, a one-story wooden building with camping infrastructure, which he built in the middle of a forest roughly twenty kilometers away from the town of Pucón.

"The forest captures and keeps on attracting you." That is how, in his words, John explained the power of forests in making him decide to dedicate his life to studying and protecting them. The power of forests resides in a form of fascination over which one has little control and which does not exhaust itself; one's interest is constantly renewed by the changing forms of forests themselves.

Miguel, whose trajectory we will hear more about in chapter 5, is an experienced tour guide. He was born into a farming family, to later specialize in ecotourism and become one of the park managers in charge of Cañi Sanctuary, a private protected area located in the surroundings of Pucón. Even though he spent his youth not far from Cañi Mountain, where the homonymous protected area would eventually be established, he paid attention to this mountain only later in life: "I came to Cañi when I was eighteen, and I've been working here for twenty-two years. It's been quite a transformation to have the chance to work where I live. I think it's the greatest experience a person can have." Miguel might have lived around this forest from an early age, but he became utterly changed by his evolving relationship with it.

The transformative event of the arrival at a forest or a mountain is recounted by environmentalists with an emphasis on the unique agential features of specific places. Among them, forests figure as places that, more than any other, can prompt a transformative experience. For many environmentalists, forests are special because they are endowed with regenerative potential for water and soil, and consequently for the plants and animals dependent on them. The biodiversity hosted by forests is the clearest indicator of their regenerative power. Like farming populations living across southern Chile, environmentalists draw a clear line between native forests (*bosques nativos*) and monocrop timber plantations (*plantaciones*) known for their depletive effects on soil and water. The dichotomy between the two conceals the anthropogenic character of frontier forests in favor of their representation as pristine spaces but remains a powerful articulator of the exceptional regenerative power of forests. In one interview, Carlos, a forest engineer with experience in different ENGOs, identified some of the potentials of native forests: "They generate canopy, food for animals and mushrooms; they generate life. Besides serving as a source of water, forests are also a source of inspiration, culture, spirituality, and a connection with something that we don't know exactly what it is, but it matters to us." The enigma of forests, their opacity and mystery, and the rich diversity of life forms they host explain their unique abilities to not only inspire but also direct human knowledge in ways that nonhuman life is valued and celebrated.

In environmentalist discourses, the forest is "a locus of truth and meaning" (Pike 2017, 112). Its transformative power is made evident through its opposition to anthropogenic spaces, cities in particular, which are blamed for removing humans from their true nature as beings deeply affected by other species. The trope of dystopia helps the imagination of everyday urban life as an "undesired world that must be avoided and mobilized against politically" (Krøijer 2020, 49). It is also fundamental to the essentialization of forests as utopian places where authentic humanity can be uncovered through subjective experiences of *rewilding*, a term indicating the process of reconnecting with nature common in more radical versions of environmental activism. The image of human authenticity assigned to forests generates another feeling central to the experience of environmentalism: that of grief for the possible future loss of wilderness (see Cunsolo and Ellis 2018) and with it, the possibility of recovering our true human status. Loss, as Ogden reminds us, is not simply an absence, but rather a "disposition of alarm and resignation" (2021, 6) potentially generating attentiveness toward a world understood as fragile and surprising at once. Loss can be felt as hopelessness, but also as a sense of awe toward a world that can be lost, but has not been just yet.

In environmentalism, the transformative power of forests on human subjectivity stems from the agential qualities of forests themselves encountered under unpredictable circumstances. This, however, is just one side of the story. For forests to be able to keep on transforming humans and constantly revealing to them the world anew, humans need to cultivate a certain predisposition expressed emotionally through sentiments such as curiosity and wonder. Such a predisposition presupposes the intentionality of the latter to embark on a lifelong learning process through which the transformative power of forests becomes durable. Learning in environmentalism is an embodied and perceptive activity. In Lorimer's definition, conservation consists of "tentative and skillful processes of 'learning to be affected' by a target organism or ecology, disciplining one's body to tune in to its forms and dynamics" (2015, 9). In forest activism, learning requires concrete experiences aimed at heightening perceptions of human relatedness with nonhuman life. In environmentalist circles in Chile, such experiences would typically include walking around forests, meditation techniques, and to a lesser degree tree-climbing, a typical manifestation of anti-logging advocacy. A medidative activity that I learned about during my stays in southern Chile is *Gaia Reiki*. Like Reiki in general, this healing practice consists of the transfer of energy through the movement of the body coordinated by a supervisor. In addition to traditional Reiki, this version encompasses direct contact with the land through walking barefoot in the open air.

Of all meditation activities, forest bathing is certainly the most popular. *Shinrin-yoku* originated in Japan in the 1980s as a therapeutic and meditative activity that would later become popular across the globe (Antonelli et al. 2022). I had the opportunity to experience forest bathing once, in a forest located further north in Chile than the ones discussed in this book, though it shares many of their ecological features. This outing was my first weekend away since the COVID-19 pandemic began in 2020. Like many others at that time, I was wary of crowds and people in general, so visiting a national park with my wife, Bernardita, seemed like the perfect escape. The forest bathing session lasted just under an hour, during which we explored a small section of the forest. Guided by a soothing voice reminiscent of yoga or mindfulness practices, the guide encouraged us to walk slowly, sit on the ground, and touch it. I quickly became aware of the temperature changes that occurred with simple actions like sitting or standing, the constant but unseen bird songs, and the myriad of insects crawling around my feet. As someone who enjoys walking and tends to move quickly, I initially felt frustrated by the limited distance we covered. My eagerness and anxiety to explore the forest, heightened by months of strictly imposed lockdown, made the slow pace particularly challenging. Yet, as the section was moving on, I began to enjoy paying attention to the thoughts that were often surprisingly and unwillingly popping in to my head after seeing insects crawling up on my feet or hearing birds singing. If I remember correctly, my thoughts were preoccupied with the relationship between life and death, a reflection prompted by the sights and sounds of the forest.

In environmentalist practices such as those described so far, direct contact with forests is helpful in developing an attentive perception of more-than-human relatedness through the adoption of new visual, auditory, and olfactory perspectives, which the very sensorial complexity of forests provokes. For many environmentalists, the perceptive transformation brought by forest engagements can affect not only relations with nonhumans, but also relations among humans, thanks to a general awareness of relatedness and empathy that these experiences are expected to foster. For a few years,

Andrés, a forest engineer by training, has been working for a large foundation running meditation workshops and spiritual retreats inspired by New
Age philosophy within a campsite a forty-minute drive from Pucón. For him,
environmental education can spur long-lasting desired effects on human
perceptions and behaviors: "If I don't have an adequate relationship with
myself and other people, I cannot claim to be a good environmentalist."

Curiosity, wonder, astonishment, surprise, and awe are common sentiments stemming from forest engagements. While these feelings can be difficult to control, they often arise from a predisposed openness to the world—a
willingness to engage deeply. This perceptual openness facilitates the perceptive and ethical transformation of the self, which is central to environmentalism. One concept that is particularly germane to this perspective on
forest engagements is *enchantment*. Enchantment describes the compelling
power of certain relationships to evoke new experiences of surprise and curiosity and, paradoxically, to continually renew these experiences through
their repetition. As discussed by Jane Bennett (2001), enchantment has long
served as a marker of traditional and religious societies in opposition to
Weber's understanding of modernity as a historical condition characterized by a generalized feeling of disenchantment from the world, understood
as inherently mechanistic and thus transparent to technical and scientific
knowledge. While mainstream narratives of industrial modernization have
relegated enchantment to the realm of tradition, the experience of enchantment itself has never fully been eradicated. As a result, the assertion that
"we have never been disenchanted" holds true. Enchantments, as Bennett
reminds us, are "already in and around us" (2001, 174), because they cannot
be reduced exclusively to a human attribute or intention. Certain beings and
places, like forests, are capable of enchanting us more than others through
their abilities to expand or bracket our perception of the world.

While enchantment is an inherent quality of certain beings and individuals, its realization depends on human skill, through which one becomes
predisposed to be enchanted by certain beings or places. Environmentalist
enchantments possess unique qualities that set them apart from other forms
of enchantment, such as those arising from religious rituals. A significant impact of environmentalist enchantment is its ability to alleviate fear. While enchantment can be a source of comfort, it is not always so; fear—often stemming from a lack of control within an enchanting relationship—can inhibit
perception rather than enhance it (Bennett 2001, 174). In environmentalist

enchantment, fear is partially dissolved through the intentional cultivation of feelings such as awe and curiosity, which are more helpful in animating love for nature. The suppression of fear in environmentalist enchantments is indeed the most striking difference between environmentalists' representations of forests and those held by landholders and foresters in southern Chile, which stem mostly from cautionary tales about the dangers of forests and mountains. Another central quality of environmentalist enchantment is its emphasis on self-learning. A first encounter with a forest might generate awe, but it is the continuity of further encounters that is responsible for the enchantment that a forest might induce. In line with its Latin etymology, *in cantare*, literally, "to sing toward something," and with the customary association of this term with the world of magic and ritual, enchantment requires repetition. To be enchanted enables the acquisition of a perceptive attentiveness focused on the slow transformation of the other, as the only way to see something changing is to see its continuity and repetition through time (Bennett 2001, 40). Enchantments are generally enabled by reproducible techniques and technologies (see Gell 1992). The contemplative practices described a few paragraphs earlier are the most common techniques through which the power of forests is revealed in environmentalism. Other techniques are representational, and they aim at making us predisposed to perceive certain beings and places as more enchanting than others. This is the case for the circulation of images and discourses on the danger of the extinction of certain species, typically labeled as *charismatic* or *flagship* in capturing the attention of conservationists (Igoe 2017, 5). These include the black rhinoceros (*Diceros bicornis*) in eastern and southern Africa or the south Andean deer (*Hippocamelus bisulcus*) from the Chilean and Argentinean Patagonia, also known as the huemul.[10]

Enchantment is central to environmentalism. Without these enchantments, self-learning, personal transformation, and the renewal of ethical commitments to nature protection would be unattainable. But despite its significance, enchantment remains a disputed notion in environmentalism, as there are multiple ways of being enchanted that necessarily provoke opposing feelings within environmentalist circles. The debated nature of enchantment appears clearly in a historical dichotomy within global environmentalism: that between science and spirituality. From its beginnings, the environmental movement has turned to religion as a source of inspiration for the valorization of nonhuman life beyond scientific and utilitarian parameters. Arguably the most enduring leitmotif in environmentalism is the idea of the *sublime*, which has its roots in Romanticism. The sublime involves the possibility for the individuals to experience emotional and aesthetic closeness with the divine and supernatural through contact with wilderness (Taylor 2010, 46). This idea still influences how frontier regions, such as Patagonia, are represented today (Mendoza 2018). The most explicit connection between religion and environmentalism is to be found in twentieth-century nature religions (see Albanese 1991; Bloch 1998; Taylor 2010), which consist of malleable sets of ritualistic practices inspired by Western New Age philosophies and Indigenous and Buddist cosmologies geared toward the worship of nature as the impersonification of a sacred entity or divinity. Around frontier forests in southern Chile, adherence to new nature religions is often sporadic and restricted to a minority of environmentalists. A few camps and temples, mostly associated with Buddist, Hare Khrishna, and New Age communities, are scattered around the forested landscape. These spiritual communities are generally moved by the belief that closeness to nature is a necessary condition for spiritual self-realization (Zunino and Huiliñir-Canio 2016, 12).

While nature religions do not completely define the forest protection movement, the religious characterization of a deep love for nature is widespread around southern frontier forests. The attribution of sacredness to endangered ecosystems (Milton 2002, 104) and the recurring theme of sacrifice, especially in radical actions like forest occupations, illustrate how religion influences environmentalism as an underlying force, even when not explicitly acknowledged (Pike 2017, 19). Catholicism can also serve as a platform for environmental religiosity, as in the case of the association of life and water, which in many ways underlies the spirit of protest against hydroelectric projects in Chile (see McAllister 2020, 130–131). However, discomfort with institutionalized religions, particularly Christianity and its historical connection with anthropocentrism, explains why many environmentalists prefer to talk about *spirituality* rather than *religion* in depicting their relationship with nature. The term *spirituality* is particularly helpful in emphasizing the subjective nature of environmentalist life projects, often depicted as journeys of self-discovery and personal growth (see Taylor 2010, 7).

In line with the malleability of nature spirituality, activists also borrow and rewrite Indigenous cosmological notions to express more general ideas about the spiritual power of nature. During a community workshop, an attendee responded empathically to the intervention of a Mapuche landholder who was critical of the negative impact of commercial forestry: "The forests inspire all of us here because they have many spirits. The ngen that our Mapuche friends talk about, they are real, absolutely. There is an energy that gives life and diversity to the entire world." As discussed in the previous chapter, in Mapuche cosmology, ngen are powerful and sometimes mischievous master spirits associated with natural features. They require careful and respectful engagement with humans. In environmentalist narratives, they may turn into more general spiritual forces.

The inclusion of Indigenous cosmologies into environmentalist discourses is not exempt from critiques of cultural appropriation or Western essentialization. A clear example is the view of some environmental activists who at times discredit Mapuche foresters as inauthentic, as their commercial practices are incompatible with their role of nature guardianship. At the same time, the translation of Indigenous and environmentalist notions can strengthen shared interests in nature protection among the two collectivities. In fact, the reference to ngen spirits by the workshop attendee was met with praise and approval by Mapuche landholders sitting next to him.

Despite the popularity of nature spirituality in the environmental movement, its role remains highly contested. For many environmentalists from southern Chile, spirituality has no place in the design of informed strategies about environmental protection and might even work to discredit environmentalism in the eyes of political interlocutors and broader society. On at least a couple of occasions, I heard how divergences in the roles of science and religion can turn into conflicts and divisions within an ENGO. In an interview, Mario, an experienced activist who has participated in the implementation of several conservation projects around the town of Pucón, recalled a controversy that took place several years earlier. Tensions among members of an ENGO arose following the decision to build a hut to be used by scientists monitoring wildlife populations within a private protected area: "They believed that this shelter was being built on a sacred mountain, a pristine place, but it was far from being the reality." The mountain, which local ENGOs were working to protect and later rewild, had traditionally been used for forestry and livestock husbandry. Like spirituality, trust in science is also a matter of controversy. While ENGOs rely extensively on scientific reports to demand protection against environmental threats, they are often led to question the impartiality of scientific expertise, particularly in the context of controversies over the impact assessment of development projects (Berglund 1998, 168).[11] Nature spirituality is central to the articulation of environmentalist enchantments and, by extension, to developing a political commitment to nature protection. However, despite being portrayed in modern narratives as part of a disenchanted worldview, science is not excluded from generating its own forms of enchantment. As we will explore in the following chapter, conservation science involves engaging with the world in ways that can evoke feelings of awe and surprise, even amid the repetitive routines of data collection.

Environmentalist enchantments unfold in the midst of different and apparently incongruous experiences. They can be experienced as part of personal journeys of self-knowledge, involvement in disruptive forms of eco-activism, and consumption of wilderness experiences. Once turned into commodities, environmentalist enchantments become more easily accessible to an increasingly large population of consumers in the booming ecotourism industry. As commodities, environmentalist enchantments can function as new processes of capital accumulation responsible for the growth of the real estate market in increasingly gentrified rural areas. However, conservation economies do not mark the end of eco-activism or the ethical potential of environmentalist enchantment, as evidenced by the intertwined paths of eco-activism and entrepreneurship among environmentalists in southern Chile.

FIGURE 7 Pucón with the Villarrica volcano in the background (Photograph by ByDroneVideos/Shutterstock.com)

Green Productivism and the Political Economy of Enchantment

Green productivism is a model of economic transition for frontier regions based on the presumption that sustainable growth is best spurred by ecologically sustainable forms of capital accumulation such as tourism and conservation investment, particularly in carbon payments rather than resource extraction (Mendoza 2018, 12). In green productivism, the state holds a central role, participating in place branding for upcoming ecotourist centers and providing funding mechanisms to the tourism industry. Green productivism, expectedly, has multiple and contradictory manifestations. The growth of tourism entrepreneurship and the real estate market has brought new employment and infrastructural improvements in frontier areas. It has also inspired new conservation initiatives and rejections of agro-industrial projects within a local population increasingly antagonistic to them for ethical as well as economic reasons, given their potential negative impact on tourism. However, farming populations can also experience a more negative side of green productivism, resembling the broader phenomenon of overtourism. Employment opportunities are seasonal and more likely to be enjoyed by a younger, transient population from urban areas. At the same time, the gentrification of rural land into residential units has made living costs increasingly difficult to manage. Southern Chile has become a major draw for lifestyle migrants, primarily middle and upper-class urbanites from Santiago (see Hidalgo and Zunino 2012; Marchant and Rojas 2015). Over the past two decades, the number of people moving to rural areas around towns like Pucón has steadily increased, with a notable surge during the COVID-19 pandemic when remote work became more feasible for some professions. These lifestyle migrants are often attracted to residential complexes known as *comunidades ecológicas* ("ecological communities"), which feature natural green spaces and adhere to strict eco-friendly construction standards. However, residential growth and gentrification are not limited to well-known towns. A land rush is now occurring in more remote areas of southern Chile and Patagonia, driven by the liberalization of the real estate market. This has made relatively inexpensive small residential plots (*parcelas*) available, which small-scale buyers view either as future investments or potential sites for holiday homes, contingent on future infrastructure developments like roads and electricity.

Along with real estate development, ecotourism is the other key driver of green productivism. The deep global economic impact of ecotourism is explained by the fact that this is not simply a commercial specialization in the tourism industry, but rather an influential discourse on the ethical and economic value of wilderness, inspired by the language of sustainable development and the counterculture movement of the 1960s and 70s (Fletcher 2014, 93). As defined by Fletcher, ecotourism is sustained by "a cultural or discursive process, embodying a particular constellation of beliefs, norms, and values that inform the activity's practice and that are implicitly propagated via ecotourism's promotion as a strategy for sustainable development and environmental conservation in communities throughout the world" (2014, 3). The commodification processes at work in ecotourism (see Büscher and Davidov 2016; Ojeda 2012) are driven by the transformation of wilderness into a consumable product, shaped by ideals of authenticity (West and Carrier 2004). This often involves presenting pristine environments where farming activities are no longer deemed appropriate—despite their historical continuity (see Carrier and Macleod 2005).

Ecotourism differs from mass tourism because it encourages low-impact infrastructural interventions in underdeveloped areas (Fletcher 2014, 11). While ecotourism facilitates projects of rewilding through the establishment of private protected areas where services are offered, predictably, it is still responsible for urban transformations, particularly those associated with higher demands for accommodation. The reconfiguration of remote landscapes as accessible wilderness is enabled not only by material changes to transport and housing infrastructure but also to the development of a particular gaze among locals and tourists alike, which favors attention toward pristine biodiversity hotspots. As Urry and Larsen remind us, the tourism industry is sustained by the ability of market and state actors to create "resources, techniques, cultural lenses that potentially enable tourists to see the physical forms and material spaces before their eyes as 'interesting, good or beautiful'" (2011, 2). The ecotourist gaze prompts consumers to feel attracted to places approached a priori as wilderness. These places are the object of place branding as well as material interventions in the landscape (Fletcher 2014, 150), such as paths and borders designed to focus attention on biodiversity hotspots and panoramic sceneries. As shown by Mendoza, the sublime, a sentiment that is historically associated with elite adventurous experiences of wilderness, has not been erased with the growth of the tourism industry but rather become safely available to a larger public (2018, 54).

In the public arena, ecotourism is generally treated as a panacea for both poverty and environmental degradation in remote areas (see Das and Chatterjee 2015). Such a view is common among environmentalists living around southern frontier forests. For them, ecotourism is a political and economic force capable of making conservation an attractive source of employment and entrepreneurial opportunities for local landholders and, in turn, instilling environmentalist values in rural society at large. In an interview, Nancy, an activist and entrepreneur with a large trajectory in forest conservation in Chile and abroad, explained why thinking of nature protection as a secondary social issue in comparison with rural poverty fails to capture the essence of the environmental movement: "In Chile, some people say that it is a luxury to worry about the environment. However, when someone establishes a new protected area, they are also planting a new concept about the environment and society, whose impact will be felt by all those living around it." In various discussions, the positive economic and social impacts of conservation on rural communities are often framed in terms of empowerment (*empoderamiento*). Empowerment through ecotourism involves fostering both political commitment to nature protection and entrepreneurial creativity among local farming residents. This concept of empowerment is explicitly contrasted with the traditional disempowerment associated with state dependency, known in Chile as *asistencialismo*. Environmentalists frequently critique state involvement in conservation for two main reasons: First, the state's involvement in nature protection is always secondary to its historical alliance with the agribusiness industry, and second, genuine commitment to conservation requires proactive individual efforts rather than reliance on the state's effectiveness in enforcing environmental protection.

Central to green productivism is the creation of values that are at once commercial and ethical. As once explained by Pablo, a member of a ENGO from the town of Villarrica, the establishment of new private and public protected areas around the town of Pucón have helped cement environmentalist values for the entire population: "With all these new parks, the economic value of land around here has changed a lot. However, a more intrisic value has also grown. Many farmers are today proud of the nature surrounding them." The commodification of wilderness inherent to green productivism has evidently problematic underpinnings, attested by the impact of gentrification and other forms of economic exclusion. Yet the fact that many environmentalists are both political activists and entrepreneurs or workers active in the local tourism industry tells us of the depth of the intersections between green productivism and eco-activism. While eco-activism can often take the form of an individualized recreational activity with little social impact (see Erickson 2011), in towns like Pucón, advocacy for forest protection is also sustained by a desire for a new, more eco-friendly, economic strategy that could represent a viable alternative to historical dependency on agribusiness. Trust in the positive effects of small-scale entrepreneurship on economic growth and nature protection reflects the principles of entrepreneurial activism (İpek 2023). This approach, observed among some microentrepreneurs, involves viewing their commercial activities as part of a larger political struggle (see Lewis 2019).

In the frontier forests described in this book, visitors can choose from a wide variety of activities, including rafting, volcano trekking, leisurely forest walks, and horse riding. This chapter has paid more attention to meditative and educational activities offered by ecotourism entrepreneurs because they are perhaps clearer examples of the potentials of environmental enchantments made available in ecotourism in encouraging attentiveness to ecological relatedness and even a political and ethical commitment to nature protection. Adrenaline-filled activities, like rafting, might have less of an impact on the hit-and-run visitor to frontier forests, but they nonetheless contribute to the consolidation of a widespread belief among eco-activists and entrepreneurs that wilderness provides uniquely enriching experiences and its protection is urgent, not only if green economies are to flourish but also for the persistence of nature's ability to enchant us. The success of ecotourism is sustained by its ability to make environmentalist enchantments available to an increasingly wider public. In green productivism, the enchanting effects of wilderness can be normalized as momentary and replicable experiences that, qua commodities, can be consumed as events in themselves. However, experiences such as those enabled by ecotourism can also generate forms of enchantment that translate into a durable ethical commitment to conservation and an affective relationship.

The political economy of enchantment is ambivalent ground for the articulation of environmentalist values. The commodification of wilderness experiences remains a key articulator of environmentalist engagements with nonhuman life, but it does not define them in their totality. The incomplete commodification of the wilderness experience can be understood by examining the inherent nature of commodities. While nonhumans turned into commodities rarely enchant us beyond their socially accepted economic values, for Bennett (2001, 115), their commodification lacks the totalizing power that both critics and supporters of capitalism seem to assign to it. One can hardly encounter a pure commodity—even more so when the commodity consists of an experience. While Marxist demystification remains a fundamental heuristic tool to uncover relationships and biographies of production and thus avoid the naturalization of commodities, it is also analytically indispensable to look at the ethical and political effects of the enchantments that the objects of commodities, such as commodified wilderness experience, can generate (2001, 113). When nonhumans are collectively categorized as nature and turned into experiential commodities, encounters with them may lose the potential to inspire the sustained, intentional attentiveness to the world that enchantment evokes. However, beings and experiences that are commodified always retain aspects that go beyond their commodity status. While the commodification of wilderness experiences might encourage a lifelong appetite for enchantments with nonhumans, it can also mark the end of a relationship of enchantment that, once consumed, is depleted or exhausted.

Precarious Ecocentrism and the Question of True Humanity

In this chapter, I characterize enchantment as a central experience of environmentalism. Environmentalist enchantments continuously invigorate life projects driven by the desire to be surprised and affected by the very nonhumans whose protection one feels responsible for. Despite the diversity of these environmentalist endeavors, they are united by a common aspiration: to continually refine and transform one's perception of the world and sense of self in ways that allow nonhumans to reveal something new about themselves, the world we inhabit, and ultimately, ourselves. In environmentalism, the ultimate aim of this lifelong journey of self-learning is to uncover a more authentic humanity: one that has been obscured by urban civilization and inattention to nonhuman life.

The ideal outcome of this process is the development of a relational self that embodies the principles of ecocentrism rather than anthropocentrism.

Both terms are commonly used in environmental activism. Among environmentalists in southern Chile, ecocentrism and anthropocentrism may not always be explicitly mentioned, but their main premises are recurrent themes of conversations. The term *ecocentrism* has been historically conceptualized as an understanding of the world that recognizes the essential equality of all ecological relations. Its central principle, identity, was first articulated by Arne Næss as part of his ethical and ontological proposal of deep ecology, which many environmentalists in southern Chile cite as a major philosophical influence. In deep ecology, identity is based on the idea that humans see shared substance and feelings in nonhuman others (1989, 174). Only by seeing ourselves in nonhumans can we fully recognize the value of all forms of life.

I propose that the experience of ecocentrism is essential to the formation of the environmentalist self, yet it remains precarious because humanity is often conceptualized as either destroyer or guardian. The intentional pursuit of ecocentrism is inherently paradoxical, as it seeks to transcend anthropocentrism while still being rooted in human intentions and actions. Even though the principle of identity makes morality a preconscious predisposition based on the direct perception of commonalities across the human-nonhuman divide (Milton 2002, 75), identity requires a moral intention to first approach nonhumans as others in order to later perceive them under a new light. For Argyrou (2005, 157), the paradox of ecocentrism lies in the fact than an individual needs to become a fully conscious subject with new perceptive attention to nonhuman life in order to live in a world where the subject/object divide implicit to anthropocentrism is no longer at work. Albeit moved by a political and ethical aspiration of overcoming anthropocentrism, ecocentrism portrays humanity at once as a condition inserted into and dependent within the broader web of life and the external cause of its disruption. In de Steiguer's definition of ecocentrism, this school of thought "maintains that the world was originally in a natural state of equilibrium unambiguously intruded. Since then, the intricate web of life has been broken through a succession of degenerative disruptions that will ultimately lead to the destruction of the world itself" (2006, 15).

Naturalism constitutes the primary ontological base of Western environmentalism even when the experience of ecocentrism is essential to environmentalist self-making. As proposed by Descola, naturalism is an ontological scheme "defined by the continuity of the physicality of the entities of the world and the discontinuity of their respective interiorities" (2013, 173). Under naturalism, humans are exceptional for their interiority and subjectivity, while their corporalities have animal-like qualities. In environmental activism, ecocentrism is an ethical rendition of the world that has historically been articulated in opposition to dominant versions of Western naturalism, which are driven by a desire for human mastery. However, eocentrism aligns with a naturalist view of the world, as it reinforces the idea of nature as a self-evident entity, thus merging the existence of nonhuman subjects into this broader category. In doing so, it attributes to nature a transformative power that can reveal human authenticity, suggesting that true human nature is uncovered through engagement with the natural world.

The idea of nature in Western humanism has been the main target of critical reflections, perhaps the most notable of which is ecofeminism, with its critique of the essentialism of nature as a transcendental entity on whose behalf certain humans, mostly men, can speak with more authority than others (Gaard 2017, 30). Protecting nature rather than specific nonhumans and the constructive relationships on which their vitality depends has problematic political implications. For Latour, ecological politics "does not speak about nature and has never sought to do so. It has to do with associations of beings that take complicated forms—rules, apparatuses, consumers, institutions, mores, calves, cows, pigs, broods—and that it is completely superfluous to include in an inhuman and ahistorical nature" (2004, 21). In his proposal, environmental activism should be concerned with the dissolution of nature and the recognition of nonhumans as different subjects imbricated in political affairs.

While the political value of deconstructive critiques of environmentalism can be debated, the tensions between ecocentrism and Western naturalism present clear challenges. This incongruity complicates the ability to develop effective strategies for care and protection that are attuned to the specific, situated nature of ecological relationships impacted by both gradual and sudden forms of human-induced environmental destruction. While critiques are essential to reveal the inherent and perhaps unavoidable contradictions within Western environmentalist ontologies, they often neglect the profound effects that environmentalist ideas and practices have on the redefining of humanity as an inherently ambivalent category at the core of environmentalism. Among environmentalists, humanity is an irreducible condition that one might desire to dissolve within an ecocentric world, but that continues to be ontologically framed as outside nature. This sentiment is captured in the words of Andrés, an active figure within the environmental movement and ecotourism industry in Pucón:

> The human being is a destroyer of equilibrium. Everywhere we enter, we make a mess. The forest is no different. What we are trying to achieve is for humans to become an entity capable of collaborating with the forest, rather than causing its imbalance. We want to be part of the forest, but leaving a space for nature to be nature.

The core motivation of any environmentalist life project is the desire to become part of the forest, or nature more broadly, even when such a possibility is impossible. In *environmentalist alterhumanism*, this sought-after connection with nature is essential to the process of self-making, where one learns to experience the affective powers of nonhumans on us and, in turn, become politically committed to the protection of nature as the site of true humanity. This particular form of *becoming human through and with nonhuman others* is built upon the ambivalent position of humanity defined at the interstices of ecocentric aspirations and acknowledgment of anthropocentrism as the dominant condition of a world. Even when ecocentrism is a precarious and paradoxical way of being in the world that can never be fully achieved, its experience is essential for environmentalists to learn to pay attention to how one can experience and make sense of their humanity through relationships with nonhuman others.

* * *

In this chapter, I have described some of the sentiments, practices, and values that characterize the life of environmentalists living around southern frontier forests. Their work and legacy are central to the historical conformation of a conservation frontier since the 1990s, where the value of nature has shifted from being a resource to be extracted to an experience to be consumed. I have also examined some of the contrasts and overlaps between resource and conservation frontiers unfolding in the same geographical spaces affected by settler expansion at the turn of the twentieth century. The changes that come with the consolidation of conservation frontiers range from capitalist accumulation responsible for new inequalities and exclusions to the effective forging of political and ethical commitments to the protection of nature. Within the political economy of enchantment that structures human life in conservation frontiers, desires for self-transformation through exposure to nature's affective power, the momentary vision of an ecocentric world, and the acknowledgment of anthropocentrism as the dominant perspective converge to form a distinct individual and collective way of *becoming human through and with others.*

In the next chapter, I continue to explore how attentiveness to nonhuman life plays a central role in the configuration of humanity and its alterity in conservation. This time, the reader will hear about the experiences and values that move conservation scientists in their attempts to show a new perspective on forest environments: that of birds, whose acts and relationships direct us to new ways of thinking about life, death, and the sustenance of a fragile world.

Chapter 4

The Birds' Forest

*Conservation Science and Avian Life in
the Shadow of Human Disturbance*

During the years I spent regularly visiting protected areas in southern Chile, I had the opportunity to meet several ecologists whose field sites overlapped with many of the localities described in this book, or at least were geographically similar. Eager to find out more about the role of science in the establishment and consolidation of conservation frontiers, I began to meet with avian ecologists with field experiences around the towns of Pucón and Currarehue. Birds, as I learned in these conservations, can reveal much about the nature of a forest as the site of multispecies interactions. Many structural features of forests, such as the key role of dead trees in the configuration of a habitat for migratory avian communities—or *guilds* as they are known technically— would go otherwise unnoticed without a focus on the triadic relationship linking humans, birds, and trees. As my interest deepened, I asked Sebastián, a colleague from the Pontificia Universidad Católica de Chile, if I could join the fieldwork team he was coordinating at the time to learn more about the practice of avian ecology itself. A few weeks later, I was in Pichares, the hamlet where the base of Cañi Sanctuary is located. This time, Martín, a fellow social scientist, and I had the opportunity to visit a restricted area of the park, typically off-limits to visitors and accessible only to scientists, guides, and local residents. We joined three interns, who at the time were in their final year at college, and their supervisor Jessica, a junior ecologist from Canada, in a two-day fieldwork session. This fieldwork was part of an international collaboration between avian ecologists from Chile and Canada, two of the few countries that are home to temperate rain forests. Martín and I met the research team at an intersection in the proximity of the park. After reaching a wooden gate, we began walking along a path. It was a surprisingly cold and foggy day for summer, something that made the walk more tolerable given the camping gear and the heavy instruments we were carrying.

As part of a research project on nesting behaviors in forests, one of the main objectives of this campaign was to survey trees with previously known nesting cavities, identifiable by fluorescent tags clipped onto trees with GPS coordinates. Once a cavity was retrieved, team members would begin to monitor activities within and outside the nest through the *piper*, a term used by researchers to refer to a wireless monitoring system with an extendable plastic pole reaching over ten meters. Using the piper requires strength and precision, given the considerable weight of the pole and the small size of the tree cavity, sometimes only a few centimeters wide. The holder carefully moves the tip of the pole, to which a small camera is fixed, into a tree cavity to observe the nest therein on the monitor. Any abrupt movement could damage the nest, or even destroy the eggs. Throughout the two days of field-work, observations were accompanied by emotional comments on the status of each nest. With excitement and awe, the observer would tell the rest of the team about the quick movements of featherless tiny birds who had just hatched from their eggs. Or with disappointment, they would report the presence of scattered twigs and feathers, suggesting that a nest known to host a few hatchlings had been predated by another bird species.

The emotions rising from the experience of entering an otherwise in-accessible place to observe powerful life processes such as birth and death did not distract the team from the most tedious and yet crucial part of the process—that of taking notes, so as to transmute their observations into the printed forms that would later become the bulk of the data for the en-tire project. Any observations made while using the piper or simply walking through the forest were accompanied by educated guesses about bird calls or sightings. These forests are home to abundant populations of the small but highly effective predator the American kestrel (*Falco sparverius*), the colorful austral parakeet (*Enicognathus ferrugineus*), and the chucao (*Scelorchilus rubecula*) with its high-pitched powerful chirping. They also host species scarcer to this region of Chile, such as the Magellanic woodpecker (*Campephilus magellanicus*), one of the largest woodpeckers in the world, distinguished by the bright red plumage on its head and often spotted because of its rhythmic, reverberating knocks high up in the trees.

In thinking retrospectively about my observations of these field activities, I cannot help but draw an obvious analogy between my interlocutors' research and my own. Despite evident differences, our research activities equally depend on subjective experiences and often volatile observations that we would eventually struggle to make sense of and turn into more generalizable accounts of human-environmental relations. In his ethnographic account of marine biology, Helmreich writes: "If marine microbiologists are engaged in a kind of oceanography—a word that speaks to the immensity, if not impossibility, of writing down the ocean—ethnography shares the similarly difficult task of writing up an account of a people's practices . . . that can speak beyond an instance of fieldwork" (2009, 21). Despite speaking from and about a place, avian ecologists working around frontier forests in southern Chile see their message as a cautionary tale about the precariousness of forests and the different forms of life they host beyond their field sites. Central to the work of avian ecologists is understanding how bird behaviors can reveal new relationships in which human actions are embedded, often without our awareness. "Seeing like a bird" is an often understated aim of avian ecology. Such a perspectival shift is crucial for recognizing the highly dynamic yet enduring connections that link human labor, bird territorialization, and the structural affordances of forests, all of which co-constitute humans, birds, and forests as what they are.

This chapter focuses on the last and most recent of the four expressions of alterhumanism depicted in this book. Here, I offer an ontological and ethical representation of humanity and its alterity as it emerges from avian ecologists' experiences of perceiving bird behaviors and imbricating them with relational narratives about forests and their dwellers. This version of humanity and its alterity, which I refer to as *ecologist alterhumanism*, originated at a historical intersection between science and conservation in Chile during the 1990s. Since the expansion of private and public protected areas during this decade, ecological research in Chile has increasingly moved away from questions specific to zoology and botany to concerns over human-wildlife conflict and conservation science more generally.

Becoming human through and with nonhuman others is an ongoing pro-cess shaped by complex, ambivalent relationships. In this dynamic, humans are seen both as a *disturbance*—a term used to describe the external and potentially destructive effects of human labor—and as *part of nature*, re-flecting the ecological status often assigned to humanity by avian ecologists. *Ecologist alterhumanism* revolves around the open-ended question of what humans become when seen from the perspectives of birds, challenging the traditional boundaries between species and rethinking the human condition through interspecies relations. Characterizing forests through the perspec-tive of birds means to recognize the elusive and yet durable consequences of human actions on the constitution of forests, in particular on their structural features responsible for directing avian behaviors. The emergence of a new understanding of the world, enabled by the articulation of new avian per-spectives, redefines humanity in more relational terms. This shift highlights the slow and often unexpected consequences of human labor on nonhuman life, particularly concerning the structural complexity of forests, which is vi-tal for essential avian behaviors, like the use of tree cavities for nesting. New awareness of the impact of human actions on forest life prompts a critical re-flection on the ethical type of cohabitation that humans should ideally adopt. As we will hear more about in the following pages, avian ecologists' ethical reflections often lead to diverse strategies for community engagement. These range from collaborations with environmental policymakers to workshops with local schools, all aimed at raising awareness about the dangers of certain human actions in the forest. At the same time, they celebrate Indigenous and farming knowledges about avian life and its protection as examples of how healthy interspecies cohabitation is not only possible but already practiced.

The evolving portrayal of humanity as both disturbance and part of na-ture in conservation science stems from a specific way of engaging with the forest, which I refer to as *emplacement*. This term describes the condition of being shaped by place—a spatial construct that brings together animate and inanimate entities, histories, and even thoughts, forming a collective and meaningful whole (Casey 1996, 24). For avian ecologists, place is the primary access to the world they study, but also a category that matters beyond their emplaced experiences. Place guides the perception of ecological relations as the objects of scientific enquiry. Through observations akin to birdwatching, ecologists learn not only to perceive birds, but also to be affected by them, allowing them to become aware of new relations within the forest world. The

FIGURE 8 Preparing the piper to inspect a nesting cavity (Photograph by the author)

situatedness of knowledge production (see Haraway 1988) and the affective influence of nonhumans in guiding attentiveness and sensitivity toward the world (Despret 2004, 112) are central to a scientific practice that challenges the notion that disengagement is necessary for objectivity. As Barad reminds us, even in science, "knowing does not come from standing at a distance and representing but rather from a direct material engagement with the world" (2007, 49). Emplacement involves not only the way conservation scientists gain ecological understanding of the world but also an epistemic process that transforms specific localities into transposable types of places. This enables comparisons with similar environments across the globe, such as categorizing diverse ecosystems under the broader classification of temperate rain forests. Relating and circulating data across different types of places (see Latour 1999; Walford 2017) is how place is constituted in ecology, and interdependent subjects, such as birds, humans, and forests, are defined and inserted within durable relationships.

To begin exposing the role of emplacement in the definition of humanity articulated in conservation science, let me sketch the phenomenological overlaps between birdwatching and avian ecology.

Birdwatching, or Learning to See the World Otherwise

For the avian ecologists I met, their paths toward a professional career in science began with their gradual involvement in birdwatching (*observación de aves*), an activity that in many cases has continued interruptedly as a life project of self-learning nonetheless useful to the improvement of many of the observation methods employed in avian ecology.

While birdwatching is now an important part of scientific training for many avian ecologists, it wasn't always accepted as a legitimate practice. In the nineteenth century, the ornithological community largely dismissed birdwatching, seeing it as unscientific compared to more formal methods like specimen collection. This rejection highlights the process of *boundary work*, where certain practices are excluded in order to define and protect what counts as scientific expertise (see Gieryn 1999). Over time, birdwatching became recognized as valuable, but that early dismissal illustrates how the boundaries of science are often contested and negotiated. At the time, ornithologists were indeed struggling for the recognition of their specialty within natural history, so that lines had to be drawn between the growing phenomenon of amateur birdwatching and the more traditional practice of avian species description (Birkhead and Van Balen 2008). In countries such as the United Kingdom, birdwatching was enjoying an unprecedented popularity thanks to technological developments in the optical sciences, such as those associated with binoculars, that facilitated field observations and official discourses celebrating nature as national heritage (Macdonald 2002, 19).

In Chile, the rise of ornithology was embedded in the nation-building project following independence from Spanish rule in the early nineteenth century. Natural historians from Europe were hired by governmental institutions to provide encyclopedic depictions of the many uncharted territories that made up the new nation (Walters 2003, 105). Eventually, birdwatching developed a loyal base of practitioners, as it did in other countries. Throughout the twentieth century, birdwatchers began to congregate into different organizations promoting bird protection, such as the Chilean chapter of the International Council for Bird Preservation (ICBP) established in 1940 or, during the 1980s, the *Unión de Ornitólogos de Chile* or the "Chilean Union of Ornithologists," also known as *AvesChile* ("Chile Birds").[1] Parallel to the growth experienced by birdwatching, ornithology has consolidated as a specialty within the biological sciences, thanks partly to an expansion of research agencies and funding in Chile since the 1990s. With the consolidation of ornithology as a professional science came a shift from a more traditional, species-oriented approach to one inspired by ecological frameworks (see Lazo and Silva 1993) like those guiding the research of the scientists whose work and ideas are narrated in this chapter.

In conversations with avian ecologists, a recurrent theme was the origins of their interests in birdwatching, in most cases linked to comforting memories of the past associated with birds, such as weekend strolls with their parents in parks or discovering new animals while avidly reading children's encyclopedias about animals (see Pizarro and Larson 2017). But while emotional connections with birds might have triggered an initial interest in birdwatching, it was a desire for self-improvement and new knowledge that made my interlocutors decide to turn this practice into a lifestyle. Self-discipline and an almost obsessive attention to detail is frequently mentioned as a fundamental skill if one wants to become a *birder*. Self-discipline compels birders to be skeptical about first impressions and always double-check distinctive characteristics for each species (such as colored spots), known as field marks. The acquisition of this skill requires an incessant routine of learning about species' features through the field guide, the most valuable tool of any birder besides binoculars. While learning the visual and auditory skills necessary to capture bird movements and sounds remains essential for birdwatching, knowledge acquired from field guides makes taxonomic recognition relatively immediate. Such a knowledge can turn into a "gateway (and sometimes obstacle, actually) to more immersive, holistic, and more-than-categorical relationships between humans and other beings (as well as other humans)" (Appel and Bird-David 2023, 1). The emergence of modern birdwatching rests on the adoption of a new type of "seeing" (see

Law and Lynch 1988), which no longer entails an unconscious, organic vision, but rather "a discriminating, knowledgeable gaze" by a citizen-scientist
who has developed "a learned, keen faculty through a process of critical self-
analysis" (MacDonald 2002, 63).

In the experience of many birders, the selective gaze developed through
this activity becomes naturalized as an innate form of perceptive attention.
My interlocutors have described their daily hearing and visual perceptions
as constantly and unreflexively attracted to movements and sounds in the
sky. As recounted by Sebastián, "Birdwatching became for me a daily activity.
You acquire something that becomes impossible to switch off. Regardless of
where you are, you listen to and look for birds in the sky all the time."

The combination of irreflexive perceptive openness and knowledge of
pre-established categorizations became clear to me during one of my earliest involvements in this practice. Before doing research for this book, I had
no experience with or knowledge about birdwatching. Roberto, an amateur
birder working at that time as an ecologist at my university, was kind enough
to introduce me to the practice. Even though surveys are best taken during
the morning, when birds are more active, Roberto agreed to meet with me
and two other colleagues of mine on a cold winter afternoon to show us how
birding (*pajarear*) works in the field. We visited two lakes, as birds concentrate in high quantity and diversity around bodies of water. A survey generally begins with observers taking note of locations and starting times in their
field notebooks. Armed with binoculars, Roberto started to get glimpses of
the birds surrounding him. In case their presence was difficult to detect, he
would carefully listen to the bird calls to guess their provenience. During brief
pauses, Roberto wrote down species and numbers of individuals. Censuses
are formally ended when observers are satisfied with their observations, or
simply tired. Avian surveys can be taken either in groups or individually, but
even in the second case, they are never simply individual activities. While in
the past birdwatchers submitted data on species distribution and localities to
central databases run by ornithological societies, today many of them report
their observations on eBird, the largest online open access database of avian
observations, which is constantly updated with data by scientists and amateur birdwatchers across the globe. Upon uploading his survey data, Roberto
concluded his survey, which lasted a bit less than half an hour.[2]

The pleasure of birdwatching derives not only from improving knowledge
of avian life and contributing to a dedicated community but also from reaching

personal milestones. In line with the long tradition of species-oriented ornithology, unprecedented recognitions of rare species bring great joy and pride
to any birdwatcher. At some point during the survey, Roberto enthusiastically
began to focus his binoculars on a distant spot in the lagoon while drawing our
attention: "It's a *cauquén de cabeza gris!*" He had just spotted the endangered
ashy-headed goose (*Chloephaga poliocephala*), endemic to the Southern Cone
and characterized by a thick gray, white, and brown plumage. "It's difficult to
explain how beautiful it is for me to see this bird. I've been wanting to see one
for a long time," Roberto added. His emotion about this first-time encounter
was contagious, and I feel fortunate to have witnessed this moment.

For many of my interlocutors, the incorporation of birdwatching into
ecological research began as early as their university experiences, first as
undergraduates and then as PhD students. While becoming an expert in
avian ecology does not formally require experience or an ongoing practice of
birdwatching, in most cases that I have known, research methods employed
in avian ecology encompass many of the learned skills of birdwatching that
are unlikely to be acquired quickly in the course of a research project. Birdwatchers' skills, emotions, and predispositions—in particular the passion
of their focus on birds—help them run surveys as precisely as possible, but
also enjoyably. As indicated by Despret, research in animal biology allows
for encounters not marked by simple empathy—in other words, a unilateral
projection of one's desire to feel connected to the object of such desire—but
rather by the unfolding of a relationship of attunement through which both
animals and humans are constructed as emotional beings (2004, 127). In
science, animals embody "the chance to explore other ways by which human
and nonhuman bodies become more sensitive to each other" (2004, 114).

Among the avian ecologists I met while preparing this book, an affective
engagement with birds was often viewed as a necessary aspect of developing
a scientific career rooted in a profound commitment to nature protection
and a personal investment in self-learning. While birdwatching and avian
ecology are experienced as complementary ways of perceiving and feeling
the world, there is a crucial difference besides the perhaps more obvious
distinction between the professional and amateur characterization of these
activities. Training in avian ecology entails a shift of attention from bird
behaviors to the environmental conditions that shape avian life and the processes of territorialization in which avian guilds—groups of bird species that
share similar ecological roles or behaviors—engage.

Jaime, an avian ecologist from my university, once recounted his first steps in this field. Early on in his undergraduate program in forest engineering he took courses in zoology and forest conservation, while also organizing avian censuses with fellow students who would become future research partners. To Jaime, training in avian ecology meant learning to approach birds in an ecological sense. Birds serve as *proxies*, meaning they reveal connections within ecological networks that are often difficult to identify, such as the relationship between dead trees and birds, which plays a crucial role in nesting. In his words, "the forest is my true passion, even more than birds. Ultimately, what I am interested in is the relationships: how birds interact with the forest. I look at the life histories of birds to understand the life of a place."

Through repeated encounters with birds, avian ecologists learn not only to categorize species, but also to perceive the world around them from new perspectives inspired by the observation of bird behaviors. The question of how a tree looks to a bird is perhaps the most obvious example of how avian ecology prompts the imagination of the forest world as lived by different avian guilds. Like other organisms studied in science (Helmreich 2009, 58), birds can carry important messages about threatened ecosystems, such as native forests. For birds to reveal something new about the world they dwell in, their behaviors need to be anchored to specific ecological niches endowed with structural affordances capable of guiding their behaviors. The practice of avian ecology prompts practitioners not only to shift their representation of birds from species to agents with abilities of territorialization, but also to emplace relationships linking trees, birds, and even humans in specific localities that are later turned into replicable types of place, a translation central to the comparative endeavor of conservation science.

Emplacement in Avian Ecology

The fieldwork activities I described at the beginning of this chapter were part of a research project that aimed to gather new evidence on nesting behaviors in and around Chilean temperate rain forests. Three main methodologies were implemented. The first one was designed to record entries for species population and distribution within selected forested stands, namely a group of trees with shared similarities, including species and age (Ibarra et al. 2017a, 412). This field activity is the one that most closely resembles avian censuses carried out by birdwatchers. The second methodology served to gather data on nesting cavities, such as distribution of nests and tree species. Nesting cavities were spotted by visually following the flights of adults from species known to be nesters and by searching for evidence of recent wear around cavity entrances (Altamirano et al. 2017, 2456). Observations on the interiors of the cavities were carried out either by sight for nests that were easily reachable, like those located on fallen trees or, more frequently, through the piper that I described earlier. Data obtained through observations of cavity interiors included numbers of breeding species and changes in nests recorded over time, in particular whether they had been predated or abandoned after birth (2017, 2456–7). The third methodology consisted of a plotting strategy designed to produce a habitat inventory for the local forest based on the horizontal and vertical distribution of tree canopy, undergrowth, and forest floor. As I will explain at length later in this chapter, this methodology is essential to the identification of those structural conditions ideal for bird reproduction.

Identification of birds and cavities follows pre-established international standards of practice. However, their search is made possible by perceptive skills similar to those used in birdwatching. Frontier forests of southern Chile are exceptionally dense, so hearing is essential to bird recognition. While cavities can be discovered randomly by catching a glimpse of a bird in flight, a scientist with untrained hearing has little chance of detecting a bird's presence. To carry out research around southern forests, one needs to polish one's hearing, *afinar el oído*, as Jaime once explained: "There must be at least 800 cavities per hectare in these forests; you simply do not have time to check each cavity you see with a camera. You need to follow adults, and the only way to do that is by hearing them. Sometimes you can go around a tree and try to hear chicks. I would go as far as saying that the first approach is almost always auditory." In science as a whole, technology does not lead to complete disembodiment, even though the legitimacy of scientific research has often relied on a strong denial of the importance of "the sensory body as a primary research tool" (Knorr-Cetina 1999, 95). In avian ecology, such a denial is not relevant, because human perception is not a problem per se, and the key challenge remains how to transform field observations into replicable data.

As for ecological research in general, human interference with wildlife behavior is an intrinsic occurrence and a risk to be controlled. Unlike birdwatching, where a bird's presence can be actively sought through bird calls, avian ecology is guided by the general ecological principle of detachment, which posits that data collection should be carried out by limiting observers' interference, such as the application of scents or the use of red clothes believed to attract birds. Detachment posits an inherent paradox: that of actively engaging with wildlife to observe animal behaviors while simultaneously creating distance between scientists and animals to maintain ideal conditions for natural behaviors (Candea 2013). However, the relationship between engagement and detachment in ecological research can also be understood as one of productive tension allowing for new observations of changing animal behaviors. As proposed by Candea, "although forms of engagement and detachment can curtail or truncate one another, they also extend one another and make one another possible" (2010, 255).

During the research project on avian ecology, I became familiar with the productive role of the tension between detachment and engagement exemplified by the possibilities offered by the piper, the tool which I described at the beginning of this chapter.[3] Out in the forests, the piper needs to be handled with care to avoid harming any birds. Intrusion into cavities can cause stress among recently hatched chicks and can even cause them to fly away before being fully prepared. Upon entering a cavity, the camera probe can also damage nests and even destroy eggs. In one circumstance, I witnessed the distressful uncertainties that the use of pipers can cause among ecologists. During the monitoring of a cavity, one of the interns found that the chicks were relatively mature and could fly away at any moment. Unfortunately, he struggled to see the cavity clearly. To record the data correctly, the team would have needed to push the camera probe further into the cavity. Team members began discussing whether they should leave the cavity or stay a bit longer. Since the presence of the probe had already stressed the chicks, the team leader, Jessica, took the final decision to move the probe only a few centimeters ahead and then remove it very quickly, even though it might have meant that those observing the monitor had very little time to count the chicks. Technologies such as the piper seem more aptly described as intervening in, rather than overcoming, the embodied relations between the perceivers and the perceived (Barla 2019, 109). Reliance on technology is not taken for granted; it is continually evaluated through context-specific questions regarding data accuracy, the necessity of preserving the natural state of wildlife through disengagement, and the ethical implications of using certain tools on nonhuman beings.

Uncertainties about the disruption of the natural status of wildlife highlights the situated nature of scientific research. Unlike laboratory settings, where data gathering conditions are standardized and considered less significant, fieldwork requires researchers to adapt to the natural environment's pace in order to accurately engage with it. Haraway's invitation to recognize science as situated knowledge (1988) resonates deeply with the significance of affective relations in the practices of avian ecology and the conservation sciences more broadly. Drawing upon feminist perspectives questioning the validity of universal claims of transcendence in science, Haraway suggests that relativism might be a misleading alternative to the universalizing claim to objectivity in science. Relativism as "a way of being nowhere while claiming to be everywhere equally" (1988, 584) hinders the comprehension of the situated nature of knowledge production, scientific one included. For Haraway, "The alternative to relativism is partial, locatable, critical knowledges" (1988, 584). In avian ecology, the situated nature of scientific knowledge is made explicit through reflections on the power of place in directing scientists' observations. This perspective highlights the capacity of scientific knowledge to illuminate specific locations, unveiling the unique agential qualities that characterize ecological assemblages and their effects on different nonhuman populations.

In science, place matters for different reasons. There are places of choice for science: namely, those biodiversity hotspots that are more capable of highlighting histories of environmental degradation than others (Moore 2019, 22). Place also matters as an emotional connection for conservation scientists, who develop relationships over the years animating the search for new questions and apprehensions as they emerge from these localities. The beauty of southern forests in Chile, their richness in biodiversity, and the histories of conservation activism were crucial factors for many of my interlocutors to keep choosing the Cañi natural reserve as their field site over the years. Place can also matter as an analytical category: in other words, a model of emplacement that engenders specific forms of relatedness among different forms of life. Frontier forests in southern Chile correspond to a particular ecological category of place, the Valdivian temperate forest. The diversity of tree species and the abundance of understory that define this particular ecological niche provide researchers with the opportunity to observe unique interspecies processes of territorialization that would be difficult to study in other rural areas of Chile. As once explained by Sebastián, "The heterogeneity of these forests makes it possible for many different species to find their micro-habitat and co-exist in a place with many resources."

In contrast with the traditional ideal of disembodiment in science, place is a category central to ecological analysis even when it is not explicitly recognized as a key heuristic. As seen earlier in this book, the category of place brings to the fore phenomenological questions of perception—that is, how places give us access to the world—as well as ontological queries about the agential nature of certain localities—that is, how places make the world we dwell in. Place is ontologically prior to space, as every knowledge of the world emerges from adopting a particular position in space. The agency of place lies in its ability to gather things, experiences, and thoughts in ways that they become inextricably linked among themselves (Casey 1996, 24). Emplacement, as I defined earlier in this chapter, refers to the condition of being entangled in relationships that not only occur within a place but are also shaped by it.

In the ecological sciences, emplacement serves both as a basis for observations and as an analytical accomplishment capable of producing representations of particular types of place. Birds are endowed with the power to characterize places in auditory terms (Pizarro and Larson 2017, 191). As indicated by Whitehouse, "For birds, sound-making is also place-making; it is an act of territorialising space, of making relations with other birds and continually re-weaving the context of their lives" (2015, 58). By becoming attentive to birds' place-making, avian ecologists learn to recognize place as a more multifaceted arrangement of relations and perspectives than it might initially seem. Place-making, or *territorialization* as it is more commonly known in ecology, is the process through which birds contribute to shaping places that, in turn, influence their behaviors. In the history of ecology, the concept of territory has evolved from being seen solely as a contested space for competing over resources to a context where "acts of territorialization" create diverse senses of belonging among birds (Despret 2022, 93). In other words, place is not merely a container of limited resources for which birds compete, but the outcome of dwelling behaviors that come together to form collectivities, known in ecology as *avian guilds*. Avian ecology is predicated on an epistemic practice remindful of what Stengers has defined as "thinking through the middle," a form of thinking that does not ground ideal horizons and instead renounces any attempt to "disentangle something from its particular surroundings" (2005, 183).

The centrality of emplacement in the experience of avian ecologists serves as a reminder of the situated and embodied nature of scientific knowledge—a reality often overlooked in the pursuit of objectivity. Emplacement also makes a compelling case for ecology as, essentially, a process of relating and situating subjects such as birds in the forest. To make a place visible and intelligible, avian ecologists need to follow as much as articulate the relationships that provide forests or any other place with specific agential abilities. They are aware that their data speaks of and from a particular place. To find common patterns across different sites with similar ecological structures, observations need to be converted into comparable data sets. This process of abstraction is crucial for the representational work through which avian life, forests, and humanity are defined as subjects, allowing their interactions to be understood in more predictable terms within specific types of places.

Relating Data, or How Birds, Forests, and Humans Are Defined

The world brought to the fore by avian ecologists is built around the primary role of birds in indexing relations of mutuality in which humans are inserted but are also capable of disrupting. By connecting birds with one another and with other inhabitants of the forest world, previously unnoticed relationships—many of which involve humans—become visible and eventually turn into a concern for conservation. In the research projects on avian ecology that I have described so far, the relationship that matters most is the one between forest structure and bird behaviors. Forest structure refers to distribution of tree canopy, undergrowth, and forest floor. In avian ecology, relevant forest features also encompass cavities, the number and proportion of tree species, and the levels of decay for trees where cavities are located (Altamirano et al. 2017, 2457). Some forest qualities, such as levels of canopy density and distribution, are categorized on the basis of international conventions assigned to specific types of forest (Ibarra et al. 2017a, 420). Other indicators for forest structures are numerical, as in the case of estimated number of individual trees per species.

Data on forest structure is gathered mainly through a methodology known as plotting. In the research projects described in this chapter, plotting consists of the demarcation of a 140 meter transect, separated by a minimum distance of 20 meters away from the next (Ibarra et al. 2017a, 412). Observations of forest density and species within a plot are later compiled into a habitat inventory. Plotting requires researchers to record geometrical data as precisely as possible in conditions where measurements can only be approximations. I had the chance to participate in the plotting of a couple of sections of Cañi Mountain.

As I remember it, plotting was without a doubt the most physically demanding research activity in avian ecology. Once the research team reached a tree with a previously detected cavity—recognizable by the presence of a pinned florescent orange tag—two team members put a rope around the tree and from there began to walk away from it along a cardinal axis with the help of a compass. As they walked away from the tree, struggling to move through thick understory while avoiding being stung by nettles, they were placing poles for each rope at one, five, and eleven meters from the surveyed tree. At each of the points, a team member held the pole, which was three meters long, and started counting how many times vegetation touched the pole from the bottom to the top. Zero touches meant that at one of the three distance points there were no nearby trees or understory plants. If a pole was touched four times by vegetation, either another tree or undergrowth, it indicated that the measurement had been taken in a dense part of the forest—the most common scenario for plotting in the temperate rain forests of southern Chile.

"This is all very scientific," joked one team member while trying to throw me the end of a rope so that I could extend it to the eleven-meter point. Team members were expected to report what species of trees they observed within the transect and estimate the possible distribution of understory and tree canopy for the entire transect. This estimate was intended to complement the measurement of plant distribution calculated with the poles. As this measurement is inevitably an educated guess, it is never recorded by an individual researcher, but rather discussed by all the team members, who must eventually agree on a percentage through comparisons with other plots. While helping with plotting, I ventured one estimation, trying to calibrate my guess to the other few plots I had previously visited. I settled for 90 percent, a figure reduced by the rest of the team to 80 percent.

In discussing the type of scientific precision required in avian ecology, my interlocutors showed little concern that their measurements fell short of total precision. The very conditions of forests make any search for perfect measurements unrealistic, so that mistakes in the recording of data can occur at any time—for instance by handwriting numbers unclearly in the field notebooks or by mistyping them in Excel tables later. The successful gathering of data on forest structure depends on trusting other team members' personal skills; conversely, teamwork is necessary to adjust individual estimations. Habits of rigorous transcription are necessary to ensure that data can be analyzed and verified for years to come. Given the nature of academic career trajectories and uncertainties about the continuity of projects dependent on precarious funding, junior scientists participate in research only for a limited time, and then move on to different projects. This constant modification of the research team prompts researchers to establish protocols of data collection and analysis easily replicable by new members.

In a context where data is drawn from estimations and observations that rely on learned skills, scientific accuracy must consist of other factors than an increasing precision in the quantification of bird movements or canopy density. During a conversation with Roberto, I approached this discussion by asking a very blunt and perhaps naïve question: "What is good data in avian ecology?"

"Good data," Roberto replied, "is that which allows me to reach robust conclusions based on findings that can be statistically validated. In ecology, you need to adapt to the place you're carrying out research and look for types of data that make sense there, just like you, as an anthropologist, have to change your interviews whenever you are in a different place." Good data, he explained further, must first and foremost comply with the sampling protocol previously established by the research team in compliance with existing international standards of statistical representativity for specific habitats and fields of ecological science. Data that does not fit within established categories has no use. Good data, therefore, consists of measurements that are attuned to other measurements in the same field; they fit within categories that make comparisons with data across different research settings possible. Accuracy ultimately lies in the categorization and repetition of measurements rather than the precision of measurements in the field. As seen at the beginning of this chapter, encounters with some species represent milestone achievements for bird watchers. Videos capturing rare species through camera traps or regular cameras can result in publications highlighting little-known behaviors or interactions with another species.[4] However, the characterization of individual species remains a secondary interest in comparison with a more resolute focus on behaviors and relations involving avian guilds. Rather than in its nature as a potential discovery, the value of any data lies in their ability to join others in showing a pattern for bird behavior.

The establishment of samples that can fit replicable categories is how ecological science engages with a world inevitably marked by the indeterminacy of nonhuman behaviors. As Deleuze and Guattari suggest, finding order in apparent chaos might be the very motivation of scientific pursuit: "Science cannot avoid experiencing a profound attraction for the chaos with which it battles. If slowing down is the thin border that separates us from the oceanic chaos, science draws as close as it can to the nearest waves by positing relationships that are preserved with the appearance and disappearance of variables" (1994, 205). In science, a variable is any measurable factor, trait, or condition that can change over time, causing a transformation in other entities and the relations they are imbricated with. Examining the processes by which data is selected and compared among atmosphere scientists in the Brazilian Amazon, Walford has drawn attention to a transformation of what scientists define as raw data—that is, data coming from an instrument and that has not gone through a quality control process—into certified data, which constitute the basis of scientific findings. All the effort that a research team "puts into collecting raw data in the first instance generates neither data nor error, but rather the endless potential for constantly creating the relation between them" (2017, 76).

The stabilization of data requires a type of relational work capable of transforming observations into variables inserted within a more durable arrangement of relationships, such as those linking forest structural features and birds. For variables to be put in communication across different field sites, relationships need to be articulated around common denominators, such as the standards used to define variables in forest structure. Latour has drawn attention to this point by characterizing ecological data as *circulating references* (1999). As suggested by its etymological roots in the Latin verb *referre*, meaning "to bring back," circulating references are representations of nature that are taken from specific contexts and translated into more general analytical frameworks. Through their circulation, these references are stabilized as facts. A reference, for Latour, "is not simply the act of pointing or a way of keeping, on the outside, some material guarantee for the truth of a statement; rather it is our way of keeping something constant through a series of transformations" (1999, 58). Objectivity in ecology therefore rests on the possibility of turning observations into data that can be transposed across analytical frameworks without being completely transformed into something new. Ideas of the *global* and *local* in science, such as assumptions about the universality of certain patterns in bird behavior, are never given; rather, they need to be performed in ways that render them mutually dependent (Simonetti 2019, 245). Relating data ultimately relies on epistemic movements described by Tsing as able to "make one's research framework apply to greater scales, without changing the research questions" (2015, 38).

The research questions posed by avian ecologists working around the frontier forests of southern Chile are diverse. Yet they converge on one challenge—that of identifying the most durable and regular types of relationships connecting forests, birds, and humans as they emerge from a particular habitat: the temperate rain forest. In reading peer-reviewed journals and outreach documents published by my interlocutors, my attention was drawn to three recurrent conclusions that illustrate the existence of three fundamental relationships upon which all others depend. The first conclusion concerns relations among birds enabled by the use of nests. Temperate rain forests of southern Chile are inhabited by the largest proportion of tree cavity nesters (57 percent) of any forest system. This high proportion means that birds do not have to compete over cavities, either natural or, to a lesser degree, created by primary cavity nesters, like woodpeckers who excavate their own nests (Altamirano et al. 2017, 2459). Birds from different species constantly reutilize cavities left by others. Even if the predation of cavities is common in these forests, this research finding portrays a scenario of solidarity, or at least non-competition, among birds. The resonance of this finding was such that it made national headlines in 2016, when it appeared in the scientific section of the most widely read newspaper in Chile, *El Mercurio*, under the headline, "The birds of the Chilean forest cooperate among themselves by recycling nests" (Ibarra et al. 2019).

The second conclusion concerns the key role of large decaying trees in offering protection to birds. Of the nests surveyed by the research team, 75 percent corresponded to non-excavated cavities found in both standing trees and ground snags (Ibarra et al. 2017b, 7). Since large decaying trees take several years to form, species richness is typically higher in old-growth forest where one can observe a higher availability of structural attributes and microhabitats for multiple species (Ibarra et al. 2017a, 416). Dead trees, therefore, have a second life, as they become the preferred home for many avian species.

The third conclusion concerns the impact of logging on avian life in and around temperate rain forests. By causing the removal of critical nesting substrates, such as tree snags, logging can reduce functional diversity in forests—in other words, the number of functions for local animal populations offered by a particular habitat (Ibarra et al. 2017b, 2). Logging negatively affects the population of specialist species with skills less adaptive to degraded forests, while favoring "winner" species that spread more easily across different habitats (Ibarra and Martin 2015, 425). Logging can thus act as "anthropogenic habitat disturbance" capable of provoking biotic homogenization through the ecological removal of specialist species and the consequent spread of generalist ones (2015, 419).

These three research conclusions bring to light three relationships of interdependence that link forests, birds, and humans. They highlight the importance of cavities in fostering non-competitive behaviors among birds, the positive role of dead trees in strengthening the reproduction of avian life, and the negative impact of human activities that are only apparently innocuous, such as the selective removal of old-growth trees. The articulation of such relationships also allows the definition of otherwise indeterminate subjects, such as birds, forests, and humans, who can be inserted into broader narratives about ecological balance and threats posed by human actions. In avian ecology, the agency of birds is always collective. It is defined by the abilities of multi-species collectives, generally addressed as avian guilds, to use the forest structures in different modalities and in doing so characterize forests according to their role in ensuring and preserving the vitality of different populations. Observing the relationships between forests and birds reveals the nature of the former as an assemblage equipped with a unique agential ability to guide other forms of life by providing environmental conditions for specific acts of mobility, reproduction, and subsistence. As noted by Despret, birds territorialize as much as they are territorialized by the space they inhabit and transit, so that it should be assumed that a "milieu or environment itself also 'behaves,' that it *allows* itself or *refuses* to be appropriated" (2022, 102).

For some of my interlocutors, forests are endowed with an unstable expression of vitality, changing over the years in line with modifications to climatic and environmental conditions. I remember how, in one instance, a team member compared the particular year of their fieldwork with past ones: "The forest is crazy this year; lots of birds have come out." While forests can be less or more vital, the vitality I am talking about does not equate to typical expectations of living and dead. Standing but dead trees, as well as decaying ones and fallen ones, can be sources of vitality for other forms of life, such as birds, that thrive in old-growth forest thanks to cavities used for refuge and nesting. As Sebastián once explained to me, it might be the case that "trees sustain a much more diverse life when they are dead than alive." He added that for some trees, the decaying process begins while they are still growing; in some cases, it might last decades, or even centuries.

Relating data is a process of categorization from which forests and birds emerge as interdependent subjects. However, there is another subject whose agential potentials are framed through the act of relating data. Observations of forest structure and the historical impact of human activities lead to an overall characterization of humans as uniquely capable of acting both as an external source of disturbance upon forests and as an internal feature of dynamic ecosystems, such as frontier forests in southern Chile, which are historically produced by less destructive practices of logging and grazing. In avian ecology, the term *anthropogenic disturbance* is used to describe the negative effects of logging on bird populations, particularly those that lead to a reduction in the heterogeneity of forest structure and, consequently, the decline of suitable nesting conditions. While disturbance seems a human peculiarity, humans can also partake in relationships with forest and avian life through practices that are transformative without being responsible for the demise of those forest conditions ideal to the flourishing of avian life. Logging, for instance, can help the formation of dead trees essential to bird reproduction, as much as it can cause the removal of forest features without which avian life cannot thrive. For this reason, in conversations about forest ecology with my interlocutors, humans were also described as "part of nature" (*parte de la naturaleza*), despite the irreparably depletive consequences of human labor. The notion of anthropogenic disturbance entails the existence of forests partly as wilderness endangered by logging and agricultural activities and partly as the result of accumulated human labor from the past. The temperate rain forests that constitute the main focus of avian ecologists roughly correspond to the more popular category of *bosque nativo*, native forests where endogenous species concentrate. As we know from earlier in this book, among environmental activists, settlers, and Mapuche farmers, native forests cannot be planted and therefore are defined in opposition to timber plantations (*plantaciones*), known for their negative ecological impact on water and soil depletion. In Chile, research on avian ecology within timber plantations was a classic field of study in the 1980s and 1990s. Attention focused on the question of whether commercial plantations, at that time in their maximum historical expansion, could be apt environments for avian life. Research generally indicated that plantations might work as hubs for avian guilds—more so than pasture and agricultural land—but they lacked the species richness of native forests that made them ideal habitats for avian guilds (see Nájera and Simonetti 2010). As recounted by Cristián, an ecologist and university professor living in southern Chile, the dichotomy between native forests and plantations did little justice to the study of the majority of mixed forest environments: "Research on native forests versus exotic plantations polarized the debate. I feel that small-scale farmers were left in the middle, receiving no attention. Research on native forests impacted by human activities is essential to the study of complex ecological networks built around the human-nature interface." So in defining native forests, avian ecologists face a dilemma. They need to recognize the impact of human disturbance on frail ecosystems while acknowledging that local farmers have contributed to the emergence of forests; agro-forestry landscapes host diverse avian guilds, with some species adapting more easily to agricultural areas and others to old-growth forests.

The triadic relationships that help frame birds, forests, and humans as subjects with specific labor potentials and abilities for place-making is at the core of the expression of alterhumanism emerging from the relational work carried out by conservation scientists in southern Chile. *Ecologist alterhumanism* orbits around an ontological condition of *becoming human with nonhuman others*, defined by the shifting characterization of the human as both disturbance and part of nature. In conservation science, the process of becoming human involves a dynamic articulation of humans as both part of and apart from nature. This ongoing characterization is enhanced by attentiveness to nonhuman beings that can uncover subtle and often overlooked relationships, such as those between birds and forests. These interactions reveal essential principles about the vitality and diversity of more-than-human life. This two-fold characterization of humans in conservation science is valuable for fostering awareness of the profound yet fragile connections between humans and forests. This point resonates with other scientists' representations of human-environmental relations, as in the case of marine biologists who, as described by Helmreich, "see the ocean as intimately connected to the human world, providing the ecological context within which we and other living things originated and persist. . . . [T]he ocean exists for them as an ultimate other, an entity with a force and a logic that might endlessly overwhelm or wash away our attempt to represent or control it fully" (2009, x).

By drawing an analogy with how avian ecologists represent forests, I see forests as compositions of frail relationships, such as those linking birds to trees, that can be captured only partially by the scientific gaze. From this partial gaze emerges a representation of the forest as both an entity on its own, which can be destroyed by human actions, as well as a set of relationships in which humans can partake in non-depletive terms. Throughout this book, the ethical dimension of alterhumanism has been discussed in reference to questions and concerns over just coexistence with nonhuman others. In the version of alterhumanism that emerges from the practices and experiences of conservation science, the ethics of becoming human alongside others revolve around recognizing that human labor is intricately woven into subtle and often indistinct relationships. In concluding this chapter, I will examine some of the ethical considerations that avian ecologists encounter as they contemplate the public implications of their work, particularly regarding potential legal restrictions on activities by farming communities.

"Human Disturbance" and the Message of Conservation Science

As early as my first meetings with avian ecologists, it quickly became apparent that a key motivation for pursuing a career in ecology was the opportunity that applied science offers to address social and political challenges, such as defending biodiversity threatened by agro-industrial expansion or promoting traditional agricultural and horticultural practices as alternatives to more depletive, short-term strategies. These motivations are far from isolated; they are part of a deeply rooted historical debate in Latin American scientific communities, often divided between those in favor of a more politically engaged science and those defending scientific autonomy and thus prone to accusations of elitism and apathy toward pressing social issues in the region, such as poverty (Barandarian 2018, 34–35). Projects in avian ecology, like the one I have described, are typically driven by a strong belief in the transformative potential of engaged science. As a result, they often include various efforts to enhance the public impact of research and to influence public debates about conservation.

A more authoritative and yet indirect way of impacting public policy and debate on forest conservation is through evidence-based recommendations to policymakers. Following a widespread convention in conservation science, my interlocutors typically include a recommendations section in their peer-reviewed articles or in policy papers distributed among forest officers and other stakeholders. Among them, two recommendations are recurrent. The first one concerns the ecological significance of large dead and decaying trees and understory for the reproduction and continuity of avian populations. Recommendations point out the need to include minimal restrictions on the otherwise unregulated removal of understory and large decaying trees in management plans and in certifications of sustainable forestry by external agencies (Altamirano et al. 2017, 2454; Ibarra and Martin 2015, 425).[5] However, the recommendation to preserve these ecological features can be controversial and cause rejections among foresters. Suggested restrictions on dead tree removal openly contrast with guidelines in forest management plans provided by the forest agency, CONAF. Permission to remove decaying and dead trees has long been considered the most pragmatic method to effectively mediate logging restrictions with farmers and loggers. As dead trees were thought to have less ecological value than living ones, approval of their removal would meet landholders' needs and appease tensions with no discernible negative ecological impact.

The second recommendation, which is more sensitive to the concerns of small landholders regarding increasing environmental restrictions, involves a broader critique of strict conservation models that impose total bans on local forestry practices. Research on bird-forest interactions indicates that while clearcutting significantly reduces biodiversity, selective logging poses a comparatively lower risk of anthropogenic disturbance (Ibarra et al. 2017b, 1). Complete bans should thus be enforced only for clearcutting, while selective logging should be tolerated, but regulated. Forest officers and avian ecologists are familiar with the plight of many farmers in southern Chile. The imposition of extreme prohibitions would eventually push residents living around endangered forest toward illegal logging and the abandonment of agricultural activities that have become unviable because of increasing restrictions.

For their messages to be taken more seriously, avian ecologists' engagement with public institutions often requires more than the typical skills of scientific writing. My interlocutors regularly attend meetings with representatives and actors from state forest and agricultural agencies, which in some cases may have even funded their research. This activity requires no small degree of communicative and diplomatic skills. Officers, many of whom are trained in forest ecology, are eager to receive feedback on their conservation initiatives from ecologists. However, recommendations on biodiversity conservation often clash with the economic priorities of current forestry development policies. As clearly put by Jaime, "Many officers are thinking about trees, not the forest." A focus on the role of individual trees as ecological and economic resources implies that conservation plans should concern first and foremost the quantitative preservation of trees, rather than the general ecological features that make for the sum of the trees they contain.

Public impact, as imagined and practiced by most of my interlocutors, cannot be reduced to advisory strategies targeting policymakers and other state actors. Bird conservation remains a controversial issue between local populations and environmental agencies (see Falzon 2020), given its effects of restricting activities such as hunting and logging. The relationships between avian ecologists and residents of the southern Andean valleys are inevitably embedded within broader dynamics of economic and political inequality, which are especially pronounced in rural Chile. These relations are also marked by the association that many residents around the towns of Pucón and Villarrica draw between scientists and conservation actors, who are accused of being insensitive to their concerns in the name of nature preservation. In conversations with avian ecologists, I was told how some landholders were enthusiastically willing to collaborate with scientists, for instance by reporting bird observations and actively participating in outreach activities. But I have also heard of residents preventing access to their property or charging ecologists for passage on their way to field sites—an occurrence that is extremely rare in rural Chile. Ambivalent relations with local farmers and loggers remind avian ecologists that effective environmental protection cannot be ensured simply by the threat of environmental regulations; a cultural shift is needed among those living in close proximity to the nonhuman communities that ecologists strive to study and protect. This need drives the emphasis on community-based environmental education, a consistent element of any research project among my interlocutors. For them, such community engagement efforts are most effective when they actively involve local landholders in the process. Therefore, they cannot consist exclusively of a one-way transfer of expertise. When designed as knowledge exchanges, these activities can serve to celebrate local and Indigenous knowledge about interspecies relations and divulge local ecological theories that could even inspire new scientific questions.

An educational project carried out by some of my interlocutors exemplifies the possibility of a dialogue between local and scientific knowledge. Beginning in 2018, Sebastián and other colleagues ran a project titled *Mis Abuelos Me Lo Contaron* ("My Grandparents Told Me"), consisting of a series of workshops held at different schools located around the town of Pucón and Villarrica, as well as educational trips to forests involving pupils younger than twelve years old. In both workshops and field trips, ecologists, schoolteachers, and local elders, mostly from Indigenous Mapuche communities, taught pupils about local history, avian life, and environmental education in general. The project was designed primarily to encourage pupils' curiosity about local forests, including their ecologies, cosmological relevance, and histories of transformation (see Ibarra et al. 2022). Around rural areas in southern Chile, pupils have increasingly adopted more sedentary lifestyles, venturing less and less into the forests—once the settings for activities involving entire households, such as mushroom hunting. Rural out-migration, abandonment of agricultural work associated with increasing employment in the tourist industry and, in the case of residents of Mapuche communities, assimilatory pressures, have all contributed to the decline of intergenerational transmission of local knowledge of forest and avian life.

The valorization of local knowledge in avian life has further materialized in the involvement of many of my interlocutors within a small and yet expanding field of research in Chile, known as ethno-ornithology (see Rozzi et al. 2003).[6] This term refers to an interdisciplinary field of enquiry focused on cultural representations of birds, practices of birdwatching, and the history of ornithology, associated mostly with Indigenous and traditional societies (see Tidemann and Gosler 2012). In publications on ethno-ornithology, my interlocutors emphasized the importance of a sustained dialogue between the ecological and social sciences to strengthen avian conservation

(Ibarra and Pizarro 2016, 2). An effective dialogue presupposes the recognition that local narratives about avian life are more than cultural representations serving as background information for the implementation of more culturally sensitive conservation projects. As Sebastián once stated, "The narratives that we articulate about Cañi Mountain and the birds who live around here are the core of our research. However, they are transformed as we gather narratives from the people living around here."

By letting scientific research be affected by local knowledge about forest and avian life, ecologists learn to recognize the possibility for local engagements with forests to be more than anthropogenic disturbances of avian life. While the threats to avian life posed by humans remain the main target of scientific communication, the other message is that humans are not bound to be only an external source of disturbance. Outside the realm of industrial forestry, human use of timber resources can materialize into relations of interdependence and mutuality even when the prospect of anthropogenic disturbance looms large. In their publications, my interlocutors emphasize that small-scale forestry might reduce timber volume, but it does not necessarily reduce the complexity of forest structures that are crucial for the availability of nesting cavities. Shifting representations of farmers' labor allow avian ecologists to avoid the reductionist trap of the wilderness idea, which, as Cronon reminds us, "tends to cast any use as ab-use, and thereby denies us a middle ground in which responsible use and non-use might attain some kind of balanced, sustainable relationship" (1996, 25).

The alterhumanism that emerges from conservation scientists' engagement with forests does not converge on a moral imperative. Rather, it highlights the ethical significance of a representational challenge: how to recognize humanity as a disturbance for nonhuman life but also as a non-depletive force in the making of forest environments. In ecologists' alterhumanism, an ideal way of *becoming human through and with nonhuman others* presupposes attentiveness to nonhuman life as a condition necessary for humans to be more than disturbances. Learning to be affected by nonhumans, such as birds, entails a renewed awareness of the often barely visible chains of effects of human actions and the responsibility that this entails. To claim responsibility for the effects of human actions on avian life means to recognize their durability in spite of their discreet visibility and apparently isolated nature. Through the relational work of turning observations into data and connecting them, avian ecologists stabilize human-forest-bird interactions under more durable forms. As argued by Yusoff, responsibility toward nonhuman life entails a concern for "how to secure forms of recognition as lasting commitments and how to understand the durability of intra-actions" (2013, 210), a term that Barad has coined to refer to those interactions that are constitutive of the beings partaking in them (see 2007). Making relationships durable, regardless of the elusiveness of embodied encounters with nonhuman life, as in those unfolding in avian ecology and even birdwatching, requires us to recognize that human actions are inserted into histories that always exceed the present—such as those responsible for the afterlife of trees and their regenerative potentials for avian life.

* * *

This chapter concludes the first section of this book, where I have characterized four manifestations of alterhumanism emerging from different histories of engagement with frontier forests. Settlers, Indigenous Mapuche people, environmental activists, and ecologists' versions of humanity and its alterity are not cultural modes of recognition for nonhuman life. They emerge historically as ontological and ethical affirmations of what it is to *become human through and with nonhuman others*. Such affirmations are articulated from experiences and reflections on the effects of the two intersecting trajectories—that of settler colonialism as well as conservation—responsible for the making of the conservation frontier in southern Chile. Alterhumanisms do not exist as self-contained ontological claims about humanity and its alterity. Through intersections and comparisons of multiple ways of *becoming human though and with nonhuman others*, different human collectives frame their particular histories of engagement with frontier forests. Differences between alterhumanisms are not simply comparative abstractions of collective practices and ideas. They are also hierarchical, being produced and arranged by power relations such as those between state actors and farmers, spurred from the recent history of conservation in this region.

In the second part of this book, I characterize the power of conservation as capable of directing existing ways of engaging with nonhuman life without compromising those alterhumanisms emerging from collective histories of life along conservation frontiers. As a form of instituting power, conservation is a transformative force, prompting human collectivities to adapt practices and values to new discourses on human subjectivity. First, we will explore the impact of conservation projects led by environmental organizations on the formation of new landscapes and the ideal subjects intended to inhabit them. Next, we will examine the rise of contested forms of citizenship and Indigenous sovereignty stemming from state-sponsored participatory conservation initiatives involving Mapuche communities. These two scenarios illustrate the transformative power of conservation on various populations, as well as the resistance of alterhumanisms to being shaped by this power.

PART II

Remaking the Human
in Conservation

Interlude

Saving Nature, Remaking the Human

Conservation is a major force in the shaping of the contemporary world. Even when its impact appears limited to remote areas, turned into epicenters of new green economic models, conservation poses one of the most compelling challenges to the expansion of the agro-industrial complex around the globe. The material effects of conservation are clear, yet always ambivalent. Conservation enables new forms of enclosure under the moral imperative of preserving nature (see Grandia 2012; Isla 2005; Kelly 2011) while encouraging the protection of commons threatened by infrastructural and agro-industrial projects. There is, however, another impact of conservation, one that is perhaps more opaque but with deep ramifications for broader debates on the future of humanity on earth. Like very few other phenomena in the twentieth century, conservation has transformed how we think of nature and humanity. If we look closely at the role of conservation in the emergence of new discourses on ecological relations and the practices affecting them, we soon realize that more than nature, it is the human that is the ultimate target of the ethical and ontological transformations promised and engendered by conservation. In conservation, the human is an undefined epistemic object awaiting redefinition through embodiments and discourses. Its redefinition draws upon critical reflections on the limits and possibilities of both anthropocentrism and ecocentrism as the two default modes of coexistence with nonhuman others. The human is also a situated and plural material condition to be disciplined, directed, and finally transformed through the adoption of new values and behaviors associated with an ideal, environmentally minded type of human individual.

Power relations in conservation emerge not only from experiences of dispossession and activism but also from attempts to rewrite normative meanings of humanity and from prompting different populations to conform their behaviors to those norms. For conservation to become an uncontested solution to both ecological degradation and poverty, local populations need to adopt mainstream discourses on conservation as their own, while their behaviors must change to be attuned to the values and practices of the ideal citizen, entrepreneur, and activist projected by these discourses. I refer to the notion of discourse as mostly drawn from the work of Foucault, who defines this phenomenon as a form of power responsible for the historical consolidation of ideal human subjects made possible by changes in values and behaviors that a discourse encourages them to adopt (1982, 2002). To see discourse as a form of power means to recognize that power is distributed in ways that institutions cannot always fully control, and yet it can be effective in disciplining human behaviors without necessarily resorting to violence or coercion. A discourse, such as the celebration of mastery over nature in settler colonialism, presupposes a subject with specific potentials and behaviors (as in the image of a successful settler), which individuals and collectivities are expected to reproduce. Subjectivization is the process through which individuals transform themselves with the ideal subjects that institutions and dominant discourses promote and naturalize in their minds. Through techniques of knowledge production and circulation (such as training programs and regulatory mechanisms on agricultural activities, in which human behaviors become objects of self-discipline), conservation prompts the formation of environmental subjects, defined by Agrawal as individuals "who have come to think and act in new ways relative to the environmental domain being governed" (2005, 7).

Discourses and practices of conservation are necessarily met with adoptions, adaptations, and refusals among those living and working around protected areas (see Blaser 2010; Cepek 2011; West 2006). There is a clear analytical need to examine the logic of power responsible for projects of subjectivization. However, there is also a more empirical concern to highlight: the often-unpredictable effects of such projects, which rarely unfold as the teleological transformation of individuals into subjects reflecting consistently expected values and practices. Subjectivization is never a straightforward process. Foucault has warned against the analytical limits of taking this process too far in his late advocacy for an empirical approach encompassing not only a focus on the internal rationality of power-knowledge complexes but also the resistance that they encounter: "Rather than analyzing power from the point of view of its internal rationality, it consists of analyzing power relations through the antagonism of strategies" (1982, 780). Attention to the resistances generated by historical projects of subjectivization sheds light not only on power relations but also on the alternative ways of being in the world envisioned among those who antagonize and those who are affected by these projects. To characterize conservation as an uncertain project means to recognize the ontological recalcitrance of ways of becoming human that conservation, as other discursive forces, attempts to remake. Subjectivization lacks the teleological nature that simplistic readings of the power-knowledge dyad might assign to it, because ideas about humanity and alterity emerge not only from institutional projects of knowledge transfer but also from embodiments through which the category of human is redefined and demarcated from others. This is indeed the underlying premise of alterhumanism that I have pursued in this book.

In my characterization of the power of conservation as an uncertain project geared toward the material and the discursive remaking of the human, the notion of *instituting thought* proposed by Esposito (2020) appears as an inspiring descriptor. Instituting thought refers to the particular power that ideas hold in fostering processes of world-making. Instituting stands as an alternative to two traditional models of political ontology, in which politics either intervene in existing processes of world-making or are a constitutional force present in all forms of world-making: The first, commonly associated with existential phenomenology, is founded upon the relegation of politics to a successive process concerning ontogenesis, which is consequently treated as a pre-political process; the second, best exemplified by some versions of affect theory, sees politics as embedded within the very process of world-making and thus extends political agency to virtually all relations that imbricate humans and nonhumans. The idea of instituting thought entails an alternative scenario whereby human thought is assumed to be a creative force endowed with the power of instituting entities and relations in a world that is nonetheless always more than the product of our thinking. Unlike the act of constituting, which presupposes a unilateral process of creation, that of instituting refers to the demarcation of different forms of life that come along with the act of qualifying the world that surrounds us. The power to institute is never an ex nihilo act. In Esposito's words, "the instituting creation is always conditioned by bonds and given situations that channel action towards a ditch already excavated in part. However, to be conditioned does not mean to be determined, as the created meaning is not to be completely explained by pre-existing ones" (2020, 168).

The outcome of instituting thought is the emergence of something that potentially already exists. Meanings emerge from other meanings, but they are also capable of transforming what they emerge from rather than being simply created by them. To characterize conservation as a form of instituting thought means recognizing that the transformations engendered by this project are capable of reconfiguring existing relationships among humans and with nonhumans rather than creating new ones. Affective engagements with human and nonhuman others are productive of a certain ontological security that is socially shared and cannot be simply erased and replaced by new discourses on nature.

In Part II of this book, I examine the power of conservation with an emphasis on its instituting potentials and the projects of subjectivization that it spurs. With the human question in mind as the center stage for my depiction of the power of conservation, I will offer a perspective complementary to materialist interpretations of conservation, capable of revealing both the emergence and dispossession of ways of *becoming human through and with nonhuman others* as caused by the material and discursive power of conservation. I define the transformative effects of conservation on the lives of farming populations from southern Chile as *unfinished subjectivization*, in other words, the uncomplete but relentless process of becoming specific subjects under the opportunities offered by conservation politics and economies. There are many projects of subjectivization affecting one's life as one goes through different experiences, from educational programs to self-development as a worker as we navigate different settings and labor regimes. Those enabled by conservation are animated by an expected horizon, in which farming populations conform their values and behaviors to an ideal model of an environmental subject capable of bringing together an ethical commitment to nature preservation, trust in the emancipatory effects of the new green economy, and desired engagement with the state apparatus inspired by an ecological definition of citizenship.

In the next two chapters, I explore the power of conservation discourses in engendering unfinished processes of subjectivization by focusing on two desired transformations of human belonging and ethics from the perspectives of NGOs and state institutions. Chapter 5 focuses on the unfinished transformation of farming populations into environmentalists in the southern Chilean frontier. Here, I depict the types of collaborations and conflicts between local landholders and administrators of private protected areas that arise from the establishment of wilderness enclosures. Attention will be paid to the mediations of controversies over agricultural labor and movement across protected areas. In chapter 6, I explore the effects that mobilizations and claims by Mapuche landholders over state-protected areas hold on the articulation of ideas and practices of environmental citizenship and aspirations of Indigenous sovereignty. Becoming ecological citizens is the result of institutional action, but it is also a reflexive experience in which Indigenous landholders creatively articulate new forms of relatedness to protected areas.

There are many other unfinished processes of subjectivization enabled by conservation, and a book would not be an adequate space to fully disclose them. The two unfinished subjectivizations presented in the following pages should be taken as exemplary of a particular method of subjectivization associated with the emergence of conservation frontiers, which privilege participation over coercion as inherent to the model of community-based conservation. Before moving on to the depiction of these two processes, it is worth remembering the particular ideological scenario into which conservation in Chile has historically been inserted.

A Note on Neoliberalism

September 11, 1973. The presidential palace, La Moneda, is on fire. In what was considered simply unimaginable until that point, fighter aircraft had bombed the entire building, with soldiers looking on from a distance. At that point, it was "mission accomplished" for the group of army, navy, and air force officials backed up by the CIA and responsible for one of the most violent coups d'état in Latin America during the convoluted years of the Cold War. In that same palace, the democratically elected socialist president Salvador Allende met his death, most likely through a self-inflicted gunshot as an alternative to certain murder at the hands of troops soon to be storming the presidential offices.

In the wake of the coup, some households, particularly in the affluent eastern districts of Santiago, celebrated the downfall of a three-year government marked by escalating political conflicts. These tensions were intensified by conservative media, boycotts orchestrated by transport entrepreneurs, economic turmoil, and acts of terrorism carried out by radical right-wing militias. In other homes, people were in utter shock and began to fear for their lives or those of their family members. A systematic deployment of state terror soon followed the coup, with the imprisonment, torture, death, and disappearances of thousands and thousands of left-wing militants and sympathizers, including even a few dissident military officers. Many found refuge in embassies or were conceded exile in the months and years following the coup. In the countryside, farmers who had actively participated in the land reforms that started in 1964 but accelerated under Allende's Unidad Popular government saw their hopes of land access crash. Instead, they became the preferred target of state repression. The goal of the new government was to extirpate the "Marxist cancer" from Chile, as it was declared by some of its members. Under the leadership of General Augusto Pinochet, the military dictatorship would rule the country for seventeen years.

The seventeen years of dictatorship was not yet another case of military rule in the unstable context of Latin American democracy. They gradually turned into one of the most extreme experiments in political economy in the world, a true "silent revolution" as celebrated by Joaquín Lavín, a presidential candidate of the 1990s and one of the most influential figures of the Chilean right after the end of the dictatorship. Neoliberalism in Chile never unfolded as the gradual process of restoring natural attitudes of economic freedom from excessive labor regulation, as envisioned by its supporters. Neither the radical policies of privatization of state enterprises and resources nor the laissez-faire reforms of agricultural and industrial production would have found support among the general population for such a long period of time as that in which the dictatorship restructured economic governance in the country without much public scrutiny. Pinochet's military dictatorship paved the way for the introduction of radical economic reforms designed by the "Chicago boys"—a group of economists trained at the University of Chicago under the guidance of Milton Friedman (see Cárcamo-Huechante 2006).

The consequences of neoliberalization were particularly evident in environmental governance, a field that was entirely restructured by the privatization of natural resources and the growth of primary exports benefiting, for the most, wealthy investors with connections to Pinochet's government. The growth of the forestry industry was, for instance, enabled by the transfer of state-owned land and reforms such as 1974's "Decree Law 701" (*Decreto Ley no. 701*), which introduced tax exemptions and subsidies for replantation that used fast-growing species such as eucalyptus (*Eucalyptus globulus*) and Monterrey pine trees (*Pinus radiata*), destined for the transnational market. A free market, some might say, but one that could only happen through state violence and privatization of commons. Neoliberal reforms also contributed to the retreat of state regulation and the welfare system, leaving the private sector with unprecedented freedom in the provision of pretty much any good, from housing to education. The "Chilean miracle," as it was branded by Friedman himself, was in reality a scenario in which gross economic growth was happening, albeit very slowly, while extreme poverty (aggravated by the deficiency of welfare support) was rampant and inequality was out of control.

The whole country found itself completely vulnerable to international economic crises. The 1982 bank crisis had two notable effects: Firstly, the military government opted quickly for what they thought was the most reasonable response, namely the state rescuing private banks; secondly, a spike in poverty led to an unprecedented rise in protests all across the country, ultimately forcing out the military dictatorship. The popular struggle for the return to democratic rule culminated in 1988, when the end of Pinochet's government and later general presidential elections were sanctioned through a referendum that the opposition to the dictatorship won with 56% of the vote. Transition to democracy was also enabled by a series of negotiations involving the recently reestablished political parties, entrepreneurs, and members of the military regime, whose main leaders were offered guarantees of immunity in case of future prosecution for their involvement in human rights violations (see Garretón 1994).

The first democratically elected government since the 1970s was assumed in 1990 under the leadership of centrist president Patricio Aylwin. Over the next thirty years, post-dictatorship governments guided by the center-left coalition *Concertación de Partidos por la Democracia* ("Coalition of Parties for Democracy"), in alternation with two right-wing governments led by entrepreneur Sebastián Piñera, brought about steady economic growth and unprecedented rates of social mobility. They also introduced several reforms designed to offer some welfare support to marginalized sectors of society. To many, those three decades were the most affluent in Chilean history, and the image of the country as a healthy democracy with modern and efficient state infrastructure and an entrepreneurial mindset was cemented within and outside Chile (Paley 2001).

Despite improvement and expansion of the national welfare system, something welcomed by the majority of the Chilean population, neoliberal attitudes favoring corporate involvement in the provision of basic goods and services and the management of natural resources (Tecklin et al. 2011) have continued to pervade the design of governmental policies. This is also thanks to the law-making implications of the dictatorship-era constitution of 1980, which recently failed to be replaced in two consecutive constitutional referendums. High levels of household indebtedness associated with the consumption of even basic services such as health and education, persistent levels of inequalities, and precarious labor regimes are the other side of the Chilean success story (see Han 2012). Despite cyclical crises of neoliberal ideology, exemplified in the eruption of protests and riots in 2019 initially provoked by rising living costs, Chile continues to be a textbook case of neoliberalism. Structural continuities between the military dictatorship and the later democratic era explain much of the pervasiveness of neoliberal ideology in the everyday lives of millions of Chileans.

The remaking of the human through conservation, the main focus of the second part of this book, is inevitably influenced by the pervasiveness of neoliberal principles of human personhood and, in some cases, their refusal among the different dwellers of the conservation frontier in southern Chile. But what are we talking about when we say *neoliberalism*? This notion is often applied too loosely to nearly every aspect of contemporary global capitalism, to the point that it has weakened socially and historically situated debates on the manifold manifestations of this phenomenon (see Ferguson 2010; Venkatesan et al. 2015). Despite its somewhat loose usage, neoliberalism is a specific historical phenomenon, consisting of the consolidation of a particular economic ideology and its application worldwide. Its origins can be traced back to the 1960s, when a restricted group of self-defined liberal economists from different countries launched their attack against the then-popular Keynesian political economy while advocating for market deregulation and a major presence of private initiative in the public sphere (Harvey

2007, 20). In a few decades, neoliberalism became a dominant influence in both public debate and policy design across many parts of the globe.

As first noted by Foucault (2008), neoliberalism is not only an economic agenda, but a new understanding of selfhood built upon a sturdy trust in self-discipline and accountability. Under neoliberalism, as argued by Rose, "liberal strategies of government ... become dependent upon devices ... that promise to create individuals who do not need to be governed by others, but will govern themselves, master themselves, care for themselves" (2006, 150). We do not need to see neoliberalism only in the irreparable retreat of public goods and state presence encouraged by the dominant discourses in favor of privatization. Attention can and should also be drawn to the emphasis placed on the positive role that market freedom plays in the resolution of social challenges, or in the welcome transformation of citizens into knowledgeable consumers capable of taking advantage of state support as well as market opportunities (Schild 2007). Neoliberal understandings of the self and society advance a view of individual agency centered on the rearticulation of social relations as alliances based on market rationality (Gershon 2011, 540). Within this historical configuration of the self, the role of the state is to create and preserve an institutional framework in which human well-being is thought to be best advanced by liberating individual entrepreneurial freedoms and skills.

The desired principles and values imbuing the imagination of new normative versions of the human in conservation do not respond to universal guidelines but emerge from specific historical contexts, in which the very meanings of humanity and nature are always under dispute. In Chile, hopes and actions among those implicated in the politics of conservation unfold against a neoliberal background in which ideals such as economic freedom, self-accountability, and trust in the empowering possibilities of wilderness consumption are celebrated as much as contested. Through different conservation experiences, such as those that I depict in the following two chapters, questions over the roles of both the state and the market in the constitution of the conservation frontier and its subjects are articulated in ways that remain inexorably open.

Chapter 5

Becoming Environmentalists

Enclosures and Mediations in Nongovernmental Conservation

"We hope that things can be done in one day and we can enjoy them the day after. The Cañi [Sanctuary] has taught us that it's never like that—only after twenty-five years can we see the benefits of conservation. The story that the environmentalists told us—that we could live off trees—sounded like a fairytale then, but we can finally see it now. Today it's more valuable as a standing tree than a chopped one." With these words, Miguel, one of the park administrators of Cañi Sanctuary, began his speech during a community workshop held at the base camp of this protected area. Cañi Sanctuary occupies most of the 1,525-meter-high Cañi Mountain, rich in endogenous species such as a deciduous beech known as *lenga* (*Nothofagus pumilio*) and the endangered monkey puzzle tree, araucaria (*Araucaria araucana*). With a history tracing back to the early 1990s, this sanctuary is the first privately protected area in the country. Among conservation practitioners in Chile and abroad, "the Cañi" is praised as a success story in community-based conservation. In Miguel's speech, "we" refers to most of his neighbors from the hamlet of Pichares, whose lives have been deeply and, for the most part, positively impacted by the establishment of this protected area.

During the 1980s, when tourism had just started to look like a thriving economic force around the southern Andes, Pichares found itself in the middle of a busy tourist route, connecting the lake resort of Pucón to an area at the border with Argentina renowned for its hot springs (*termas*), natural parks, and secluded hotels. First came paved roads and electricity. Then came economic opportunities in the form of seasonal employment and services to tourists. Today, Pichares is a hamlet of roughly one thousand people. Most houses, typically one-story wooden buildings with gardens around them, concentrate along the main road running through the flat and fertile valley of the Liucura River, which is also the main entrance of Cañi Sanctuary. As in most rural areas across southern Chile, social gatherings take place in two small evangelical churches, a medical outpost, a public elementary school, and the building of the local neighborhood association (*junta de vecinos*), indistinguishable from other houses. Unlike other rural villages in the area, Pichares is also home to other, less usual buildings, including an educational farm open to visitors, an organic restaurant with a program of live music during the summer, mostly attended by tourists from Pucón, and a Hare Krishna camp, with a rotating population residing in one large house and tents in the backyard during the summer. As we know from earlier in this book, an increasing number of middle- and upper-class ecotourism entrepreneurs and professionals, attracted by the chance of living an outdoor lifestyle, have relocated to rural areas around the towns of Pucón and Villarrica.

The new Pichares, born out of the ecotourism boom, typifies the sort of achievements and frustrations that dwellers of the conservation frontier in Chile have experienced over the last three decades. The promises brought by conservation and ecotourism are slow to materialize; even worse, they might never be fulfilled for some. A few residents have found employment in new businesses set up in the area, while others have decided to actively seek revenues from tourism, for instance by renting out rooms in their houses to tourists during the summer. Many of them have enthusiastically embraced conservation values as part of a new ethical process of self-making and, in some cases, as inspiration for new economic opportunities to seize. However, there are other residents who see a threat in conservation projects, as new protected areas effectively restrict their movements and agroforestry activities. They see how eco-friendly urbanites have capitalized on most of the entrepreneurial opportunities in the area and, in some cases, are uncomfortable with attitudes that they perceive as classist. And of course, residents for whom conservation remains a siren song are nowhere to be seen in community workshops designed to celebrate the positive economic and ecological impact of conservation.

This chapter explores the divergent effects that community-based conservation has had on farming populations from southern Chile through a focus on the adoption and refusal of conservation values and practices. Becoming environmentalists, I will show, is an unfinished project of subjectivization, whose depiction requires attention to the effects of wilderness enclosures on embodiments and representations of the forest world as well as broader ontological and ethical configurations of humanity and its alterity among farming populations. Attention also needs to be paid to negotiations and mediations inspired by the model of community-based conservation through which environmentalist actors, aware of the exclusionary potentials of protected areas, engage with dwellers on the conservation frontiers in the hope that the project of becoming environmentalists can bring about positive ethical and economic changes to frontier populations.

Nongovernmental conservation has emerged at the crossroads between the democratization processes of the 1990s, which materialized in the rise of a large and heterogenous environmental movement, and the consolidation of neoliberal green productivism as a model of development for remote areas characterized by high biodiversity and promising potentials for the tourism industry (see Holmes 2015; Huiliñir-Curío et al. 2019, Meza 2009; Ogden 2021; Undurraga and Aguirre 2023). One of the main ideological manifestations of neoliberalism is a general critique of state efficacy and a consequent trust in market-driven actions to tackle pressing social issues. Neoliberal conservation materializes in the opening of new market spaces linked with ecotourism, corporate social responsibility investments, and payments for ecosystem services (see Arsel and Büscher 2012; Bakker 2010; Igoe 2017; Igoe and Brockington 2007; Ojeda 2012). The unprecedented growth of private protected areas during the last three decades is perhaps the most visible consequence of the success enjoyed by neoliberal models of conservation. Nowhere is this clearer than in the recent historical phenomenon of *green grabbing*, a critical label for processes of land accumulation put in motion by large land acquisitions for conservation purposes (see Fairhead et al. 2012; Holmes 2015). While private protected areas work as vantage points from which to understand the mechanisms of dispossession triggered by conservation, there is more to nongovernmental conservation; it is a project inserted within histories of environmental activism in which natural resource extraction, and even capitalism, have often figured as adversaries. Although nongovernmental conservation is ineluctably marked by the prospect of dispossession, its practitioners, inspired by democratic ideals of participatory conservation, rely on collaborations and mediations to lessen the alienating consequences of establishing protected areas.

A common argument in debates about dispossession through conservation is that local support for (or opposition to) conservation projects depends on how unequal the impacts are on individuals. This often results from the economic constraints on resource extraction and the opportunities for new revenue, mainly through ecotourism. In a partial departure from resource-based approaches to dispossession through conservation, I argue that farmers' divergent experiences of dispossession are engendered only partly by the economic consequences of the newly protected areas. Dispossession caused by wilderness enclosure also affects farmers' embodied engagements with the landscape, since it is through the landscape that they conceptualize both forests and human labor, as well as articulate their sense of belonging. Insights from anthropology and geography have emphasized the nature of landscape both as an ideological representation of the surroundings imbued with moral and aesthetic meanings and as embodied knowledge stemming from dynamic and sensory engagements with an environment (see Cosgrove 1984; Hirsch 1995; Mitchell 2002; Olwig 2005; Waterton 2013). The idea of landscape helps me to recognize how the material and ideological changes brought about by wilderness enclosures affect people's embodied knowledge of the local environment and their ethical concerns over it. In this light, dispossession can take the form of erasures of those specific forms of engagement with landscapes that are constitutive of a sense of belonging, in this case as campesinos living around frontier forests. At the risk of oversimplifying multiple overlapping landscape experiences, I compare two models of landscapes made visible by controversies over access and natural use rights in and around protected areas. A conservation landscape is informed by imaginaries of wilderness incompatible with human labor and domestication (see Rasmussen 2019). The other landscape type that I have in mind is drawn from experiences of forest domestication among colonos and farmers in general. The temporality of *farming* landscapes contrasts with that of *conservation* landscapes, since the results of human labor are thought of as precarious and temporary achievements rather than as irreversible changes toward degradation.

Although conservation landscapes work to erase and delegitimize existing experiences and representations of forest environments among farmers, the two landscapes can in theory entangle. Mediations performed by park administrators through the means of community-based conservation can help to reduce the impact of dispossession. They can do so by making the boundaries of wilderness enclosures more porous, thus allowing for forest-ers' and cattle ranchers' movements across forests and agricultural environ-ments, with the result of reshuffling conservation and farming landscapes. The mediations I depict in this chapter (Mazzarella 2004) are discursive and material actions, dependent on media capable of instituting a condition of in-between-ness, where multiple human and nonhuman agents can dwell.

Conflicts and mediations over wilderness enclosures are central to un-derstanding the unfinished nature of becoming environmentalists among farmers living in and around frontier forests. Their subjectivization into en-vironmentalists does not unfold in a vacuum, where discourses on nature are produced, circulated, adopted, and refused. Among farmers affected by nongovernmental conservation, embodiments of wilderness enclosure in-tervene in life trajectories in which the ethical and ontological process *of becoming human through and with nonhuman others* are elaborated from the very experience of engaging with forests as a space for precarious do-mestication, but also more recently as new wilderness. In chapter 2, I have characterized understandings of humanity and its alterity among small-scale settlers from conservation frontiers as *settlers' alterhumanism,* a model cen-tered on the precarious experience of domestication around frontier forests. In this chapter, I explain the unfinished nature of becoming conservationists by focusing on the permeability and recalcitrance of alterhumanism to novel institutional projects of subjectivization.

A Brief History of Protected Areas in the Southern Frontier

Although the history of conservation in southern Chile is far from being a lin-ear trajectory of paradigm shifts, it is shaped by the social and environmental consequences of three major phases: settler expansion and deforestation; a consequent state involvement in natural resource extraction, regulation, and protection; and the more recent emergence of environmental activism and ecotourism. Publicly celebrated for fueling the country's modernization, settler expansion also opened an unprecedented debate on deforestation and the need for environmental legal restrictions. In the early twentieth century, naturalists recently employed by scientific institutions to carry out the first flora and fauna inventory in the country were the most vocal advocates for the introduction of forest protection, particularly in southern regions (see Wakild 2017). Thanks to their public esteem as scientists, they successfully lobbied early twentieth-century governments to create legal mechanisms for the establishment of protected areas, the first of which was the Malleco National Reserve, located in the southern region of Araucanía in 1907 (Pauchard and Villaroel 2002, 319).[1] As I will show in greater detail in the next chapter, the institution of national parks was functional to the project of nation-making along the settler frontier (Sepulveda and Guyot 2016, 4).

As more and more state-owned land was declared conservation areas, squatters—a category including displaced Mapuche individuals—and *colonos nacionales* who had not been benefited with land auctions were denied the possibility of claiming ownership rights through proven use, as required by colonization laws of the time. The establishment of national parks as wilderness enclosures was not unique to Chile. Known by different expressions, such as the "fences and fines approach" (Hutton et al. 2005) or "fortress conservation"—a term coined by Brockington alluding to the military language behind classic conservation (2002)—preservationist models were predominant in environmentalist discourses for much of the twentieth century. In Chile, this conservation model remained unchallenged until the 1990s, when environmental organizations began to experiment with more participatory strategies, and under their pressure state institutions, such as CONAF, followed suit.

Over the course of the century, the acreage of state conservation areas in Chile steadily increased. Today, 21.3 percent of Chilean territory corresponds to public protected areas, one of the highest percentages in the world. These areas are administered by a central agency, SNASPE (Sistema Nacional de Áreas Silvestres Protegidas del Estado), with the forest service, CONAF, acting as the institution in charge of operations on the ground. The growth of national parks over the last twenty years was triggered by an expanding environmental movement and governmental initiatives aimed at positioning Chile as a global ecotourism destination. However, the state was not the only protagonist in the recent conservation boom. Since the late 1980s, private protected areas in Chile have grown in number, reaching an extension of roughly 2 percent of the national territory. Through donations or alliances with the state, many of them have been gradually incorporated into the centralized park system (see Tecklin and Sepulveda 2014). The most recognized private protected area in Chile is the Pumalín Park, founded in 1991 by U.S. businessman and philanthropist Douglas Tompkins. Initially subjected to criticism from policymakers who saw it as a hindrance to agribusiness and infrastructural projects targeting remote rural communities, and even as a breach of national sovereignty, given its extension over an entire section of the country (Holmes 2015, 856), to this day environmentalists hold the Pumalín Park in the highest possible esteem for pioneering the rewilding of Patagonia. Following Tompkins's tragic death in a kayaking accident in 2015, the Tompkins Conservation Foundation donated all their 530,000 hectares of properties to the state in 2018, under the condition that they would be incorporated into a broader regional network of public parks across northern Patagonia (Montes 2019).

Support for private protected areas has been sustained by different legal reforms, such as the 2008 Law on Native Forest Recovery and Forestry Development, which introduced easement measures for owners of forested properties with a high percentage of endogenous species, and the more recent 2016 "Law of Conservation Right" (*Ley 20.930, o de Derecho Real de Conservación*), which formalized the status of natural and urban properties as protected areas regardless of future changes in ownership. Despite official support by the state, public funding to private protected areas remains scarce. Most private protected areas are dependent on philanthropism (see Beer 2022) and tourism entrepreneurship (see Huiliñir-Curío et al. 2019), making them more prone to be developed as business opportunities rather than nongovernmental projects run by civil society organizations.[2]

The management and legal status of private protected areas in Chile needs to be seen as part of a larger global trend. Private protected areas have a long history, whose origins might even be stretched as far as hunting reserves used recreationally by the European aristocracy during the Middle Ages. Their central role in the implementation of conservation projects, however, is more recent. The swift growth of private protected areas across the globe in the past four decades is strongly linked to the emergence of neoliberal conservation. This phenomenon is ideologically built on a critique against the central role of the state, deemed ineffective in ensuring the fulfillment of economically sustainable conservation projects, and arguments in favor of mechanisms encouraging private investment in conservation as a solution to environmental degradation and poverty in marginal areas (see Arsel and Büscher 2012; Bakker 2010; Igoe 2017; Igoe and Brockington 2007; Ojeda 2012). The most spectacular examples of private conservation are green grabs. They consist of large land acquisitions for conservation purposes typically supported by international philanthropism and corporate responsibility funding (see Fairhead et al. 2012; Holmes 2015), which, like land grabbing in general, have come under critical scrutiny in academic and political debates for their role in dispossessing farming populations unable to retain their property.

While neoliberal conservation is an ideology undeniably functional to the consolidation of private protected areas, it would be highly misleading to reduce all nongovernmental conservation projects to instances of neoliberal capital accumulation. Private protected areas are indeed incredibly diverse, ranging from large land acquisitions that fit well into the definition of green grabs to smaller private protected areas run by NGOs as self-sustainable projects, working as critical platforms from which participatory experiments in conservation can be designed. Unlike the administrators of national parks, whose very existence is justified as a defense of national heritage and common goods, or those of private parks run with no interest in the local social effects of conservation, environmental NGOs are compelled to design participatory mechanisms capable of curtailing the effects of enclosure and social exclusion on their neighbors. These mechanisms, which for the most part consist of educational activities and negotiations over protected area restrictions, belong to a broader model of conservation known as community-based conservation (Agrawal and Gibson 1999; Mendoza 2018, 110). This model is built on the premise that "local populations have a greater interest in the sustainable use of resources than does the state or distant corporate managers, that local communities are more cognizant of the intricacies of local ecological processes and practices, and that they are more able to effectively manage those resources through local or 'traditional' forms of access" (Brosius et al. 1998, 158).

While community-based conservation has emerged as a dominant paradigm since the 1990s, it has not simply replaced fortress conservation models. Indeed, it is routinely questioned by some conservation actors as well-intended but ineffective in reversing environmental degradation cycles (Büscher and and Fletcher 2020). Equally important is the fact that community-based conservation is certainly not a magical spell against the dangers of dispossession. Educational and participatory schemes might be genuinely embraced by park administrators in their attempts to foster rural populations' empowerment through conservation. However, they can also serve as strategies for consensus-building (Mendoza 2018, 111) and be implemented instrumentally as communication strategies to enforce conservation enclosures and all the prohibitions targeting local agro-forestry practices that come with them. The ambivalence between farmers' dispossession and their empowerment characterizes the history of many private protected areas run by ENGOs. This is one of the many lessons that the story of Cañi Sanctuary can teach us.

Paving the Way for Nongovernmental Conservation in Chile

The beginnings of Cañi Sanctuary trace back to 1989, when rumors began to spread about a possible land acquisition of part of the homonymous mountain by a New Zealand logging company (see Keller 2001). A group of environmentalists from England and the United States, some of them residing around the town of Pucón, decided to take action to prevent further commercial exploitation of the already degraded forests around the top of Cañi Mountain. This group of activists, both foreign and Chilean, with the support of the Ancient Forest International Foundation, an organization focused on the protection of endangered forests along the Pacific coasts of North and South America, gathered enough donations to purchase five hundred hectares from two landholders corresponding to the higher sections of Cañi Mountain. Soon after the acquisition, an NGO (the "Lahuen Foundation" or *Fundación Lahuen*) was instituted to manage the newly named *Santuario el Cañi* ("Cañi Sanctuary"). Donations proved essential to the establishment of Cañi Sanctuary, but it soon became evident that they could not ensure its economic sustainability in the long run. The dilemma of whether the sanctuary should turn into a tourism enterprise or continue to rely on donations became urgent a few years after the sanctuary foundation, when the park's administrators had to tackle their most important challenge to that date: a decrease in international funding. A decision was taken, one with no precedent in Chile: to open the sanctuary to tourism under the management of locals trained as tour guides. Although the ownership status of the sanctuary remained unchanged, in 1999 its administration was handed over to six residents, most of them from the adjacent hamlet of Pichares.

Soon after the change in administration, guides began to coordinate their actions around a new organization named Grupo de Guías Cañi. The main duties of the organization, still active, are overseeing entry fees, offering hiking tours, coordinating training activities for prospective guides, and running reforestation programs (Keller 2001). Over the years, considering the limited amount of employment that a self-sustained project of this sort could bear, only two of the original group of guides have continuously worked as park administrators. In their demanding activities, guides are assisted by a rotating group of ecotourism interns (*practicantes*), most of them students enrolled in tourism degree programs from a couple of universities in central Chile, with which the sanctuary has developed a training agreement. During the summer months of January and February, when most hikers visit the area, interns are expected to work at multiple entry points and to keep track of the park visitors.

Among conservation practitioners and experts in Chile, Cañi Sanctuary is a paragon of participatory conservation. Being the first case of a locally managed conservation project in the country, its consolidation has required creative and strenuous efforts by the new park administrators, who have faced all the difficulties of the vanguard. Generating new revenues was key to keeping the sanctuary safely accessible to visitors. Labor and materials were needed to maintain fences and paths and build at least one mountain hut where visitors and guides could find refuge during bad weather. Revenues were essential to pay salaries for park managers and interns.

Among the many challenges park administrators faced upon turning Cañi into an ecotourism project, ensuring a constant flux of visitors was certainly the most pressing. The sanctuary had many of the ingredients necessary to become a tourist attraction: The Cañi mountaintop offers visitors one of the best views in southern Chile, opening out onto lakes and snow-capped volcanos. This mountain also hosts one of the closest araucaria forests to the lakeside town center of Pucón, only twenty-five kilometers away. Yet all these ingredients do not automatically ensure an influx of visitors, and the sanctuary is in competition with other similar attractions nearby, including Villarrica National Park. For this reason, much of the administrators' initial time and energy was invested in promoting the sanctuary as a tourist attraction. Over the years, Cañi Sanctuary has figured as a natural attraction in several tourist guides and TV shows. The media presence helps capture the attention of summer visitors with little knowledge about the area, but it is not enough to ensure a more stable influx of guests, especially those who could visit the park regularly and bring more people in by word of mouth. Through different alliances and agreements, park administrators have turned Cañi Sanctuary into a hub for training programs in ecotourism, for summer school programs for international students, mostly from the United States, and as a field site for scientists and academics, including many of the avian ecologists who featured in chapter 4.

Turning Cañi Sanctuary into an economically sustainable tourist project was one of two main goals for the park's administrators: As with any other conservation project, this private protected area would not be considered to have fulfilled its mission unless it effectively contributed to the rewilding of a forest threatened historically by logging and agricultural activities. For forest regeneration to take its course, the administration considered it urgent to bring all logging and farming activities to a halt. Prohibitions against logging were quick to become effective. Across southern Chile, logging on someone else's property is rare, being condemned as equivalent to robbery. This censured activity might happen on a field long abandoned, but certainly not on a property with such watchful owners as Cañi Sanctuary. Once the protected area was established, logging therein ceased entirely.

Prohibitions against other agricultural activities were less effective. Around southern Andean valleys, there are two activities that commonly take place within forested plots other than an individual's own: extraction of non-timber products and grazing. The first activity concerns mostly the gathering of mushrooms and nuts from the araucaria tree, the *piñón*. The biennial araucaria nut collection (*piñoneo*) is undoubtedly the most important of all harvesting practices for its symbolic and commercial significance. The araucaria nut is recognized as a quintessential customary food for Mapuche people, especially for those living in mountain areas and identifying as *Pewenche*— literally, "people of the araucaria tree," the *pewen*.[3] Araucaria nuts are also a cyclical source of food and income for non-Indigenous farmers (albeit less so than for their Mapuche neighbors), like those constituting the majority of neighbors of Cañi Sanctuary. Additionally, around the sanctuary, araucaria nut collection is an informal economic activity disconnected from big retail networks, unlike other areas in southern Chile more abundant in araucaria trees and thus more visibly affected by the recent commercial success of *pi-*

ñones, a customary food staple recently turned into a gourmet product. Nuts are occasionally collected for domestic consumption, albeit remarkably less so than in the past, since, according to most of my interlocutors, people in the area have adopted a more sedentary lifestyle because of employment in the tourist service industry and a decline in agricultural self-employment. Gatherers are generally expected to ask landowners for permission to access their properties but, in practice, they can collect and commercialize araucaria nuts freely. The logic at work here is that landowners, including the state in the case of national parks, do not have exclusive rights over these products, meaning any commercial gain for gatherers is a direct compensation for their demanding labor.[4]

Despite the potentially disruptive effect of nut collection on tree germination processes, this process appeared to be a minor ecological danger to park administrators in comparison with forest grazing, the second and perhaps more economically relevant agricultural activity taking place around southern forests. While the ban on *piñón* gathering was soon lifted, forest grazing, to this day, is the main target of prohibitions and a source of latent conflicts between park managers and neighboring cattle ranchers. As we know from earlier in this book, cattle owners—both Mapuches and colonos—are used to taking their animals into forested areas to prevent overgrazing on their property during the summer, when higher areas of forest are free of snow. Despite its gradual decline, paralleling a crisis of small-scale agriculture, summer transhumance (*veranada*) is still an essential strategy for coping with grassland depletion. For cattle owners, forest grazing has a positive impact not only on their personal economies, as they can then let their pastureland regenerate, but also on the woods, which the cattle keep "clean" by feeding on the undergrowth. As shown in the first chapter of this book, among smallholding settlers, for forests to be productive as well as healthy through time, the action of keeping a "clean wood" (*bosque limpio*) needs to be routinely performed. This action consists of the elimination of undergrowth, something that can achieved through forest grazing, the removal of dead trees, and the logging of trees that stand too close to each other, bringing about competition for resources among them.

Not surprisingly, early administrators of Cañi Sanctuary held a very different perspective on forest grazing than local cattle ranchers. Cows typically forage leaves from younger trees, which results in permanent damage from both trampling and browsing. Cow manure can also harm tree seed germination, as it might cause the spread of foreign species within the endogenous forest. While the negative consequences of forest grazing, mainly soil erosion and nutrient depletion, have been documented in different areas of the world, ecological research has also indicated that moderate rates of this activity might have little impact on forest regeneration and may even help control grasses that would otherwise outcompete tree seedlings (see Buffum et al. 2009). The degree to which forest grazing can be tolerated and the adequacy of a total ban is a divisive topic, not only in southern Chile—and not only between farming populations and conservation actors, but also among conservation actors from grassroots organizations and state institutions.

During the first years of Cañi Sanctuary, to prevent the intrusion of cattle, park administrators took a radical decision: The sanctuary was to be almost entirely surrounded by barbed wire. Fencing off a mountainous area as large as this was unheard-of in the area. For farmers in southern Chile, fencing is a costly activity, so fences are normally erected around specific grazing areas to better supervise cows and around small, cultivated plots of land to protect growing crops. As long as it is not accompanied by logging or crop removal, movement across land is seen as a right and a norm for good relations among neighbors, so the sanctuary's restrictions against the circulation of cattle were met by some local ranchers with deep resentment. In some cases, their discontent spilled over into quarrels when they were caught trespassing or intentionally destroying fences to let their cattle through.

Smallholders experienced the restrictions on grazing as an attack on their livelihoods, shaped by the importance of cattle in various social and economic spheres. Cattle ownership is indeed considered by many to be the essential marker of belonging as a campesino. As once put by Ingrid, a resident from Coilaco in her fifties, "If there are no domestic animals, why would one live to own fields?" For most landholders, Mapuche and non-Indigenous alike, the presence of cattle is a compelling feature of the domestic economy, even when most of them typically own only a small herd as a consequence of the long, chronic crisis of family farming and its abandonment in favor of employment in the tourism industry. A head of cattle, colloquially referred to as *animal*, represents a major asset, more so than wood. The sale of a cow is always a much-welcomed and anticipated injection of cash, corresponding to at least the value of three months' minimum salaries.[5] Given its high status, the slaughter of a cow and its consumption marks important life events, such as weddings and funerals.

Among nearby landowners and farmers, enclosing Cañi Mountain is remembered as a contentious topic from the very beginning. Some of them, particularly younger ones who are more sympathetic to the relatively recent conservation boom, feel the restrictions might be unfair to some landowners, yet are necessary. In the long run, these restrictions will contribute to the preservation of forests, as well as to the consolidation of ecotourism in the area, with the consequent creation of new entrepreneurial and employment opportunities. Other residents recognize that forest regeneration is a welcome prospect, but question the effectiveness of the restrictions, which were particularly strict at the beginning, in ensuring this goal. For them, a totalizing ban on non-timber activities is an arbitrary measure that might not necessarily lead to forest regeneration. A ban of this sort could even trigger unintended consequences, including the possibility that animal predators such as mountain lions or foxes might get closer to the homesteads in search of food, leaving farmers with little option but to kill them in defense of their domestic animals. Others believe that fencing is not only ineffective, but also a sign of bad neighbor relations, while recognizing that private owners are free to do whatever they want and that their rights should be respected. Finally, some cattle ranchers maintain to this day their refusal to comply with property access restrictions.

Enclosures and Paths in the Making of a Conservation Landscape

Disapproval of wilderness enclosures among farmers in southern Chile has several explanations. The first concerns the negative material effects of enclosure. By prohibiting access to grazing areas, cattle owners run the risk of being unable to properly feed their animals. Another plausible explanation concerns farmers' resentment toward conservation actors. As is often the case in conservation activism (see Berglund and Anderson 2003, 5), restrictions on agricultural activities are experienced by rural residents as a reiteration of class discrimination, as they are imposed by wealthier and more educated individuals. During an interview, Mauricio, a forester in his sixties living in the proximity of Cañi Sanctuary, expressed very clearly his concern over the consequences of environmental discourses on local youth: "Some-

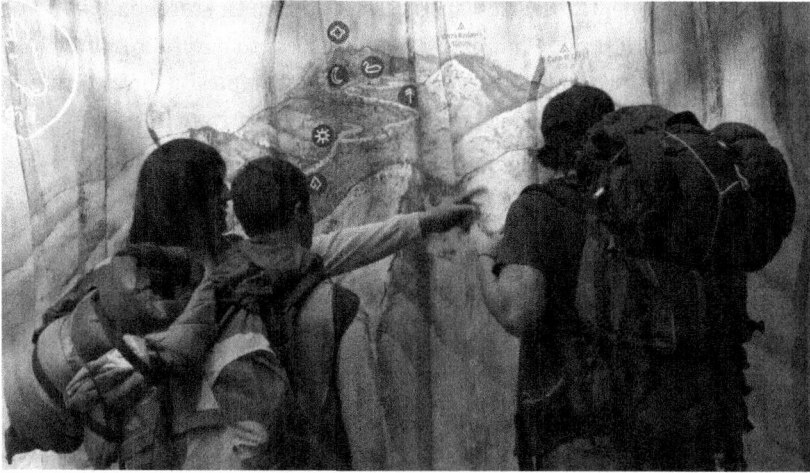

FIGURE 9 Welcoming hikers (Photo capture from documentary *Cañi*, directed by Josefina Buschmann)

times, environmentalists come by, mostly fanatics. They plant stupid ideas in the heads of the most ignorant of us. As they don't live like us; they have no idea how things work here." In Mauricio's words, environmental ideals are simply incommensurable with life as a campesino. To these two explanations (one more economic, the other more symbolic), we can add a third: Among dwellers on the conservation frontier, disapproval toward wilderness enclosure originates in changes brought by conservation to the experiences and representations of forests built around the activity of husbandry. As cattle ranchers experience and know the forests as part of their movement across this space along with their domestic animals, they are the ones among the residents who find conservation infrastructures particularly hostile.

Wilderness enclosures are the means through which dispossession takes place through conservation. As proposed by Kelly (2011, 683), the establishment of protected areas as commons can be available for investment and framed as a form of primitive accumulation, an expression coined by Marx in reference to the foundational moment of capitalist history when the producers were divorced from the means of production through the commodification of once common or unclaimed resources, land particularly. This includes such areas' later conversion into potential capital in the form of environmental services, spectacles, and genetic storehouses. At the same time that local populations are denied access to natural resource use, these resources become available to other markets, typically through public bids for tourism and other mechanisms allowing for private investment (see Brockington and Duffy 2010).

Dispossession triggered by wilderness enclosures, however, is not restricted to resource access. It can also take the form of erasures of those embodied experiences that are constitutive of a sense of belonging as campesinos. The enclosure of Cañi Mountain did not bring any major disruption to forest grazing. While some cattle ranchers have continued to carry out forest grazing within the protected area, others have simply chosen other locations. But even when prohibitions do not translate into tangible material losses, dispossession still takes place in ways that deeply affect local populations. Dispossession, I propose, also concerns the experience and meaning of landscape held among local residents. A new landscape is imposed upon other ways of perceiving and emotionally connecting to forests among residents. When we look at the erasure of farmers' perceptions of landscape and the values associated with it that are constitutive of their belonging, the prospect of dispossession becomes clear without having to be translated into tangible economic losses.

To illustrate how changes brought by conservation enclosures affect ways of experiencing and representing the forest world, I draw upon the analytics of landscape, a way of engaging with the surroundings in which phenomenological and representational approaches to space converge. Since the 1980s, customary understandings of landscape as a self-evident spatial demarcation containing easily accessible cultural and natural features have been questioned from multiple angles. One of them consists of the deployment of Foucauldian critiques aimed at unveiling the ideological origins of certain historical representations of space generally functional to the normalization of social hierarchies, as those concerning land access in rural areas are sublimated into idyllic images of the countryside (see Cosgrove 1984; Mitchell 2002; Olwig 2005). The landscape, as Cosgrove reminds us, is not the world, but a way of seeing the world, expressing ideological and cultural values in any given historical society (1984, 13).

The landscape notion, however, cannot be reduced to a discursive collective representation of the environment. Phenomenological approaches to the landscape have stressed how the articulation of dynamic representations and understandings of the environment also depends on embodiments and perceptions that are in some cases socially structured and shared (see Hirsch 1995; Ingold 2000; Tilley 1994). Largely inspired by Merleau-Ponty's collapsing of corporeity and subjectivity (1962, 134), these approaches to landscape have highlighted the concomitant corporeal and ideological nature of the environment's signification. Embodiments do not take place on a neutral background to be signified *ex novo*, but in a space that is already permeated with meanings. By establishing connections among a landscape's features, bodily activities such as walking, hearing, and seeing imbue it with meanings. This is how landscapes are formed at the intersection of, on the one hand, individual experiences of embodiment, which necessarily reflect cultural forms of mobilities, and, on the other hand, collective representations of local surroundings, which in turn are based on power-laden discourses of how nature and society should be (Hirsch 1995, 4). Landscapes, as Tilley reminds us, work as multiple and partial representations of the world; they order the connections between individuals and their surroundings, articulated through biographic encounters with past and present activities that have spatially left their mark (1994, 27).

A definition of *landscape* as both representation and embodied knowledge of the environment entails that the same space can be the setting for multiple and conflicting landscapes. Aware of the risks of reducing the complexity and diversity of environmental engagements among frontier populations in southern Chile, I draw a basic distinction here between two types of landscapes that, for lack of better terms, we may call *farming* and *conservation*. Upon the persistence of the former rests the unfinished nature of becoming environmentalists among rural dwellers affected by conservation. In defining a *farming landscape*, I draw upon the significance of the domestication of forests among settlers and, more generally, non-Indigenous farmers living around Cañi Sanctuary. A farming landscape speaks to the existence of a set of experiences and perceptions shaped around an understanding of domestication as an activity capable of bringing about positive changes to forest vitality. Among colonos and farmers in general, an ideal landscape corresponds to a "clean wood" (*bosque limpio*): in other words, a forested area where the understory is kept under control and trees do not compete for resources. In contrast with "forests"—a concept often referred to as *selva* or *monte*—"clean woods" can be controlled and maintained by humans for their own benefit.

Aesthetic and moral valorizations of clean woods reflect a specific view of humanity—one that I framed earlier as settlers' alterhumanisms, centered on the ideal role of domestication to ensure human and nonhuman vitality within the precarious project of settlement. As we know from chapter 1, among settlers at the historical margins of the colonization project, *becoming human through and with nonhuman others* is a process of ontological demarcation and articulation of social belonging built around a desired yet precarious domestication of the forest world. For most farmers living around Cañi Sanctuary, the representation of forests emerges from one experience in particular: that of navigating the constantly changing and intricate assemblages that make up forests along with domestic animals. Farmers' access to and movement within the forest is made possible by improvisational skills developed in practices such as forest grazing, nut gathering, and—to a lesser degree—recreational activities. Movement through the forest does not rely only on the presence of established paths, but it is structured around temporary openings in the underbrush created by farmers and domestic animals. The roaming and grazing of cows unfold without much direction from the owners, bringing unpredictability to which part of the wood will be cleared the most.

Conservation has enormous transformative potential for the perception and representation of rural landscapes. As West et al. remind us, "protected areas have become a new cosmology of the natural—a way of seeing and being in the world that is now seen as just, moral, and right" (2006, 255). This new way of seeing and being, however, is not to be taken for granted and needs to be constantly activated through specific embodied experiences. *Conservation landscapes* are built through material and representational acts—alongside narratives emphasizing the dangers of future biodiversity loss—designed to foster wilderness experiences marked by feelings of awe (Fletcher 2014, 150). As suggested by Rasmussen in his analysis of Peru's protected glaciers, represented as both pristine and degrading places of anthropocentric concern, conservation landscapes "imply a shift in orientation in time from preserving what is and what was (for potential educative display in the future) to countering what might become that future" (2019, 1382). These landscapes "are made by strategic erasures and essentialisms" (2019, 1382), so that inscriptions of past human activities that have shaped forest environments (see Mathews 2022) are expected to become imperceptible. Design matters in conservation for its ability to arrange landscape experiences so that, similarly to the experience of visiting a museum, features of an otherwise open landscape are made readily available to the social and ecological imagination (Heatherington 2010, 67).

Material acts consist mostly of two interventions: the introduction of barriers such as fences and the modification of paths. In the case of Cañi Sanctuary, barriers correspond to the property limits of the sanctuary rather than the entire forest, which today encompasses properties where owners can practice logging and forest grazing. Crossing property barriers corresponds only partially to a material transition from two different spaces, domesticated and wild. Accordingly, the consolidation of a conservation landscape requires other interventions capable of spurring the experience of being in a pristine environment among visitors. The design and maintenance of trails serve exactly this purpose. Generally, within any protected area, the design of trails responds to practical concerns related to the safety of visitors, as well as their potential negative impact on forest regeneration, including campfires, which is lessened by channeling visitors' movements into a limited space (Barrena et al. 2019, 12).

For administrators of Cañi Sanctuary, maintaining wilderness requires the mitigation of the effects of not only cattle ranchers but also hikers. Paradoxically, the new experience of wilderness has attracted an unprecedented presence of humans in this forest, as today, hikers outnumber by far the cattle ranchers and loggers of the past. The mitigation of the impact of these visitors rests on the calculation of a loosely defined carrying capacity (*capacidad de carga*) for the sanctuary. This notion refers to an approximate maximum number of visitors that a protected area can receive daily without being subject to a long-term negative impact. As I eventually realized, estimating the carrying capacity is more of an educated guess than the result of quantitative predictions. Often, it comes down to how many visitors can be properly supervised by overworked staff. While administrators have never been in the position of denying entrance to visitors, citing a limit to the sanctuary's carrying capacity, daily tasks include keeping a registry of visitors as a strategy for coming to grips with the times of year that visitors' fluxes swell, so that more personnel, particularly interns, can be hired.

Another strategy to protect the wilderness from its visitors is the enforcement of the ecotourism principle of "leave no trace"—*no dejes rastros* (see Mendoza 2018, 143). In brief talks held at the sanctuary entrance, guides invite visitors to remove all their traces, such as used toilet paper and plastic bags, which should be packed and brought back to town. Mitigation of visitor impact also encompasses policing activities, since the same guides instructing visitors before their trips are responsible for overseeing their activities within the protected areas. Sometimes, policing and educational efforts are not sufficient, as guides and park administrators need to remove trash and bring it back to town—something that clearly generates frustration at the lack of sensitivity and empathy among some visitors.

The design of trails responds not only to managerial needs but also to educational interests. Walks through protected areas follow a narrative articulated by park administrators and based on connections linking places treated as aesthetically and ecologically significant, such as lagoons. The educational narrative to which visitors to Cañi Sanctuary are exposed can take the form of a guided tour, but can also be a self-taught journey facilitated by aids, in particular a free trekking booklet (*guía de terreno*). The first booklet, published in 1990, was replaced by a more readable version in the late 2010s. The most recent booklet provides general information on local biodiversity and places associated with Mapuche accounts of historical events and cosmological forces present in the area. A few attractions along the main trail are highlighted, like the top of Cañi Mountain, recently renamed *Mirador Melidekiñ* (literally "Four Volcano Viewpoint" in Mapudungun), from where the visitor can enjoy a spectacular view of the volcanoes. Another is the *Estación Silencio* ("Silent Station"), where visitors are invited to keep quiet and search for endemic bird species such as the Magellanic woodpecker (*Campephilus magellanicus*), known to inhabit this particular area. The map is accompanied by quotations, most of them from poets, reminding the visitor about the spiritual connections that can be established with forests. The underlying intention behind this publication is to make the visit to this natural sanctuary a unique and transformative experience, in line with the etymology of the term *cañi*, which—despite its uncertain connection with Mapudungun terms in use today—is generally translated as *visión que transforma*, "a view that transforms."

The careful design of the paths makes walking through Cañi Sanctuary a unique experience of discovery and connection with *nature*, which can nonetheless be repeated by visitors on different occasions. Unlike the unstable old cow trails, the sanctuary paths are meant to endure because of their constant maintenance. Maintenance of paths continues to be the main concern for interns and park administrators, since paths need to be redone regularly. As once recounted by Eduardo, a young ecotourist guide, undergrowth can cover trails so quickly that sometimes it is easier to just start a new trail next to an old one than to keep clearing undergrowth: "When a trail is completely covered you start a new one next to it. You begin blocking the old one with logs and branches so that people do not mistake it for the proper trail, while cutting undergrowth next to it to open a new one." While trails are constantly made and unmade, maintenance is intended to give the trail design a certain stability over time.

Through fencing and path maintenance, the porous boundaries between farmland and forest, as experienced by cattle ranchers, are ultimately transformed into clear-cut limits separating sections of the mountain where human presence is legitimized only in the form of tourists and guides. In conservation, as Goldman reminds us, "boundary-making practices are material and discursive, epistemological and ontological, and produce certain worldly configurations" (2020, 13). Property plays a key role not only in the representation of the world, but also in structuring access to, and consequently perceptions of, the landscapes that humans inhabit and give meanings to (Delaney 2010, 13). In conservation, legal avenues to owning property are instrumental to the consolidation of certain areas as wilderness enclosures. *Conservation landscapes* are formed and grounded in compelling discursive and material technologies such as fencing, path design, place branding, discourses on environmental protection, and restrictions enabled by the language of property. Wilderness enclosures are compelling forms of territorialization, and yet they remain contested processes (Grandia 2012, 28), as they inevitably intervene and contrast other ways of experiencing and representing landscapes. Park administrators and activists guided by ideals of community-based conservation, as those involved in the management of Cañi Sanctuary, are aware that property ownership not only offers effective means to counteract environmental degradation but also creates instances of dispossession, affecting farmers' movements through the land. Mediations concerning access to protected areas and mobility therein are powerful means through which farmers' experience of dispossession can be lessened and transformed.

Mediations, or How to Cope with the Refusal of Conservation

In any conservation project, park administrators' engagement with local residents rarely follows pre-established protocols. Rather, administrators creatively elaborate context-specific strategies in response to their neighbors' reactions to participatory schemes and enforcement of regulations. Such strategies frequently look like a mix of policing of farming activities, implementation of educational programs, and negotiations, mostly concerning access and passage through the protected areas. The most important educational project in the history of Cañi Sanctuary is without a doubt the training programs geared toward the formation of ecotourist guides expected to work for this protected area and in similar projects nearby. In 1999, the Lahuen Foundation, at that time in charge of Cañi Sanctuary, started a training program open to residents from the village of Pichares. Workshops were mostly attended by youngsters in their twenties. Many of them saw these training courses as an opportunity to find employment without having to leave their homesteads or completely abandon their family's agricultural activities. Some of the trained guides eventually began to work in tourism agencies located in nearby towns, such as Pucón. Others decided to work in the agricultural sector, where they could nonetheless apply new techniques and ideas in organic farming acquired in this training program. A few of them worked for Cañi Sanctuary and later became its incumbent park administrators.

The dual position of conservation manager and local resident equipped the new park administrators with more empathic attitudes toward their neighbors. At the same time, their new responsibilities also exposed them to stressful and uncomfortable situations with those neighbors, some of them openly hostile, particularly those concerning trespassing. Miguel, one of the current administrators, explains his binary position clearly: "I can look at this issue [conservation] from two perspectives: as a farmer and as a park manager. I have been involved with Cañi [Sanctuary] since its very beginning. I listen to my neighbors a lot, as I want to better understand the clashes between conservationists and the community. If someone puts a fence where once you had free access, of course you are always going to have some kind of conflict." For him, like others involved in the management of this sanctuary, tensions with farmers are unavoidable, as conservation is inherently informed by conflict. However, a mediation for this conflict is possible once farmers' reluctance to embrace conservation practices and values is taken seriously.

In explaining local resistance to Cañi Sanctuary, park administrators exclude the possibility that farmers simply lack ecological concerns. Deforestation is as much of a worry for them as it is for conservation actors, albeit for different reasons. Neither do the administrators believe that the farmers are guided by mere economic calculations of the sanctuary's impact on agricultural activity. Prohibitions on forest grazing, as we know, do not translate automatically into a loss of profit. For guides, farmers' resistance to conservation, instead, lies mainly in the long-term effects of social exclusion and perhaps a degree of existential anxiety at such a deep change in their life conditions. Such sentiments prevent farmers from seeing alternatives to precarious agricultural employment, subsistence farming, and patronizing welfare support (or *asistencialismo*, as it is generally known in Chile). This point was succinctly made to me in one interview with a local ecotourism entrepreneur, who remarked that farmers in this area had learned "to stay poor." Such an explanation is built around a belief in the existence of an impervious custom from the past which, very much in the fashion of Bourdieu's *habitus* (1977), compels farmers to respond to changes in their social and ecological relationships by reiterating inherited practices. An explanation centered on the legacy of the past and its reiteration is consistent with an evident generational gap that park administrators usually point to in explaining that the resistance to conservation is prevalent mostly among older cattle ranchers. As once recounted by Rodrigo, a park administrator, "any study on cattle ranching carried out would immediately tell us that this activity brings little economic advantage. Farmers do it because it has always been like that." He added that older generations would simply continue to practice forest grazing until they died. The same, however, might not happen for their sons and daughters, who might start looking for alternatives to customary cattle-ranching for two main reasons: First, it is a physically demanding activity whose economic rewards are not commensurate; and second, employment in ecotourism is frequently a more viable career option.

Administrators of Cañi Sanctuary are aware that their twofold experience as conservationists and farmers with genealogical connections to the area has provided them with a privileged status and skills, useful in mediating inevitable tensions with their neighbors. Upon taking up their role as administrators, they soon realized that the strict enforcement of prohibitions could have a counter effect, increasing the occurrence of property trespassing in the protected area as an act of defiance in retaliation to perceived discrimination. Attempts by ecotourist guides to mitigate the exclusionary effects of the wilderness enclosure soon began to take the form of a gradual easement of restrictions. More so than strict policing or consensus-building strategies implemented through educational programs, a gradual increase in tolerance toward trespassing did much to repair diplomatic relations with cattle ranchers after the transfer of administrative duties at the end of the 1990s. As the prohibitions became less rigid than those of the early administration by foreign conservation activists, residents were allowed to enter the sanctuary again, for example at *piñón* and mushroom harvest times, as well as for recreational activities, on condition that they follow basic safety measures such as honoring the ban on campfires. Neighbors are not charged for entry and are allowed to use a side entrance from which the top of Cañi Mountain can be accessed more quickly. Forest grazing is still the main target of prohibitions, even though it tends to be tolerated when it involves a small number of animals. Over the years, park administrators have learned to look the other way to preserve peaceful relationships with certain neighbors.

To limit the number of domestic animals within the sanctuary, the best strategy for park administrators is to constantly maintain fences. On one occasion, park administrators and interns were repairing signage and fences that had been damaged by falling branches during recent heavy rains. When two team members realized that a few cattle were grazing around the area, they herded them toward the other side of the fence, outside the sanctuary. They later explained that their intention was to avoid trapping the animals inside the rebuilt fences; they were afraid that the animals could wander off toward higher sections of the mountains, where their owners would struggle to retrieve them. But moving the cows beyond the park limit also helped them to protect the forest from grazing.[6] This episode illustrates how the maintenance of fences serves to reinforce park boundaries to limit animal trespassing, but without engendering an unfeasible material enclosure of an entire conservation area.

While the act of maintaining fences works to make conservation barriers more effective, park administrators have redistributed their efforts along the perimeter so that areas with more visitor presence have more stable fences, while areas bordering cattle owners' properties were left with more openings. This is not only a pragmatic strategy dictated by the limited means available to park managers to maintain functioning property barriers; it is also an intentional action that could help them to mediate the presence of cattle within the sanctuary with more stubborn ranchers. During warmer months, the herds graze without close supervision—especially the animals of older farmers, who sometimes struggle to retrieve the ones that have strayed too far. This lack of supervision is one of the main reasons that limiting the animals' access to the sanctuary is a constantly demanding effort and one that can never realistically be concluded with an irreversible expulsion. The fact that conservation landscapes have never fully materialized, however, does not mean that property boundaries are ineffective in limiting the negative effects of human activities on forest regeneration. Quite the opposite, in fact: The incomplete transformation of the mountain into a wilderness enclosure is what has allowed park administrators to maintain diplomatic relations with cattle ranchers without resorting to alienating actions such as policing or top-down educational programs (which have generally been experienced by farmers as the imposition of environmental values incompatible with their livelihoods).

The maintenance of fences is not a mundane and irreflexive practice with no significant social consequences. This type of work needs to be seen as part of a broader social and ecological action: that of *mediation*. I use this term in both its meanings. On the one hand, it refers to any attempt at reconciling opposing forces from a middle position, as the etymological correspondent *mediare*, "being in the middle," implies. On the other hand, it concerns those "processes by which a given social dispensation produces and reproduces itself in and through a particular set of media" (Mazzarella 2004, 346). In depicting the relationships between park administrators and farmers in southern Andean valleys in Chile, the idea of mediation allows me to highlight the potential of material objects, such as fences, to act as outlets capable of mediating social and ecological relations. Once understood as an action capable of constantly rearticulating connections among humans and nonhumans, mediation can also be seen as a powerful means to set the necessary conditions for more-than-human coexistence. This was the case for cattle, which continue to be thought of as an invasive species by park administrators even when their presence is tolerated. Within and around protected areas, fences and paths are key outlets in the articulation of new ways of engaging with the forest world and the exclusion of existing ones among farmers, visitors, park administrators, and domestic animals.

Mediations concerning access to and use of protected areas are deeply transformative for the people imbricated in them because they can reshuffle conservation and farming landscapes, so rigidly opposed to each other in certain conservationist images of wilderness. By making wilderness boundaries simultaneously resistant and porous, mediations can elicit a set of landscape experiences and representations that might appeal to ideals of wilderness among visitors and conservation actors but that do not work toward the complete erasure of farmers' embodiments. In contrast with arguments for the usefulness of barriers in conservation (Hutton et al. 2005, 347), the history of Cañi Sanctuary teaches us that conservation can work in a more socially inclusive way, even when it apparently fails—in other words, when it proves incapable of instituting impermeable wilderness enclosures. Yet, by itself, this type of mediation is simply incapable of removing the prospect of dispossession from sight. The potential for dispossession in conservation is, to a certain degree, inescapable. The partial success enjoyed by mediation explains why, among farming populations, becoming environmentalists is an unfinished project, constantly renewed by mediations and knowledge-power technologies and always facing the recalcitrant nature of farmers' engagements with nonhuman life and the landscapes they inhabit. Against a clear-cut definition of conservation and farming interests in depicting conflicts over protected areas, we can picture a scenario in which environmental imaginaries are critically reinterpreted by rural populations in line with experiences of isolation and aspirations of development (Undurraga and Aguirre 2023, 1038).

* * *

Thirty years after Chile's earliest experiments with the paradigm of conservation-*cum*-development, residents of frontier areas continue to be baffled by the uncertain economic potentials brought by ecotourism. Only some residents from Pichares were able to initiate and then consolidate entrepreneurial projects linked to tourism, such as room rentals and food sale ventures during the summer. Most of their neighbors saw tourism simply as a seasonal cash injection into their homes thanks to the temporary employment opportunities involved. And for some, such as cattle ranchers, conservation was experienced through feelings of resentment against those environmental activists with judgmental and even classist attitudes. Among landholders from conservation frontiers, anxieties about farming are real and painful, but often not enough to abandon agricultural practices and lifestyles in order to embrace conservationist promises. To environmentalist actors inspired by the model of community-based conservation, mediation appears as the ideal means to cope with refusals of conservation insofar as they intervene not only the material manifestations of exclusions associated with wilderness enclosures but also conflicts over ecological knowledge, in particular over the experience and understandings of ecological damage and reparation.

FIGURE 10 "Close the Door" (Photograph by Martín Fonck)

Tensions over wilderness enclosures and collaborations emerging from the implementation of community-based models remind us that becoming environmentalists is an unequal and uncertain project of transformation. Subjectivization elicited by conservation initiatives is never a straightforward process, and changes brought by it can result in unintended consequences, including local disengagement with the environment (West 2006, 186), as in the case of farmers losing interest in the forests they can no longer access in the pursuit of their habitual activities.

Becoming environmentalists is an unfinished process of subjectivization, not simply for an ideological sturdiness in privileging the supposed economic and symbolic means of cattle ranching and forestry over ecotourism opportunities, but for the ontological recalcitrance of landscape experiences and representations responsible for the consolidation of multiple forms of social belonging. In this chapter, we have seen how the emergence of wilderness landscapes responds to different principles than farming ones, which reflect understandings of humanity and its alterity at the core of the model of *settlers' alterhumanism*, drawn from life histories of small-scale settlers and their struggles for domestication and endurance around the conservation frontier of southern Chile. Wilderness landscapes, as those constituted by the material and discursive means of conservation enclosures, rearrange ways of being in the forest world without leading to the erasure of other landscapes, like those experienced by small-scale settlers in their attempts to do-mesticate frontier forests. As an instance of *instituting thought*—specifically, a set of ideas with the potential for world-making—conservation is a way of seeing and acting upon the world that is also capable of redirecting engage-ment with it. It can reshape how we interact with the world, but it does not possess the capacity to create new and stable ontological frameworks for human activity.

The particular process of unfinished subjectivization that I have presented in this chapter emerged at the historical crossroads between democratiza-tion and neoliberal green productivism in the 1990s. In the next chapter, I look at another process of subjectivization, similarly inserted into the recent history of democratization in Chile. This time, we will learn about the gov-ernmental project of participatory conservation involving Indigenous pop-ulations and its impact on the formation of a new form of citizenship, built on ecological values and moral commitment to the state-run preservation of natural commons.

Chapter 6

Becoming Ecological Citizens

State Commons and Indigenous Sovereignties
in Participatory Conservation

At the end of an unpaved road that winds up the steep Maichín River valley, Ricardo's house is the last dwelling in Chile. Just a few kilometers away, marked only by a painted stone amid the forest, lies the border with Argentina. Between Ricardo's house and this border stretches the densely forested Hualalafquén National Reserve. The road ends right next to his house, where, next to a big gate, stands a large wooden sign with the logo of the forest service CONAF welcoming visitors to the national reserve. A Chilean flag flutters a few meters away. Ricardo's house serves as the park office, where visitors must leave their personal details before venturing into the protected area. Ricardo, a middle-aged man living on his own, is the heir of Chilean settlers who reached this mountainous area at the beginning of the twentieth century. I have run into him a couple of times before, while he was in the company of friends, both colonos and Mapuches. This time, we have agreed to talk about his experience as a park ranger under the more formal setting of an interview. For the occasion, Ricardo greets me and my fellow researcher Martín wearing his shirt of the forest agency CONAF, something that gave our meeting a more institutional aspect. To "wear the shirt" (*tener la camiseta puesta*) is a common expression in Chile, most likely inspired by sports rivalry, to indicate commitment to an institution or employer.

Much of our interview focused on the recent history of Mapuche mobilizations in the area and the elaboration of an agreement (*convenio*) with

CONAF introducing use and management rights to local landholders. Ricardo recounted the first takeover (*toma*) of the national reserve in the early 2000s with a hint of criticism: "They wanted a piece of land each, even when this is simply not possible." "They," in this case, refer to Ricardo's Mapuche neighbors who spearheaded the occupation of the reserve in the early 2000s and had previously described this to me as a symbolic act aimed at pressuring CONAF to recognize their use rights. What is "not possible," legally, refers to the transfer of public land within protected areas, which are inalienable state properties. Ricardo's account of the protest reasserts perhaps the most sacrosanct principles held by forest officers across Chile: The state is ultimately responsible for the future preservation of endangered forests, which belong to "all Chileans" and should be treasured as a national heritage that any citizen can enjoy. During the same interview, his tone changed whenever we discussed the effects of the negotiations and agreements that followed the protest. During the last two decades, Mapuche cattle ranchers and CONAF officers have worked together in the implementation of different activities and permits within the Hualalafquén Reserve, such as the allocation of permits for forest grazing and the maintenance of infrastructure. Ricardo had only good words to describe the agreement and its positive effects on CONAF relations with Mapuche landholders: "We have been working together very well."

The contrast between forest officers on Indigenous ownership claims versus their views on collaboration with Mapuche landholders highlights a tension between a consensus on the advantages of citizen participation in conservation and a firm rejection of ownership claims over state-protected forests. This seemingly contradictory position is a defining characteristic of state power along settler frontiers. As vehicles of state territorialization (Stevens 2014, 19), national parks have historically helped institutions to reinforce state control of indigenous territories through the regulation of settlers' migrations and the restriction of indigenous movement across frontier territories (see Peluso and Lund 2011; Rasmussen 2021; Woods 2019). The recent rise of participatory conservation as an ideal form of democratic governance and engagement with Indigenous populations does not necessarily conflict with the territorializing power of the state. Practices like consultation and co-management schemes can, in fact, reinforce the state's role as the mediator of collective claims and aid in shaping new forms of citizenship.

This is particularly evident among Indigenous and frontier populations, who are encouraged to align with state ideals of forest protection.

In this chapter, I explore the second institutional project of subjectivization unfolding at conservation frontiers. This time, I focus on the effects of Mapuche claims over protected areas and the participatory schemes of conservation implemented by state agencies on the articulation of citizenship. While participatory strategies of conservation, in particular co-management schemes, have emerged as a paradigm shift in relation to earlier, more authoritarian models of conservation, they may also evoke concerns about assimilation and the state's control over the conditions under which Indigenous populations interact with both forests and the state itself. Participatory conservation can be understood through the heuristic of environmentality, a term introduced by Agrawal (2005) and discussed earlier in this book. This concept refers to a form of discursive power that shapes individuals to align their behaviors with the roles and identities outlined by prevailing narratives about politics and the environment. In portraying the ideal subject expected to emerge from state-led participatory conservation and the behavioral and ethical transformations that frontier populations should undertake, I draw upon the notion of ecological citizenship (see Bustos 2022; Curtin 2002; Dobson 2007; Garcia and Rasmussen 2024). This expression refers to a form of belonging to the nation and engagement with state apparatus built around rights and obligations toward a more-than-human community (Curtin 2002, 296). Due to the unequal and often discordant ways different groups engage with the environment and the state, ecological citizenship is consistently "rife with tensions over ways of knowing conservation landscapes, their histories and their registers of valuation" (Garcia and Rasmussen 2024, 21).

As with other projects of subjectivization, becoming an ecological citizen is not a teleological process of transformation accepted by passive individuals. The unfinished nature of this project of subjectivization can be explained by the recalcitrance of those environmental relations informing local narratives of humanity and its alterity, as implicit to the idea of alter-humanism. In the second part of this book, the compelling and yet uncertain transformative power of conservation is defined as an instance of instituting thought or, in other words, a type of power capable of making new affective relationships with nonhumans emerge from existing ones rather than constituting them. State power in participatory conservation should not be seen merely in the creation of a clearly defined conservationist subject. Instead, it lies in the promotion of new forms of ecological citizenship through the state's assertion of moral authority over conservation commons and the delineation of legitimate claims for citizens engaged in state-led conservation efforts, especially those related to Indigenous sovereignty. This boundary work is part of a larger governance framework that I refer to as the *reason of the conservation state*. This framework focuses on justifying the preservation and expansion of state control over protected areas, regardless of the tangible outcomes of conservation initiatives.

Participatory conservation, however, is not only the instantiation of state power. It also enables the deployment of multiple strategies of power (see West 2006), a scenario depicted by Foucault as part of a critique of the supposedly univocal nature of subjectivization (1982). For Foucault, "every power relationship implies, at least *in potentia*, a strategy of struggle, in which the two forces are not superimposed, do not lose their specific nature, or do not finally become confused. Each constitutes for the other a kind of permanent limit, a point of possible reversal" (1982, 794). While participatory conservation remains an effective governmental project of citizenship formation capable of consolidating state sovereignty over frontier territories, it can also serve as the political field in which Mapuche claimants actively redefine their own rights to conservation commons and redirect aspirations of sovereignty over them. Indigenous sovereignty in this case does not consist of an extensive political project geared toward the dismantlement of state authority, but rather to the perhaps more realistic emergence of practices capable of prompting a break from dependence on the state (Simpson 2014, 10) and a consequent juridical challenge to governmental authority over relations with the environment redefined through idioms, such as care and respect (Araos et al. 2023; Pasternak 2017, 27; Postero and Fabricant 2019, 99; Trentini 2023). Among Mapuche residents of the frontier, care (*cuidado*) serves as a powerful expression of an alternative form of conservation, distinct from that envisioned by institutional frameworks. This concept weaves together relationships of both nurturing and use of forests, offering a critical reinterpretation of conservation that highlights the emotional and affective dimensions of human-environment interactions while rejecting the fantasies of rewilding. It also underscores that the process of becoming ecological citizens remains open-ended and unresolved at the conservation frontier.

FIGURE 11 Entering the Hualalafquén National Reserve (Photograph by the author)

National Parks and Land Disputes in Wallmapu

As discussed in chapter 5, the earliest national parks in Chile were created to safeguard forest resources from the rampant deforestation that followed the settlement of European and Chilean migrants in Indigenous territories. By 1912, four forest reserves—Alto Biobío, Villarrica-Hualalafquén, Llanquihue, and Malleco—were established along the border with Argentina (Pauchard and Villaroel 2002). These reserves were later designated as national parks, a change that provided them with greater environmental protection. All of these parks are located in the Mapuche homeland of Wallmapu, a region that most Chileans at the turn of the twentieth century referred to simply as *la Frontera*. Today, the national park system, SNASPE, includes 105 state protected areas divided into three categories: 42 national parks, 46 national reserves, and 18 national monuments (a category which refers to smaller territorial units, typically a lake or a mountain known as an emblematic landscape feature). Parks differ from national reserves insofar as agricultural activities are completely banned in the former, while only restricted in the latter.[1]

For Sepulveda and Guyot, border parks in the early twentieth century had a double function, to "reaffirm the state's sovereignty over resources that had to be preserved within a 'resourcist perspective,'" but also to "secure the border that separates Chile from Argentina in a period in which Northern Patagonia was more of an 'open frontier' than a strong political border" (2016, 669–770). National parks were integral to the project of *chilenización* or, in other words, the strengthening of sovereignty over borderlands, which required restrictions over mobility of the frontier's transient campesino population seasonally migrating between Chile and Argentina through unpoliced mountain passes (Klubock 2014, 19). The establishment of national parks denied squatters from both countries the possibility of carrying out agriculture and husbandry and, consequently, of staking ownership claims based on the principle of adverse possession, as was happening in unclaimed state-owned land according to colonization laws of the time. While squatters' attempts at settlement within national parks declined over time, cases of eviction took place as recently as the 1980s (Aylwin 2011, 15–16).[2]

In the 1990s, the relationship between Mapuche rural residents and the state concerning management and access to national parks underwent significant changes, mostly due to two phenomena: the introduction of multicultural reforms responsible for new institutional mechanisms for land subsidization and property conflict resolution; and the development of participatory strategies in conservation. Reforms targeting Indigenous populations have been developed primarily as a response to growing mobilizations for land restitution and self-determination rights in the 1990s. Mapuche activism dates back to the early twentieth century. Early organizations were typically led by charismatic politicians with different party affiliations but sharing an agenda marked by anti-discrimination demands and protection of collective land properties (Foerster and Montecino 1988). Later in the century, Mapuche activism was increasingly shaped by shifting alliances with leftist parties, which proved to be effective platforms in forging demands of agrarian land reforms despite inevitable disagreements over the specificities of Indigenous demands (see Correa et al. 2005, Crow 2013). During the right-wing military dictatorship led by Augusto Pinochet from 1973 to 1990, Mapuche political organizations were dismantled, only to exist as cultural projects. While the Mapuche population, like the rest of the country, were divided among critics and supporters of the dictatorship, activists involved in the agrarian reform movement were victims of state terror that included extrajudicial killings, disappearances, torture, and exile (Caniuqueo 2013). Only in the late 1980s were local organizations able to constitute an undercover umbrella organization known as Ad Mapu, which arose mostly out of a widespread concern for the pending threat of the dismantlement of collective ownership and regulations over Indigenous land planned by the military regime and later attenuated (Mallon 2005; Reuque Paillalef 2002).[3]

Undercover activism during the 1980s paved the way for the emergence of nationwide social movements in the 1990s, when the end of Pinochet's dictatorship and the consequent return of democratic rule coincided with a reactivation of grassroots politics in general. Through different strategies ranging from land takeovers to lobbying with influential politicians, Mapuche organizations mobilized for demands such as participation in decision-making over development projects, access to better and more culturally sensitive health and educational services, rights over local political representation, and reclamation of land that was historically expropriated first by the Chilean army and later by settlers. Post-dictatorship governments from the 1990s to 2020s, dominated by the center-left coalition, *Concertación de Partidos por la Democracia*, and interrupted only by two right-wing presidential tenures by Sebastián Piñera, tended to adopt a twofold strategy toward Indigenous mobilizations. In ways that resonate with the model of neoliberal multiculturalism (Hale and Millaman 2005), whereby demands posing little danger to existing market configurations are prioritized over others, post-dictatorship governments designed unprecedented multicultural reforms, including a land redistribution program designed to resolve land disputes.

However, they have also enacted controversial anti-terrorist laws criticized by human rights organizations for infringing on the civil liberties of those accused of being a terrorist threat, as well as for increasing penalties for crimes like land takeovers and arson attacks against transnational timber companies (Millaleo 2021; Richards 2013). The "Mapuche conflict," a term used by media since the late 1990s, has escalated across southern Chile. Since the 2010s, at least thirty deaths involving members of Mapuche organizations, *carabineros* (police officers), landowners, and timber company workers have been documented in connection to land conflicts and military raids in Mapuche communities. The escalation can be attributed to several factors, including the absence of a comprehensive governmental strategy for conflict resolution, the radicalization of emerging Mapuche organizations, and the growing hostility toward Mapuche rights among non-Indigenous citizens in southern Chile, which is a conservative stronghold in the country.

Although land conflicts have intensified since the 1990s, they are not a new phenomenon. Many conservative critiques of the Mapuche movement, which frame it as a recent invention of the radical left, overlook the historical roots and longstanding nature of these disputes. For much of the twentieth century, the only legal measure available to Mapuche landholders to repel expropriation of their properties by nearby settlers was to file complaints in local courts specializing in Indigenous issues, known as *Juzgados de Indios* (Di Giminiani 2018, 118). The 1993 "Indigenous Law 19,235" (*Ley Indígena 19.235*) introduced a land program run by a newly founded agency within the Ministry of Development: CONADI (Consejo Nacional de Desarrollo Indígena), responsible for overseeing numerous social policies targeting Indigenous populations. The land program has two objectives: the transfer of properties to Mapuche households according to welfare indicators and the resolution of land disputes through land transfers benefiting communities that have been able to prove expropriation of land in the past (see Bauer 2021). A land claim is an incredibly complex bureaucratic process requiring assistance from a legal team. Even when they succeed in being recognized as legitimate, they can be forestalled in CONADI offices for years before finding a resolution. Success in the land claim does not even ensure restitution of demanded territories, as the transfer of property depends exclusively on the current owners' intention to sell their properties. It is often the case that Mapuche claimants are compelled to accept an alternative property and relocate away from their demanded territories so as not to lose the opportunity for a land reparation.

Relations between Mapuche landholders and conservation institutions are deeply shaped by today's land politics, even when state-protected areas are inalienable and thus not targeted by the land program run by CONADI. As a result of this principle, land takeovers within protected areas have occurred, but they have seldom escalated into open confrontations between claimants and police forces, unlike the more frequent disputes involving privately owned properties under litigation.[4] Only in a very few cases were land swap deals agreed on by state representatives and claimants demanding the restitution of land within protected areas occupied by Mapuche landholders in the early twentieth century. These were then illegally annexed by landowners to their estates and were more recently acquired by the state as part of the creation of new parks (see Cuadra 2011).[5]

In general, claims do not target ownership change but rather access, participation in management, and authorization of agricultural activities within protected areas. A central demand is the right to prior consultation over national park activities, in particular bids for tourism, as enshrined in the Indigenous and Tribal Peoples Convention, also known as ILO 169, ratified by the Chilean congress in 2008. Claims are typically resolved through agreements (*convenios*) regularizing activities, such as summer transhumance, within protected areas and establishing co-management schemes through which local Indigenous populations can participate in budget distribution and supervision of recreational activities. The establishment of agreements between Indigenous Communities and CONAF is not only a pragmatic response to mobilizations but is also inspired by a broader commitment to citizen participation undertaken by all state institutions. Since 2002, CONAF has been implementing a nationwide plan to strengthen consultation and communication with local populations, both Mapuche and non-Indigenous, primarily through the establishment of stakeholder committees known as *consejos consultivos* (Rauch et al. 2018, 189–190). Agreements regarding access to and management of national parks arise from complex negotiations, with the most significant outcome being the delineation of rights and obligations concerning protected forests for the Mapuche signatories. To explore the effects of these negotiations on perceptions of rights, obligations, and broader citizen participation in the state, I will outline the history of one particular agreement related to the mountain settlement of Maite, which I introduced earlier in this book.

Conservation Agreements: Defining Rights and Obligations Toward Protected Areas

Established in 1912, the Villarrica-Hualalafquén National Reserve was one of the first protected areas in the country. In 1940, this area was split into the Villarrica National Park, which remains one of the most visited in the country, and a buffer zone corresponding to the Hualalafquén National Reserve. For most of the twentieth century, the Hualalafquén Reserve had all the features of a *paper park*, a protected area that appears on maps but that lacks practical means to deter extractive activities or to promote re-

wilding strategies (see Dudley and Stolton 1999). Although timber companies had been largely prevented from operating in this protected area early
on, local farmers continued agricultural activities such as summer grazing and harvesting araucaria nuts. For a long time, the reserve received
little attention from CONAF, resulting in sporadic interactions between
park managers and local residents. However, this situation changed in
the 1990s. The economic growth that followed the military dictatorship,
along with the rise of ecotourism discussed in chapter 3, led to an influx
of tourists, primarily drawn by the fishing opportunities in Hualalafquén
Lagoon. As tourism increased, park officers began to enforce regulations
that had previously existed only on paper, impacting both tourists and
local residents.

The area established as the Hualalafquén National Reserve coincided with
the land occupied by the ancestors of most present-day residents of the hamlet of Maite at the beginning of the twentieth century. At a time when the
Mapuche movement was emerging as a main actor in the Chilean political
arena and the ecotourism boom was generating hopes for economic revitalization of frontier territories, Mapuche residents from Maite began to
discuss the prospect of a land claim. Some of them were familiar with cases
of similar reclamations thanks to their involvement in the emergent Mapuche movement.[6] After months of discussion, mobilization became reality. A
few residents organized a land takeover (*toma*) in a high flat area within the
reserve formerly used for grazing. The takeover was organized with the large
summer transhumances of the past in mind. A few residents brought their
cattle to the grazing area and lived in tents for a few weeks.

Residents from Maite remember the *toma* as a peaceful event, lasting long
enough to compel CONAF representatives to meet them and discuss their
demands. Through lengthy negotiations, the agreement began to take shape.
While it included several aspects concerning access to the national reserve,
the focus of the agreement was access to the protected area for summer
grazing. Currently this agreement is part of a general management plan run
by CONAF for the entire protected area (see CONAF 2008).[7] The objective
of the management plan is to regulate summer transhumance, the extraction
of dead trees, the harvesting of araucaria nuts, and the allocation of tourism
bids. Regulation of these activities relies on a zoning scheme, through which
different permissions and prohibitions are established in zones designated
exclusively for conservation or regulated activities such as summer grazing

or recreational fishing. The management plan also encompasses guidelines for CONAF's collaboration with other governmental agencies and NGOs involved in the implementation of development projects around the national reserve, including the improvement of housing or the allocation of subsidies for agricultural activities.

Since 2006, the agreement has been subject to new negotiations every five years. Divergences resurface during renewal negotiations but have never escalated to the point that Mapuche signatories feel the need to resort to mobilization. Renewal of the agreement rarely results in major changes in the management plan. However, it does tackle important issues for both state officers and Mapuche ranchers, particularly concerning their rights and obligations toward fellow landholders, the state, and forests: Who should benefit from agreements with the state? What kind of obligations toward other claimants and the state should one be bound to? What sort of relationship should one establish with protected forests? These questions have no easy answers, so that any consensus among stakeholders included in the agreement is inevitably volatile. Uncertainties over the definitions of rights and obligations originate in the apparently ambivalent interpretations of the main rationale for use and management rights that motivated the land takeover in the first place. This rationale consists of a combination of two arguments: first, a historical argument of past occupancy and dispossession and, second, an action-oriented argument, whereby the right to the agreement is to be individually earned by committing oneself to collective activities necessary to comply with the terms and conditions of the conservation agreements.

Let us turn to the first half of the rationale to understand the implications it has for assessing rights and obligations. Landholders from Maite who have participated in negotiations with CONAF tend to justify their claim as an ancestral right, *un derecho ancestral*. This expression, frequently used in rural Mapuche communities, implies ownership rights to land based on genealogical connections that a group of landholders can assert, supported by a collective memory of past land use spanning generations. Genealogical attachment to place is expressed through a specific notion, *tuwün*, a Mapudungun term frequently translated in Spanish as a "place of origin," *lugar de origen*. As we know from chapter 2, tuwün is neither a mythical place of origin nor a place of residence with which we develop emotional connections. Rather, it evokes a locality hard to demarcate and known to be occupied by one's ancestors. Tuwün encompasses present-day Indigenous Communities, but also extends beyond current legal limits to include larger territories lost as a consequence of the confinement of the Mapuche population into small land grants known as *reducciones* (reservations) in the nineteenth century and the later expropriation of Indigenous properties by settlers. Tuwün is more than simply a place. At heart, the term matters because it is constitutive of and an extension of a person. Tuwün possesses complex agential characteristics, as it is regarded as having the ability to shape both the behaviors and physical attributes of its inhabitants (Course 2011, 46; Quidel 2020, 111). It determines several potentials for those sharing it without determining their subjectivities. It also serves as a substantive marker of identity and alterity with non-Indigenous people or winkas, whose erratic and deceitful behavior is traditionally explained as a consequence of lack of attachment to a place. Given its primary role in personal and collective identity formations, tuwün is a central motivation for land claims.

In Maite, residents familiar with local history have heard about the extension of land used by their ancestors within the Hualalafquén protected area. As we know from chapter 2, at the beginning of the twentieth century, Juan Huaiquifil led a group of Mapuche displaced families to settle around the Maichín River in what would be later known as Maite. Juan Huaiquifil is remembered as a respected cacique, as well as a rich cattle rancher. His animals occupied large sections of the Maichín Valley, including within state-owned land that would later become the Hualalafquén Reserve. He even built a house to be occupied during the summer transhumance. According to several residents, Juan Huaiquifil had amassed such a large herd of cattle that many of them became lost in the mountains and reproduced in the wild. Even today, rumors about wild cows and bulls roaming near the lake persist.

However, Juan Huaiquifil was not the only individual living and working in what is now the Hualalafquén reserve. The early inhabitants of Maite, likely known at the time as Magti, would travel to the higher sections of the valley for the annual *veranada* (summer transhumance). For many current residents, Juan Huaiquifil and other Mapuche cattle ranchers were seen as effectively owning this area, despite their lack of formal property rights. Signs of land use in the past can still be found around the Hualalafquén Reserve. Steeper sections of the Maichín Valley are rocky and punctuated by shallow caves, known in Spanish by some ranchers in the area as "stone houses," *casas de piedra*. These caves are said to have been inhabited by ancient people (*los antiguos*) before Mapuche squatters settled in Maite, a claim corroborated by traces of paint on cave walls found by an archaeological team in the 2000s. They are also known as refuges for Mapuche cattle ranchers in case of storms, having been used by residents' antecessors for this purpose since the early days of settlement in the twentieth century. Claim over the national reserve was not simply informed by emotional and historical connections, but rather by a sense of ownership and the unjust lack of its recognition in the process of state-owned land distribution in the area capitalized by settlers and, to a lesser degree, a relocated Mapuche population. Renata, a community delegate and Mapuche educator working at local schools, made this point emphatically during a conversation: "The day came. We were eight families from the community. Our plan was to recover what, one way or another, the deceased [*finado*] Juan de Dios left to us, his descendants."

Among Mapuche landholders, the collective right to access and co-manage protected areas is grounded in arguments of past ownership and ancestral connections to the land. However, the criteria for selecting individuals who can benefit from summer grazing permits and co-management arrangements operate under a different logic. Participation in the summer transhumance is subject to regulations that limit the number of cattle allowed within the Hualalafquén Reserve. Individual access rights, therefore, need to be gained. Only those ranchers who have or still partake in collective activities organized by the board of the local Indigenous Community are included in the agreement. Commitment to the community materializes through participation in meetings with CONAF officers concerning decision-making and management of the national park, labor invested to maintain the protected area infrastructure (such as fences and signs), and mutual assistance in overseeing cattle during the summer transhumance. Cattle ranchers from Maite are expected to take turns and head off animals roaming away from the grazing area during the *veranada*. Cattle rustling is a deeply feared disaster, as the economic consequences of losing a head of cattle can be significant. Commitment is not only necessary to gain individual use rights over the protected area, but also to maintain a state of alert for the entire community and foster participation in future negotiations. If community members are not involved in meetings with forest officers and local authorities, their concerns and aspirations regarding tourism and use rights in protected areas may be overlooked in the development of community engagement strategies and management plans implemented by CONAF. Residents who have spearheaded mobilizations are critical of what they see as passive attitudes among some of their neighbors: "People join in only when the plate is served." With these words, one of the agreement's advocates highlighted that in rural areas, people often adopt a passive attitude toward engaging with local authorities and show little commitment to collective political projects that do not yield immediate benefits. By contrast, families who have not actively participated in the agreement commonly express resentment toward the early promoters, feeling that they have been excluded.

For Mapuche claimants, reliance on an argument that combines ancestral land dispossession with a commitment to grassroots politics and participation in state-led conservation is pragmatic. State-owned protected forests are inalienable commons that cannot therefore be legally transferred to Indigenous claimants. Involvement in participatory conservation at least serves to give them a seat at the same table with CONAF and negotiate access and use rights within protected areas. However, collaboration with state officers in the implementation of conservation strategies has a further connotation. Among Mapuche landholders, participatory conservation entails the legitimization of Indigenous forms of conservation and care toward protected forest by the state itself and the consequent articulation of a more equal form of partnership. A new form of ecological citizenship, less passive and more critical, emerges from Indigenous landholders' involvement in state-led participatory conservation. I will delve deeper into this point later in the chapter. Before that, it is important to provide insight into the perspectives of state officers regarding co-management schemes and participatory conservation more broadly. As we will see next, participatory conservation is crucial not only for promoting environmental values and fostering a more ecologically oriented form of citizenship but also for reaffirming state sovereignty over forests as commons for the benefit of the nation.

Forests as Commons and People as Citizens: State Logics in Participatory Conservation

Across different national contexts, scientific forestry "emerged as a science of state governance and continues a close relationship [with the state]" (Tsing 2015, 218; see also Boyer 2015). In Chile, scientific forestry has offered concrete means to exercise environmental control over frontier territories. Its origins date back to the 1930s, when the first legal measures supporting the replanting of heavily deforested areas of the south were introduced (Camus 2006, 172; Wakild 2017, 38).[8] For over five decades, the implementation of scientific forestry measures has been the main responsibility of the forest service CONAF (Corporación Nacional Forestal). Founded in 1973, CONAF is a nongovernmental agency supervised by the Ministry of Agriculture and supported by a mix of private and public funding. In 1974, seemingly at odds with dictatorship ideals of a laissez-faire economy, the military regime introduced a new subsidy system aimed at encouraging private investment in industrial forestry. Decree Law 701 established mechanisms that facilitated the acquisition of state-owned land for conversion into plantations, including subsidies for replanting commercial species and tax exemptions (Klubock 2014, 243). This decree paved the way for the swift expansion of a handful of timber companies, which dominated the market through the exportation of timber to Asia and North America. Subsidies introduced by Decree Law 701 were capitalized upon by a handful of timber companies (*forestales*), which soon dominated the market with the acquisition of smaller sawmills (Klubock 2014, 244). In the 1990s, as a delayed response to the commercial challenges faced by small-scale foresters, particularly the descendants of settlers in the Andean valleys discussed in this book, commercial forestry subsidies and extension programs were extended to small landholders.[9]

To many, including most of its employees, CONAF is a small agency with a vast and diverse agenda. Its three primary objectives are fire prevention, management of protected areas, and support for commercial forestry. Its activities are supported by the more prominent and influential state agency, the "Forestry Institute of Chile" (*Instituto Forestal de Chile*), which has established strong connections with the timber industry since the forestry boom of the 1970s (Silva 1997, 470).[10] Most of the CONAF officers I met during my research for this book are extension officers (*extensionistas*), either directly employed by CONAF or temporarily contracted on an as-needed basis. These officers typically have backgrounds as agricultural technicians (*agrónomos*) or hold degrees in forest engineering, a field that is particularly popular in southern regions due to the dominance of industrial forestry. For those engineers employed by CONAF, their choice to work for the agency is often framed as an ethical alternative to pursuing more lucrative positions within transnational timber companies.[11] CONAF extension officers primarily focus on training in forest management, with an emphasis on selective logging, while also facilitating access to state subsidies for small-scale foresters (see Di Giminiani 2016).[12]

The other half of CONAF's responsibilities involves managing public protected areas. Many officers I encountered over the years perceive their institution as having a dual nature. This perspective is reinforced by the varying backgrounds and viewpoints of those involved in protected area management compared to those focused on extension work. While some managerial roles in park administration are occupied by employees trained as forest engineers or agricultural technicians from CONAF offices, a considerable number of those managing protected areas are park rangers (*guardaparques*). Gathered under an administrative unit (the *Cuerpo de Guardaparques*), slightly over five hundred rangers are employed by CONAF for the monitoring of nearly all the one hundred state-protected areas in Chile. Governmental reports identify understaffing as a chronic problem for park administration, a problem further complicated by the sharp increase in the number of protected areas in the last three decades, making Chile one of the countries with the highest percentage of protected area within its national territories.[13] Low wages and understaffing were the primary causes of a significant and prolonged strike by park rangers in 2024. Many rangers have part-time contracts and are employed seasonally, since many protected areas are closed to visitors during low seasons. Due to customary gendered stereotypes for this work and the necessity of leaving their families when vacancies are available in remote areas of the country, most rangers are young men. Only recently has this position been increasingly taken by women (Camus and Lazo 2014, 67).[14] While they can be relocated by CONAF across the national territory, many rangers are locals whose houses border the protected areas. Rangers are generally selected according to their knowledge of the local surroundings, not by their professional training. This is the case for Ricardo, whose history we heard at the beginning of this chapter. Work as a ranger typically includes keeping statistics about park entries and exits, monitoring fire use and unlawful activities by visitors (such as leaving trash within the protected area), and occasional maintenance of park infrastructure such as gates and fences.

For the forest officers I met, the value of protected forests is multiple. Southern forests are landscapes with unique aesthetic characteristics to the enjoyment of national and international tourists; they are resources significant to the life of rural populations, as they provide not only wood, but also non-timber products; and they provide ideal ecological conditions for high levels of biodiversity. These different meanings, however, converge on one definition of forests, as a natural heritage of the country that must be managed by the state as commons. The global history of conservation is marked by the role that biodiversity hotspots and landscape features hold in the discursive formation of national heritage, a phenomenon central to nation-building (Olwig 2005, 7). The classification of national parks as heritage has historically led to their separation from the social and ecological contexts in which they exist (Heatherington 2010, 67), resulting in the erasure of Indigenous peoples' histories of environmental engagement. For forest officers, protected areas are envisioned as wildernesses that must remain free of human presence to be preserved for future generations. However, they also recognize that these ecosystems have been shaped by historical human activities, which continue to influence the landscapes of frontier forests, revealing them to be more than just untouched wilderness.

The premise of participatory conservation rests on the understanding that protected areas can no longer be managed solely by policing local populations, who are viewed as more than just a potential threat. In the conversation with Ricardo described at the beginning of this chapter, we discussed what exactly is to be preserved through the establishment of a national park: "The park is fine the way it is. If they are going to allow more people, more infrastructure up there, it's going to look ugly. The more natural it is, the more beautiful. The tourists love it." Keeping national parks as beautiful as they are, he added, entails fire prevention, garbage removal, and enforcing logging restrictions. Local landholders crossing state-protected areas are not necessarily an intrusion or a threat, and domestic animals, such as cows, do not qualify as invasive species. "Cows don't do anything," he explained. Cows belong to the protected area as landscape features that can be enjoyed by visitors, most of them urbanites looking to experience nature in a loose sense. Commitment to natural heritage in this case animates a defensive stance for the protection of concrete places rather than ecological contexts.

The characterization of protected areas as national heritage is part of a broader discourse on state responsibility for the protection of commons. For forest officers, protected areas are public goods owned and enjoyed by all Chileans. As inalienable state properties, the responsibility for the continuity of these public goods in the future rests solely on the state. Such a representation of the state as an impartial arbiter of public goods means that citizens can participate but cannot take full control of state conservation, given the diversity of their interests and aspirations. Protected forests should never become properties available to local landholders, whether Mapuche or settlers, as was eloquently put by a forest officer: "If we leave them everything, no tree will be left standing." State ownership involves the representation of all citizens, and its primary responsibility in the preservation of protected areas are the two principles guiding negotiations over access and management rights with Indigenous populations. These two principles render the transfer of state-owned protected areas to individuals and the practice of commercial forestry within parks as unfeasible and non-negotiable.

The enforcement of state territorial ownership as a limit to Indigenous aspirations of sovereignty over ancestral territories responds to a particular logic, whereby the legitimacy of the state rests on its geographical expansion and continuity. I refer to this logic as the *reason of the conservation state*. I use this expression as a loose reference to the historical idiom of the "reason of state" (*ragion di stato*) introduced in the sixteenth century by Jesuit diplomat and essayist Giovanni Botero. The reason for the state has emerged historically in juxtaposition with an understanding of politics as an art of persuasion. It involves framing the preservation and expansion of state power as a goal and necessity in itself, independent of the actual societal impacts this expansion may produce. This is central to the logic of the *reason of the state*. The term *reason* "has an instrumental sense, meaning the capacity to calculate the appropriate means of preserving the state" (Viroli 1992, 4). The *reason of the conservation state* refers to the rationale whereby national parks and state authority are imbricated into a mutual relationship. National parks do not simply need the state for their protection. They are also needed by the state to enforce its legitimacy in remote areas. The preservation of the state requires the preservation of protected forests and vice versa.

The implications of the *reason of the conservation state* in negotiations over use and management rights with Mapuche communities can be observed in concrete circumstances, in which the state holds unquestioned control over specific terms and conditions of conservation. An example comes from the estimation of carrying capacity for different zones of a protected area. Such estimation is crucial insofar as it can lead to more or fewer restrictions over agricultural work. In the case of the Hualalafquén agreement, this is the only element of the management plan that does not rely on participatory strategies. It is rather based on expert advice over which neither Mapuche signatories nor CONAF supposedly have a say. For the first estimation, a college professor aided by students was hired to establish a threshold for tolerable forest grazing. Based on this estimation, CONAF managers also set the date for the beginning of the summer transhumance. Another example comes from tensions over the number and selection of beneficiaries of the conservation agreements. As seen earlier in this chapter, Mapuche claimants identify potential beneficiaries of use rights based on belonging to a community with past history of land occupancy but also individual commitment to community activities, particularly those related to negotiations with state institutions. A few years into the agreement over the Hualalafquén Reserve, CONAF representatives proposed to extend summer grazing rights to Indigenous communities located further away from the protected area. This change would help CONAF expand their community engagement actions. It would also regulate the presence of a few cattle ranchers from other localities who were already taking their animals into the reserve during the summer without formal permission. Original signatories of the agreement quickly manifested their discontent at the decision, which was eventually withdrawn. As explained by Mario, a resident from Maite with experience as a community delegate, changes like these ones ignore the history of the agreement and could bring more tension among Mapuche people: "Why do they want to bring all *Comunidades* in the valley together? Don't they understand that this would just cause problems?" Although this proposed modification to the agreement did not succeed, it heightened awareness among the Mapuche landholders involved about the precariousness of their control over the terms of the agreement.

Mapuche claims over protected areas are driven by memories of past land use, a sense of historical injustice, and enduring emotional ties to ancestral territories within state-owned forests. Rather than addressing these claims as demands for reparations or land ownership, officers are inclined to interpret them as aspirations for involvement in state actions. These aspirations are addressed through negotiations that grant use rights, designed to be minimally disruptive to forest regeneration while also maintaining the state's authority over conservation and broader control of frontier territories. Participatory conservation is an essential component of the *reason of the conservation state* insofar as it prompts citizens to participate in the

consolidation of state presence in and around protected areas without necessarily leading to a reconfiguration of conservation strategies as grassroots
actions. By establishing the possibilities and limits of citizen participation
in the management of protected areas, the *reason of the conservation state*
appears as the main logic behind the formation of ecological citizenship.
However, ecological citizenship is not the exclusive result of a state project
designed to consolidate state presence in conservation areas, discursively
and materially. As we see next, collaborations with state institutions provide
Mapuche landholders with an opportunity to critically reimagine the type of
citizenship that aligns with their aspirations for more equitable participation
in the state apparatus, alongside their desires for local sovereignty, particularly in relation to decision-making over the protection and exploitation of
frontier forests.

Reimagining Conservation Commons at the Frontier

For rural Mapuche communities, citizenship has been shaped by a long history of cultural assimilation and discrimination, fostering a widespread align-
ment with national identity. Following the late nineteenth-century invasion
of the Mapuche homeland, Wallmapu, the Chilean state granted only partial
citizenship to the Mapuche people, excluding them from electoral rights. This
exclusion aligned with the era's narrow definition of citizenship, which also
barred all women and men without formal education (Herr 2019, 99). Yet the
extension of citizenship to the Mapuche population was a priority to governments in the early twentieth century, as this process was integral to nation-
building. In frontier areas, the settlement of migrant populations was part of
the broader project of homeland-making (*hacer patria*) and implicated both
Mapuche and non-Indigenous Chileans, as seen in chapter 2. For Mapuche
populations, citizenship was a pragmatic strategy to ensure land protection
rights in the face of settlers' illegal and violent land dispossession. However,
it was also the process that facilitated forced cultural assimilation, mostly
through formal schooling designed to promote the replacement of Indigenous values and the Mapudungun language with Chilean culture. Pupils were
forbidden from speaking Mapudungun in class, and Chilean teachers from
this time are often remembered for mocking their accents. In the last thirty
years, programs of intercultural education designed to revitalize Mapuche

culture have been implemented in Mapuche areas (see Loncon et al. 2023), but for most Mapuche rural residents, formal education is still strongly linked to the trauma of racial discrimination (Hofflinger and Nahuelpan 2018).

From a governmental perspective, the cultural assimilation process was deemed successful, as it fostered a broad identification with national identity in rural Mapuche areas. This sense of national belonging is evident not only in discursive claims of identity but also through various expressions, such as enthusiastic participation in Independence Day celebrations on September 18 and the appreciation of national cuisine and music. Rural southern Chile is a stronghold of the traditional nationalist right, largely influenced by the local landholding elite, and while voting in Mapuche areas is very diverse, it tends to reflect this regional tendency.[15] Among those Mapuches adhering to conservative values, a strong identification with national values tends to accompany a more accentuated denial of Indigenous belonging and detachment from Indigenous politics. Refusal of Chilean belonging is also common but seems restricted to more radical political activists who see it as a colonial imposition rather than a complementary identity.

Among the majority of rural residents, attitudes toward Indigenous politics remain moderate and correspond to neither identification with nationalist conservative ideals nor to ideologically oriented self-denial as Chileans. Nationwide surveys have indicated that the vast majority of rural Mapuche people identify as both Chilean and Mapuche, a reflection of both a particular configuration of citizenship but also of the high level of interethnic marriages. The complementarity between Indigenous and national belonging can be contrasted with the more clear-cut divide between being Mapuche and a winka, a term that is used both as a synonym for non-Indigenous person and a derogatory expression characterizing non-Indigenous individuals as settlers and usurpers. Surveys also show that while support for the creation of an independent Mapuche state is minimal, sympathies toward other instances of Indigenous autonomy are very common (see Reyes 2022). In conversations about Indigenous identity held in rural areas, it is common to overhear statements such as, "We are the first" or "the real Chileans." To many Mapuche landholders, the condition of being autochthonous to the Chilean nation grounds rights, such as access to protected areas, that should not be extended to other Chileans.

While conservation may not initially be viewed as a primary arena for citizenship development—especially when compared to formal education—

conservation institutions, particularly in frontier regions, have facilitated interactions between farming communities and the state. These interactions are essential for shaping both perceptions of state power and feelings of national belonging. Participatory conservation is today the most effective governmental strategy to foster citizen participation around protected areas. Participatory conservation appears as a quintessential case for the process of subjectivization, whereby individuals are compelled to adopt conservationist values and practices associated with an ideal subject as it is imagined by policymakers and NGOs (see Agrawal 2005; West 2006). However, there is more to the participatory phenomenon than the irreversible imposition of alien meanings. To frontier populations, participatory conservation can also represent the source of the instrumental capture of state economic and symbolic tools, sometimes even to challenge state power, as in the case of legal claims over protected areas (Caruso 2014, 151; Cepek 2011, 512). It can also serve as a disputed political field and a creative platform from which new meanings about nature and humanity are articulated and national and Indigenous belongings are transformed (Martínez-Reyes 2016, 164).

Among Indigenous populations involved in participatory conservation, ideas and practices of conservation are adopted in ways that universalistic principles of environmentalism are reiterated but also subject to critical assessments (see Blaser 2010; Martínez-Reyes 2016). As noted by Oakley, "While categories like 'nature' and the 'environment' are not merely instrumental . . . they are also not the limit for emerging understandings and practices of environmentalism" (2020, 16). Conservation may seem to be enthusiastically accepted by Mapuche communities living near protected areas; however, it simultaneously highlights the tension between conservation practices and Indigenous cosmological principles, as well as contemporary needs. I argue that the emergence of new forms of ecological citizenship among Mapuche rural populations are driven by a desire for recognition from state authorities as equal partners. At the same time, there is a refusal to accept the state's authority over the definitions of *conservation* and the normative relationships with forests that landholders are expected to adopt. Ecological citizenship ultimately emerges at the interstice between participation in statecraft and the reclamation of an ideal engagement with forests beyond state authority, which does not simply reiterate universalistic principles of environmentalism.

Critical reinterpretations of conservation values and practices among Mapuche landholders suggest that environmental protection can be aligned with local ethical and economic aspirations. The idiom through which more sensitive models of conservation can be implemented is that of care, *cuidado* (see Araos et al. 2023; Trentini 2023). This term is commonly used in Chile to describe a way of enhancing the lives of others and feeling a sense of responsibility toward them, particularly in relationships with children and elders. The act of *cuidar* (to care for) can also extend to nature, animals, and a wide range of nonhuman entities that one feels responsible for.

As highlighted in critical academic literature on the recent consolidation of care as an ethical principle in global debates on health, work, and environment (see Fisher and Tronto 1990; Mol et al. 2010; Puig de la Bellacasa 2017), care is an ambivalent term bringing together instances of domination and control with relations of empathy and solidarity. As an ethical predisposition and action, caring entails a responsibility for the lives of others, which can manifest itself in relations where dependency and autonomy are articulated in unpredictable ways. Around southern Andean valleys, care indicates actual and ideal practices of agricultural labor that bring together protection but also exploitation of natural resources.

As suggested earlier in this book, alterhumanism among Mapuche dwellers of the conservation frontier is built upon the acknowledgment of the irreducibility of the human condition in relation to nonhuman others, as well as the rejection of anthropocentric narratives that situate humans in full epistemic and material control of nonhuman others, as in celebratory narratives about human domestication. Implicit to these principles is the existence of a dynamic hierarchy among nonhumans, who are endowed with varying degrees of autonomy and agency and, consequently, recalcitrance to human care and domestication. When applied to protected forests, the concept of care describes various forms of environmental engagement that do not align with the ownership associated with freedom in commercial extraction, nor with the conservationist ideal of rewilding. Care, then, is rarely used to describe actual agricultural practices. Rather, it is more frequently employed as a normative representation of how agriculture and forestry should be. Reimagining agricultural labor as care is nonetheless effective, as it directs landholders' attention to the potential harms they could inadvertently inflict on nonhumans whose responsiveness to human care and exploitation is hardly predictable.

In Maite, monitoring illegal logging, avoiding campfires, and inculcating in children a passion for ecological knowledge are some of the ways in which care for forests is put into practice. The co-management agreement of the Hualalafquén National Reserve has incentivized both practical activities targeting protected areas and educational projects, inspired more broadly by the principles of environmental education and Indigenous cultural revitalization. As described by both CONAF officers and people from Maite, theirs is a good relationship because it materializes in convivial and intimate moments of working together. A couple of months before the summer, when more visitors reach the national reserve, residents who actively participate in the use rights agreement check park signs and eventually relocate them or even replace them. They use machetes or chainsaws to clear bushes from the paths and facilitate the transit of both ranchers and tourists. A few years into the agreement, a local group also worked side by side with a ranger to build a wooden observation desk from where a Chilean flag flutters in the breeze. All these activities are generally described as forms of care toward protected areas.

Care is also an ethical principle that can be disseminated through education. As part of her work in cultural revitalization, Renata has been organizing an environmental workshop for school pupils called *Club de la Naturaleza*, in parallel to her courses on Mapuche cosmology and language. One of the objectives of this environmental workshop is to foster interest among the local youth in the cultural and ecological significance of keystone species, such as the araucaria tree. On one occasion, pupils were invited to participate in the maintenance of the infrastructure of the Hualalafquén Reserve. They also left decorated wooden signs reminding visitors about environmental norms along the main trails of three reserves. These signs can still be spotted along the main trail of the Hualalafquén Reserve.

The distinction between care and conservation is significant. Although both terms pertain to environmental protection, care suggests that human activities can be more than just threats to wilderness and its regeneration; they can also enhance rural landscapes. Care also serves to justify the Indigenous presence in protected areas against conservationist perspectives that emphasize the urgent need for human depopulation and rewilding as the only viable solution to natural degradation. In interactions with state institutions, care functions as a compelling argument for Mapuche communities' entitlement to protected areas. It complements their claims rooted in ancestral land connections and past ownership by emphasizing the ethical legitimacy of their historical role as custodians. In a few conversations with residents of Maite, this argument was explained in the following words, "We have taken care of these forests forever; we can do it ourselves." Amid the shifting dynamics of collaboration between environmentalism and Indigenous activism that emerged in the 1980s as a reaction to agribusiness expansion (Conklin and Graham 1995; High and Oakley 2020), the concept of care presents an alternative to both essentialized narratives of Indigenous custodianship—suggesting that non-traditional communities lack authenticity (see Nadasdy 2005)—and preservationist viewpoints that overlook the effectiveness of customary practices in wildlife regeneration. In conservation, translation is an integral process responsible for the transformation of local understandings of human-environmental relations into meanings and categories inserted within frameworks of environmental governance (see West 2005). Interpreting agricultural activities in and around forests as expressions of care carries significant critical and political implications. It highlights the limitations of environmentalism as a universal concept that can be seamlessly tailored to local aspirations and challenges the notion that human depopulation is the sole viable route to achieving just coexistence with nonhuman entities.

The emphasis on care through which residents of Maite depict their involvement in state-led conservation has significant implications for the definition of protected forests as commons. Typical definitions of commons are based on universalistic premises, whereby their value is to be preserved for the rest of the world or the nation. As commons, protected forests are in theory owned by the citizens of a country, with the state acting on their behalf. Accordingly, no group can claim an exclusive relationship with protected forests, since conservation remains a prerogative of the state acting on behalf of its citizenry. As proposed by Blaser and de la Cadena, Indigenous struggles over natural resources might be best described as processes of *uncommoning* (2017). The term *uncommoning* does not refer in this case to enclosure or privatization. Rather, uncommoning consists of reclaiming a historical relationship with nonhumans central to world-making in Indigenous contexts. As the *reason of the conservation state* continues to guide conservation agreements, for Mapuche claimants, new relations of propriety with protected forests are unfeasible. These claims over protected areas effectively compel the state to permit Mapuche landholders to engage with forests through practices that, rather than merely reiterating ahistorical customary traditions, creatively intertwine environmentalist values with revitalized cosmological principles. This engagement fosters a new mutual definition of forests and people, forming the foundation of the concept of alterhumanism. The idiom of care reshuffles protection and extraction of natural resources while articulating a definition of conservation commons in which the inclusion of Indigenous responsibilities and actions is made compatible with their preservation as public goods. It also prompts critical reflections on what it means to be an Indigenous citizen at the conservation frontier.

Ecological Citizenship and the Limits of Indigenous Sovereignty

Conservation agreements, I have argued, engender a reflexive process through which Indigenous belonging is framed in relation to both the state and the environment: While ecological citizenship is reasserted, aspirations of sovereignty are redirected toward the reclamation of historical relationships of care for forests that do not require state authority to be effective. The unfinished subjectivization of Mapuche frontier dwellers into ecological citizens can be explained by the critical effects that aspirations of sovereignty hold in limiting the extent of state authority over the terms of relations that link Indigenous communities with forests. For Mapuche landholders, conservation agreements represent not mere concessions from the state but political victories achieved through mobilizations and, more broadly, through a dialogue with state authorities.

The term "dialogue" (*diálogo*) frequently arises in discussions surrounding social conflicts in Chile, particularly those related to Mapuche mobilizations. While its content varies, it is generally assumed to be the only viable, albeit difficult path toward the resolution of land conflicts in Wallmapu. Mapuche activists see dialogue not only as a political strategy, but also as a way of doing politics entrenched in Mapuche history. Mapuche leaders have relied on negotiation practices in complement with military resistance to cope with colonial threats since the heyday of the Spanish invasion in the seventeenth century. The most emblematic form of negotiation is *trawün* or *parlamentos*, large, highly ritualistic meetings in which agreements were struck among local leaders and representatives of the Spanish crown concerning topics such as commercial exchanges across the Biobío border, the presence of Catholic missions within Mapuche territory, and the exchange of war captives (see Marimán 2002; Zavala 2005).[16] As proposed by Foerster, colonial authorities have traditionally approached peace treaties as Mapuche acts of submission, while Mapuche leaders saw them as pacts between equals (2018, 29). This difference in perspective is relevant. By engaging in diplomacy through rules imposed by the state, Mapuche leaders have been able to partly repel the Chilean state project of complete assimilation and eradication of Mapuche anticolonial aspirations (Pairican 2020, 281).

The historical faith in dialogue among Mapuche communities should not be regarded merely as an illusion or a passive response to state authority. Dialogue, as in the case of negotiations with forest institutions, is the result of political mobilization. Mapuche claimants are aware of the fragility of any instance of dialogue and the need for a constant state of alert. Denial of dialogue by state authorities usually materializes in the lack of consultation with Mapuche populations affected by private and public projects in fields such as infrastructure construction and conservation. For Mapuche activists, the 169 Indigenous and Tribal Peoples Convention undersigned by Chile in 2008, mostly referred to as Convenio 169, is a crucial legal mechanism that they can refer to in negotiations over controversial development projects, insofar as it establishes the right to free, prior, and informed consent for Indigenous people (see Millaleo 2021, 65–67). A significant recent concern regarding the effects of state initiatives is the creation of a new conservation entity: the "Biodiversity and Protected Areas Service" (*Servicio de Biodiversidad y Áreas Protegidas*), established in 2023. This service aims to enhance funding and infrastructure for park management and is anticipated to undergo a consultation process throughout 2024 and 2025.

Dialogue, of course, remains a problematic word. As proposed by Butler, "The power relations that condition and limit dialogic possibilities need first to be interrogated. Otherwise, the model of dialogue risks relapsing into a liberal model that assumes that speaking agents occupy equal positions of power and speak with the same presuppositions about what constitutes 'agreement' and 'unity' and, indeed, that those are the goals to be sought" (1990, 20). In depicting Indigenous-state relations, the idiom of dialogue presumes a problematic symmetry that obfuscates the power of the settler state in imposing which dialogues can take place. However, dialogue is not only a mystification of settler relations but can also be articulated as the result of political struggle, as in the tradition of Mapuche diplomacy, in which dialogue is valorized as an achievement made possible by overt forms of resistance. Dialogue requires conflict and vice versa. This is because, as Coulthard affirms, "without conflict and struggle the terms of recognition tend to remain in the possession of those in power to bestow on their inferiors in ways that they deem appropriate" (2014, 3).

Not all forms of resistance, however, can contribute to the possibility of dialogue. For most Mapuche landholders whom I met in southern Chile, radical acts of mobilization, such as arson attacks common in some areas of the country, are not acceptable for a general ethical rejection of violence, but also for the consequence that violence holds in denying their recognition as political interlocutors by the state and consequentially, the possibility of dialogue. The logic of dialogue through which Mapuche residents of Andean valleys frame their relations with state institutions has two significant consequences. On the one hand, a critical new form of citizenship emerges; on the other, new ways of imagining and practicing Indigenous sovereignty are articulated as more realistic aspirations rather than a utopia.

Sovereignty is not a common term in Indigenous politics in Chile, as its use is generally restricted to the more traditional meaning of state authority and national independence. Over the last few decades, Mapuche political debates have rotated around the meanings and possibilities of notions of "autonomy" (*autonomía*). Autonomy is an indeterminate political horizon. Among Mapuche leaders and writers, it does not target Indigenous statehood, but rather a set of diverse actions designed to allow Mapuche residents to hold control over decision-making processes directly affecting their lives. In practice, autonomy can materialize in the activation of Indigenous institutional spaces with no interference from non-Indigenous actors (Marimán 2012, 24–25) or in a tradition of anti-colonial writing by Mapuche collectives and authors as part of a broader process of decolonization (Antileo 2020, 274). While for some, autonomy can materialize in projects articulated through the means and resources of the state (Park and Richards 2007; Radcliffe and Webb 2015), for others, autonomy can only be achieved by rejecting collaboration with the state and taking control over dispossessed land by force without going through institutional mechanisms, a strategy that Pairican (2014) has defined as *rupturista*, "disruptive," in opposition to other forms of Mapuche activism. Some Mapuche leaders have identified "plurinationality" (*plurinacionalidad*), a model of governance developed in two other Latin American countries, Bolivia and Ecuador, as the legal framework for a definition of Indigenous autonomy that presupposes the existence of Indigenous people as collective subjects not only with cultural but also political rights (Millaleo 2021, 110).

In depicting aspirations and critical appraisals of state power among Mapuche landholders involved in participatory conservation, I use the term *sovereignty* in a broader sense than the notion of *autonomy*. It refers to the aspiration of self-governing collective life, not as an institutional project but as one performed in everyday life and geared toward the reclamation of significant social and ecological relations from alien powers, including those of the state. As proposed by Postero and Fabricant in their analysis of Guaraní activism in Bolivia, "sovereignty is embedded in local relationships, including those with the land and broader natural environment . . . it is not owned by the state, but by those who have long-standing reciprocal relationships with the lands and beings in that territory" (2019, 99). As this form of sovereignty is reasserted through the state rather than in opposition to it, Indigenous struggles center on the question of how their sovereignty can co-exist with their status as citizens (2019, 105).

Enveloping Indigenous sovereignties within the state might not lead to a full realization of independence but can lead to future scenarios where they pose "serious jurisdictional and normative challenges to each other" (Simpson 2014, 10). Conservation agreements are essential means for carving out Indigenous sovereignty within state authority. As this chapter has asserted, their effects are twofold. Conservation agreements reinforce state sovereignty over frontier spaces by promoting citizen participation and reasserting the nature of protected areas as national commons. They also offer a critical challenge to state authority over frontier spaces by allowing Indigenous communities to reclaim relations of care with forests as an alternative ethical form of engagement.

Participatory conservation illustrates how institutional projects aimed at shaping subjectivity engage with the very concept of humanity and its relationship with those we define as nonhumans. Indigenous reclamation of seemingly ambivalent relationships with forests intertwines notions of ownership and care, forming the foundation of a specific interpretation of alterhumanism. Earlier in this book, we explored how the process of *becom-*

ing human through and with nonhuman others in Mapuche frontier communities reveals an understanding of nonhuman agency and responsiveness characterized by fluid ontological boundaries and the varying potentials of domestication within the forest ecosystem. The institutional project of subjectivization inherent in participatory conservation seeks to transform frontier dwellers into citizens committed to the protection and enhancement of commons. However, this process of subjectivization is likely to remain incomplete, as the embodied relationships with nonhumans that shape our understanding of humanity resist many of the changes that institutional efforts to redefine human identities and behaviors may impose. The ongoing journey toward becoming ecological citizens serves as a poignant reminder that citizen formation is a contested arena, where Indigenous aspirations for sovereignty—especially those focused on reclaiming environmental relationships central to local world-making and restorative projects—drive engagement with the settler state.

* * *

Becoming ecological citizens represents the second of two ongoing projects of subjectivization explored in this book. The first project, as previously discussed, revolves around the adoption of environmentalist discourses and practices. The subjectivization engendered by conservation is unfinished because, as an instituting power, conservation is capable of directing, but not necessarily erasing and rewriting power-affective engagements with nonhumans. Of course, there are more such projects unfolding around conservation frontiers. In the name of economic efficiency in the new green economy, small-scale foresters are compelled to adopt managerial perspectives on forest extraction and regeneration (see Di Giminiani 2016). As a consequence of the ecotourism boom and through the institutional means of microfinance and rural development, a growing number of individuals are adopting entrepreneurialism as a desired lifestyle for its promise of freedom and a livelihood alternative to formal employment or farming, even when it is carried out under often precarious and informal conditions (Soto et al. 2023). However, a book can only accomplish so much. Instead of attempting to document all potential projects of unfinished subjectivization at conservation frontiers, it may be more beneficial to highlight the contrasting and overlapping trajectories of private and state conservation as they intertwine within a landscape shaped by various historical projects, including state territorialization, environmental activism, and the neoliberalization of social life in the burgeoning green economy.

As I near the conclusion of this book, one final question arises. A broader and more indeterminate historical process is unfolding in the background of the ongoing formation of conservation frontiers. As a matter of fact, it is more than a background, but the very motivation for imagining the conservation frontier as a refuge from industrial civilization and a site for thinking creatively and critically about new ways of becoming human. The Anthropocene represents not merely a label for industrial modernity but a profound epistemic shift in humanity's understanding, rooted in a troubling vision of a future characterized by ongoing and escalating crises. Conservation grapples with this crisis, striving to recognize the delicate foundations of cohabitation among all living beings. Thus, the pressing question arises: How can we navigate our existence as humans in the world that lies ahead?

FIGURE 12 Flower of quila (*Chusquea culeou*) from southern Argentina (Photograph by Leo Ridano/Shutterstock.com)

Epilogue

Crisis and Rewilding in the World to Come

"The quilas are flowering!" Quila (*Chusquea quila*) is a perennial bamboo found in abundance in the understory of the southern forests of Chile and Argentina. These plants are expected to flower during the spring roughly every fifteen years. Soon after blooming, quilas begin a process of decay leading to their deaths. When a large number of quilas do so at the same time, people from southern Chile take it as a portent for a bad year ahead. The ominous message of quila flowers has its origins in a specific event in the history of colonization of Wallmapu. As recounted by Spanish chronicler Jerónimo de Vivar, in 1552, the newly founded city of Valdivia was invaded by rats, who quickly devoured all food provisions. That year, the quilas blossomed.

The causal connection between rat invasions and the flowering of quilas, known to Jerónimo de Vivar's informants, has been substantiated by recent ecological studies. Rats are attracted to the seeds of the dying bamboo and, thanks to the sudden availability of this food staple, their population grows exponentially during blossom periods (Diaz 2021). While pest control measures have drastically reduced rat invasions occasioned by quila flowering, the association between quila flowers and imminent crises continues to this day. Climate crisis might play a role in the increasing occurrence of quila blossoming and the other environmental hazards they seemingly occasion. After blossoming, dying quila bamboo facilitates the spread of wildfires in the summer, which in southern Chile have dramatically increased in size and occurrence in the last two decades due to the severity of the most recent droughts, the proliferation of agro-industrial activity, and urban sprawl.

Since I first visited the Andean valleys described in this book, quilas blossomed almost every year. From extraordinary events, flowerings have become habitual images of a latent environmental crisis materializing in droughts and wildfires in the summer and flooding in the winter. These phenomena, while now routinely anticipated, continue to present significant management challenges for any government. Their scale makes effective containment and mitigation difficult, requiring not only substantial resources that might not be available but a more structural redesign of urban and rural infrastructures that no government is willing to or can actually put into action.

Three crises with different timeframes and uncertain consequences have unfolded in the background of this book. Inevitably, they have shaped many of the ideas about democracy and habitability that have guided my engagement with the politics of conservation throughout. In October 2019, during the right-wing presidency of Sebastián Piñera, Chile was caught in the midst of social unrest, with the eruption of protests and riots against rising living costs, in particular the rise of public transport fees in the capital, Santiago, and against the police brutality deployed in their response. The *estallido social* ("social explosion") was not necessarily an overt political project aimed at moving past the radical version of neoliberalism with which Chile has been historically associated. It was, nonetheless, a clear manifestation of a deep neoliberal crisis, revealing widespread disaffection with the political and economic elites at a time when the promises of social mobility and increasing opportunities for everybody seemed to be contradicted by economic stagnation, a sturdy inequality gap, and a widespread sense of vulnerability to the private sector dominating the fields of education, health, and pensions (see Luna 2021).[1] In looking for a solution to political unrest, Congress agreed to begin a new constitutional process to eventually replace the Pinochet-era 1980 constitution, which sanctioned many laissez-faire policies still at work in the country and restricted legislative debate through high parliamentary quorums, with a new document, this time drafted by a popularly elected institution.[2]

However, it was the eruption of another crisis that brought the social protests to a halt. In the space of a few months at the beginning of 2020, large weekly protests became a distant memory with the eruption of the second crisis, the COVID-19 pandemic. Exposure to the SARS-CoV-2 virus had tragic and deadly consequences, with long-term effects almost impossible to predict. Soon, attention turned to the impact on the economy and what the pandemic exposed in the social fabric of almost every country on earth. In Chile, as everywhere, poorer sectors of society were more vulnerable to the ensuing health and economic crisis. The loss of employment in the informal market and the consequent exclusion from remote work schemes or subsidies introduced as compensation mechanisms meant that many were left with no choice other than working illegally, without health and safety measures (see Di Giminiani et al. 2020).[3]

The third crisis informing many of the ideas presented in this book is longer, more complex, and with no near end in sight. The climate crisis leaves no nation immune to its effects, but, like COVID-19, those with poorer infrastructures are often the most vulnerable. The injustice of environmental collapse remains a scandalous paradox: Nations that contribute less to carbon emissions pay the higher costs of the climate crisis. Among the effects of climate crisis in Chile, the gradual advance of desertification is certainly one of the most distressing. This process coincided with a megadrought cycle from 2010 to 2019 associated with the El Niño–Southern Oscillation, a periodic variation of seawater temperatures across the Pacific in South America which dramatically affects rainfall. This megadrought, however, was unlike others in the past for its severity and the presence of other contributing factors. Water deregulation policies introduced by the Pinochet dictatorship had already led to dramatic cases of water crisis in areas where monocrop fields were introduced to meet global demands for produce such as avocados. And of course, global warming worsened these already worrisome water crises. The unprecedented recurrence of quila blossom was just one of the many revealing moments of the current crisis in Chile. News about drying lakes and rivers reminds people in Chile, as elsewhere, of a crisis that is here to stay and that will shape the world to come.[4]

The three crises (political, sanitary, and ecological) that have served as the historical background for the writing of this book might have different origins and consequences, but they share one important aspect: All crises eventually reveal the fragility of social and ecological coexistence and habitability and make obsolete assumptions about them that were once held with security. Crises might be tackled with the design of technical solutions aimed at readjusting our lifestyles to new environmental conditions, but most often they prompt the critical imagination of alternative futures and inspire radical actions capable of transforming those structural elements of economic and political processes that led us to a crisis in the first place (Cordero 2016; Gago 2017; Narotzky and Besnier 2014). The debate over the benefits and insufficiency of the energy transition in responding to global warming exemplifies the inherent tension between the critical potentials of crisis and its managerial configurations. The critical potential enabled by the experience of crisis goes so deep as to question the very notion of humanity and its implications in the current debate over the existential concern posed by climate change. The idea of the Anthropocene is built indeed on the recognition that the climate crisis is open-ended, that it cannot be reduced to a moment after which things go back to business as usual, and that the very idea of humanity needs to be radically reformulated.

The term *Anthropocene*, first popularized by Nobel Prize winner in chemistry Paul Crutzen at a conference in Mexico in 2000, attests that in the Industrial Age humanity has become a force capable of interrupting geological cycles once thought of as independent from human history. In 2024, the International Union of Geological Sciences (IUGS) rejected the status of the Anthropocene as a geological epoch mostly on the grounds that its origin was simply too recent for a consensual definition, especially considering that proponents of the new epoch converged in 1952, the year when sediments from Crawford Lake in Canada showed a noticeable change caused by residues, in particular radioactive plutonium left by nuclear bomb tests. In the IUGS's official statement, however, the idea of the Anthropocene has not been discarded, as it "will remain an invaluable descriptor in human-environment interactions."[5] Despite ongoing debates over its exact definition, the Anthropocene has been instrumental in framing the current climate crisis as a uniquely human-driven process, unprecedented in scale and impact throughout history. By opening up the possibility for human and natural history to be indissociable, the idea of the Anthropocene invites us to think of humanity as both a force of its own, particularly destructive, and one entangled with nonhuman agencies in always surprising ways (Chakrabarty 2021; Latour 2014).

The idea of alterhumanism pursued in this book is inspired by many lessons of the Anthropocene debate and the sense of crisis evoked by this notion. Alterhumanism, we have seen, posits humanity as a central category directing the articulation of human-environmental relations. At the same time, this category is plural, always in the making and dependent on affective relations with nonhuman others, providing us with the means to understand the ontological and ethical limits of human engagement with the world. I situated the empirical approach to the human question offered by alterhumanism within two historical contexts: the impact of conservation in thinking about more-than-human coexistence and, more recently, the radical redefinition of humanity at the basis of Anthropocene thinking.

In the remaining pages of this book, I want to underscore the importance of experiencing crisis and its critical potential in reimagining humanity within the Anthropocene. This approach goes beyond frameworks of human exceptionalism or purely ecocentric aims, engaging instead with the evolving question of what it means to be human as we envision future life. The Anthropocene elicits a crisis like no other as it cultivates the vision of a future built around a central image of a depopulated, rewilded world that is at once a utopian solution to climate change and its inevitable dystopian outcome. Around global conservation frontiers, many have already come to experience the rewilded world as either a worrisome prospect of land abandonment or a victory for nature and its ability to take its due course. Can rewilding be something other than the inevitable outcome of the crisis or a radical solution reinforcing the enduring legacy of wilderness conservation without humans? Yes, but under one condition: that of not forgetting that relations with the environment and among humans are in need of forms of repair that recognize the entangled nature of histories of care and exploitation, such as those that make the conservation frontier in Chile what it is today.

Living with the Crisis

My use of the term *crisis* to depict the historical background behind the writing of this book has a specific reason. Unlike other possible semantic alternatives, such as *disaster* or *tragedy*, the term *crisis* evokes two possibilities: a trust in technocratic solutions entrenched in the notion of crisis management and the disruptive imaginative potentials of crisis in rethinking once self-evident principles and norms of collective life (see Cordero 2016; Masco 2017). Managerial attitudes are more common in crises that unfold under cyclical fashions, a point extensively documented in Marxist analyses of overaccumulation of capital and market crashes. More generally, crises entail a loss of epistemic control over previously self-evident assumptions about coexistence and habitability in our daily life. As suggested by Narotzky and Besnier, the idea of crises refers to "structural processes generally understood to be beyond the control of people but simultaneously expressing people's breach of confidence in the elements that provided relative systemic stability and reasonable expectations for the future" (2014, S4).

Among the most compelling effects of any crisis is the critical reflection on their structural causes and the consequent search for new experimental solutions that could help move past it and avoid its repetition. The critical potential of crises can materialize in the rearticulation of basic ideas about coexistence, justice, and habitability that constitute the conceptual foundation of social life. As Gago reminds us, "The crisis is a privileged *locus* for thinking because there is a cognitive porosity; concepts are set in motion, and sensibilities express the commotion and reorganize the thresholds of what is considered possible and how it is enunciated" (2017, 233). For crises to be effective in fostering critical reflections capable of informing enduring social transformations, their experiences must be puzzling and work similarly to the phenomenological process of epoche, which consists of the suspension and bracketing of what is known. For Cordero,

> in historical periods in which social actors consciously self-describe as living in crisis, the concept somehow becomes an indispensable means to make sense of the conflicts, excesses and disruptions that affect social and political life. In this capacity, crisis situations are also conceived as spaces for critique, insofar as they open normative questions about the limits and acceptability of the current state of society and about the very mechanisms of normative justification through which social actors accept and maintain a damaging form of life. (2016, 31)

The experience of crisis often resembles the state of *impasse*, where one passively waits for transformations that might not happen. Yet crisis may also spark a range of emotions—like hope—that fuel the renewal of imagination and foster actions directed at shaping the future (Renfrew 2018, 81).

Like any other crisis, the Anthropocene can leave us in a state of suspension, unwilling or incapable of responding to its unprecedented challenges, or of fostering the imagination of radical futures and the actions that might make them turn into reality. The sense of impasse provoked by the Anthropocene is unique insofar as it leaves little hope for the end of its crisis without the adoption of radical changes in lifestyle and limitations to economic productivity, which might not even be sufficient. The grim projections of global warming have given rise to sentiments such as grief and themes like dystopia, which have shaped how visions of the future are portrayed in cinema and the arts (see Ginn 2015). Toxicity, environmental disasters, and rewilding are perhaps the most recurrent images of the future anticipated by the very idea of the Anthropocene. As a consequence of such a dystopian figuration of the future, the affects that have most clearly characterized the embodiment of the Anthropocene are fear, grief, and anxiety. Ecological grief (see Cunsolo and Ellis 2018) expresses not only sorrow over the irreparable loss of species but also tangible concerns about the future human habitability on earth. Ecological grief, however, is not necessarily destined to be a doleful wait for inevitable disaster. Even when it does not translate into concrete transformative actions, the experience of grief can animate hope for the future (Head 2016) by helping us to develop a new form of attentiveness toward what is lost, what can be saved, and the fragility of the social and ecological relations that give vitality to the worlds we inhabit.

The attentiveness to the world that the discomforting experience of the Anthropocene crisis can help us cultivate is indissociable from the critical reflection that the very idea of the Anthropocene sustains. Ecological attentiveness in the Anthropocene is directed inevitably toward the consequences of human production and consumption on geological and climate processes, which were previously poorly seen or even unimaginable. In bringing to light the geological dimension of human actions and their slow, dispersed, and thus hardly perceptible consequences on more-than-human coexistence, the Anthropocene has rewritten the very idea of humanity held dear in the humanistic tradition. Under the Anthropocene, the human is indissociably a force unique in its geological potentials in relation to other forms of life while, at the same time, it is profoundly entangled with them. Geological history is no longer the background to the much faster stories of human exploitation and care. In Chakrabarty's words, "Anthropogenic explanations of climate change spell the collapse of the age-old humanist distinction . . . between natural history and human history" (2021, 26). Along similar lines, Latour suggests that the Anthropocene "gives another definition of time, it redescribes what it is to stand in space, and it reshuffles what it means to be entangled within animated agencies" (2014, 16). Human history is no longer the exclusive result of affairs involving only humans. It also involves different forms of entanglements between human cultural processes and "nonhuman processes that exhibit periodic unruliness" (Connolly 2017, 68), as reflected in a growing awareness of the urgent need for climate change adaptation across a wide range of productive activities.

In rendering the human a unique geological force and one deeply embedded with nonhuman agencies, the Anthropocene reshuffles our understanding of the universalistic and particularistic status of being human. The planetary dimension of the Anthropocene notion entails a call for shared responsibility as members of the same species for the future of the earth. However, the effects of and responsibilities for the current crisis are far from being equally distributed. Industrialization—whether in capitalist or socialist forms, though primarily the former—has historically driven the reliance on fossil fuels and the exponential rise in carbon emissions over the past two centuries. Historical analyses linking capitalism with industrial development, of which Moore's neologism of Capitalocene is an explicit example (2015), have highlighted the key role of capital accumulation in the *great acceleration* and its unequal manifestations, with powerful market actors, higher social classes, and wealthier countries bearing the most responsibility for global warming. The tension between universalistic and particularistic visions of humanity in the Anthropocene reminds us that being human is a plural and diverse ontological condition. As suggested by Viveiros de Castro, Anthropocene thinking requires the practice of a radical form of ontological pluralism, dedicated to uncovering the existence of multiple ways of being on Earth while invested in "developing the new insights about the multifarious symbiotic interdependence of all life-forms" (2019, 298). The acknowledgment of humanity as both a universal ontological category with distinct geological implications and a plural manifestation arising from various processes of entanglement is a fundamental insight from the Anthropocene discourse that has particularly informed the concept of alterhumanism explored in this book.

The reason why the critical potentials of the Anthropocene crisis are remarkably different from other crises is to be found not only in the novel reconfiguration of humanity as a geological force but also in its projection of an inevitable slow collapse of human life as we know it, at least in industrial contexts. A world with declining conditions for human habitability first and then devoid of humanity and free to rewild can result in an immobilizing consciousness in the face of inevitable disaster as much as the reckoning that radical solutions are needed to cope with a crisis unlike any other in human and natural history. In the Anthropocene, rewilding represents both a potentially dystopian outcome of the crisis and a possible solution to it. The global emergence of rewilding as a key theme in the conservation and climate crisis debate has rejuvenated accounts of humanity, shifting the perspective from a morally positive view of anthropocentrism as a desirable form of engagement with the world to a negative interpretation that frames humanity as a fundamental contributor to the depletion of nonhuman life. The plural and processual characterization of humanity offered by the idea of alterhumanism provides valuable insights into how rewilding can be envisioned as a process of revitalization and repair that does not inherently require, or necessarily result in, a world devoid of humans.

The Futures of Rewilding

In 2020, during the COVID-19 pandemic, we might have had a taste of how rewilding may look in the future. In some countries, where lockdown measures and mobility restrictions were enforced, nature seemed to have momentarily reclaimed urban spaces. In a deserted Venice, with tourists and mega cruise ships gone, waters acquired a turquoise color taken by many as a sign of its decontamination, while extraordinary footage of dolphins swimming in the city canals went viral. In Santiago, videos of pumas roaming around residential areas became instant news. With very little traffic, pumas felt safe enough to venture outside the nearby mountain valleys where their population has retreated as a consequence of urban sprawl in the last century. These scenes, remindful of the distressing experience of lockdown, corroborate the main tenet of rewilding: Nonhuman life can thrive only once human populations are held back. Whether as an unintended process linked to land abandonment or a purposeful conservation strategy, rewilding sees human retreat as the necessary condition for wildlife to revitalize.

Rewilding is grounded in the belief that human depopulation enables a form of ecological recovery. However, how it can be achieved and its potential costs are the two open-ended questions, rendering rewilding a loosely defined phenomenon, open to varied interpretations and approaches. Early uses of this term can be found in the anarcho-primitivist movement, for which ecocentric self-transformation and the consequent development of a more ecologically and politically equal society could be achieved through retreat from civilization and extensive contact with wilderness. Today, most uses of this term refer to a specific set of conservation practices and values designed to help nature take its own regenerative course. In the late 1980s, environmental activist David Foreman and conservation biologist Michael Soulé popularized this term by advocating for the reintroduction of wild species into areas where their population had disappeared (Lorimer et al. 2015). As put by one of its influential supporters, George Monbiot, rewilding is about "resisting the urge to control nature and allowing it to find its own way. It involves reintroducing absent plants and animals (and in a few cases culling exotic species which cannot be contained by native wildlife), pulling down the fences, blocking the drainage ditches, but otherwise stepping back" (2014, 10).

While sharing many of the features of customary preservationist models and their more recent rediscoveries, such as the back-to-barrier movement (Hutton et al. 2005), rewilding extends beyond wildlife conservation by adopting a proactive stance to wildlife regeneration. Rewilding is based on the possibility of nature taking its own course, but it remains an experimental process, as it requires different forms of population control by park managers and scientists (Altrudi 2022), and the consequences of trophic changes triggered by species reintroduction are hard to predict (Knight 2017). As a model of conservation, rewilding today is primarily enacted through three actions: the reintroduction of keynote species, in particular big predators, aimed at transforming trophic chains in ways that allow them to resemble the ecological scenario before population decline; taxon substitution, through which extinct species are replaced by others with similar ecological functions, such as seed dispersal; and land abandonment to facilitate the return of apex predators, like wolves and pumas, in regions where human populations are declining (Lorimer et al. 2015, 41–42). Together, these actions aim to reestablish self-sustaining ecosystems that can evolve with minimal human oversight.[6]

Despite its undeniable allure, rewilding inevitably has problematic implications. Common criticisms point to the dangers of evictions from rewilding territories—an occurrence well known in the colonial history of conservation—and the compensatory nature of many rewilding initiatives, which entail that depletive agro-industrial projects can be remedied through the establishment of new protected areas. Another target of criticism is the delegitimization of local human-environmental relations inherent to the search for benchmarks—in other words, the historical moments preceding wildlife decline that rewilding initiatives aim to bring back. Inherent to the identification of benchmarks is the correlation linking human population growth with wildlife decline. As indicated by Jørgensen, the problem with rewilding, in its most radical version at least, is that it "disavows human history and finds value only in historical ecologies prior to human habitation" (2015, 487). Rewilding is destined to play an increasingly central role in the Anthropocene. It will offer practical means to curb carbon emissions through the restoration of ecosystems while simultaneously prompting the imagination of utopian and dystopian futures. This, in turn, challenges us to rethink the very way in which we dwell in the world. As more consensus on the benefits of rewilding is gathered, criticism will be even more necessary, particularly if we want to avoid repeating the same mistakes of traditional conservation, starting from the very idea of humanity as inexorably antithetical to wilderness.

Rewilding can transcend wilderness enclosures by integrating human communities as active participants in conservation efforts, rather than viewing them as separate from or detrimental to natural processes. Bearing in mind some of the implications of the idea of alterhumanism for the debate on conservation, I would like to propose that rewilding could indeed be a viable solution to promote more-than-human coexistence, but only if it abandons universalistic representations of humanity, recognizes that nature always takes its course with the participation of multiple human collectivities, and that different forms of life are in need of different forms of repair. Rewilding initiatives should be ideally implemented with particular attention to those experiences and memories of past ecological and social harm, such as deforestation and colonial encroachment, that constantly resurface and redirect relations imbricating humans and nonhumans. For rewilding to not repeat the mistakes of traditional conservation, it would need to be accompanied by another action that addresses the past while anticipating the future: reparation. Even when they encourage the recognition and closure of past injustices, reparations are always forward-looking. They serve as construction projects designed to foster world-making projects that confront the lasting, intergenerational impacts of historical harm and, in doing so, often initiate unforeseen social and ecological changes (Táíwò 2002, 5). Reparations addressing environmental harm, such as industrial pollution, are frequently structured as compensatory measures targeting affected human populations. However, a more authentic ecological version of reparation should recognize that "harm and recovery of environments and human societies are intrinsically linked" (Papadopoulos et al. 2023, 2). Albeit often thought of as projects of restoration, in practice, ecological reparations always affect "relations between people and their land, the biodiversity conserved on or through this land and the benefits communities do or do not derive from these" (Büscher and Fletcher 2000, 186). For reparations to be ecologically focused, their implementation should prioritize the more-than-human relations that they affect, offering holistic forms of restoration for all collectivities involved, both human and nonhuman.

Reparation and rewilding share a key similarity: Both reflect on past harm while acting as forward-looking transformative projects with unpredictable outcomes. Their coupling, I believe, can spur the imagination of a future where wildlife can thrive through the limitation of human activities without reducing humanity to an undifferentiated universal subject standing as an inherent threat to nonhumans. It can also help us sidestep the pitfalls of allowing conservation to marginalize communities impacted by the creation and expansion of protected areas, or of permitting the continuation of depletive human activities by leveraging conservation initiatives that provide compensation without addressing the underlying processes of environmental depletion. Ecological reparation is a key component of any alternative model to these two historical tendencies in conservation: one rooted in fortress conservation and the other that embraces a more pragmatic, yet less critical, approach to ecological compensation. In Büscher and Fletcher's proposal, alternative models should be built on the principles of conviviality (2020), a term in line with its etymology "living with," which encourages both democratic participation in conservation and the moral urgency of environmental repair.

Unprecedented crises demand radical solutions. The Anthropocene crisis has encouraged new critical perspectives on the combined effects of conservation and the profound changes in consumption habits and agro-industrial production. Other strategies to cope with the climate crisis join rewilding in revealing the inadequacy of any reformist aspiration to simply make way for comfortable adjustments to our current lifestyles and economic models. Energy transition and the degrowth movement are two approaches to the current crisis that, like rewilding, promise to curb carbon emissions and extinction processes by transforming existing models of productivity and patterns of consumption. Of course, both approaches are not free from problematic implications, such as the enduring demand for natural resources linked to the development of the renewable energy industry and the reception of the idea of degrowth in the Global South as an imposition by rich countries who have already benefited from industrial development. What makes proposals such as rewilding, degrowth, and energy transformation key contributions to the current debate on environmental crisis is not necessarily their material and economic impact, especially for the first two, but their radical call for a profound reassessment of humanity. This reassessment emphasizes humanity's dual role as both part of and separate from nature in addressing the ongoing crisis. The Anthropocene has reshuffled how we think of the human condition. It forces a recognition of the entanglements of humans and nonhumans that cannot be decoupled, and so reorients humanity's responsibility to reckon with itself as a geological force that can and does erase other forms of life. In looking for a way out of the Anthropocene crisis, we must acknowledge the reality of humanity as a destructive force as much as its profound ability to cultivate an ethics of care toward nonhumans—two positions serving as the basis for the idea of alterhumanism advanced in this book. Thinking through the Anthropocene does not mean surrendering blindly to the idea of future depopulation in an increasingly hostile world for humans, nor does it mean cultivating fantasies of wilderness reclaiming its territory. In the futures imagined through rewilding, the revival of wildlife and our continuity as a species depend on the relinquishing of domestication as the dominant human way of being in the world.

The stories of settlers, Mapuche farmers, environmentalist activists, scientists, and state officers depicted in this book remind us that from experiences of environmental decline and rewilding emerge new and multiple ways of thinking about human potentials to deplete and revitalize the world around us. Their perspectives on humanity discussed in this book through the lens of alterhumanism emphasize that, while *being human* is a fundamental viewpoint for understanding the world, *humanity* is an evolving concept shaped by various interconnections with nonhuman entities. The vitality of the world depends on humans in their capacities to be both caretakers and destroyers. This means that the myriad processes of becoming human are deeply entwined with our relationships with what stands beyond and within ourselves. By embracing this humble and ambivalent understanding of humanity, we can better comprehend the current crisis and, hopefully, it might also teach us something about how life can be imagined in the world to come.

Acknowledgments

The stories and ideas that I reproduce in this book are drawn from interviews, conversations, and shared experiences with numerous people living and working around the towns of Villarrica, Pucón, and Currarehue. While there are more people that made this book possible, I would like to express my deepest gratitude to Manuel Venegas, Roberto Sanhueza, Sidia Nahuelán, Germán Curihual, Ruth Valencia, Chelmo Curihual, Tomás Ibarra, Robert Petitpas, Teresa Quilacán, Tomás Altamirano, Marta Quilacán, Jerry Laker, Cristóbal Pizarro, Juana Pincheira, Rod Walker (RIP), Luís Fica, and Jorge Paredes. I am especially indebted to Loly Salazar, Iria Fuentes, and Mariano and Andrés Huaiquifil for their hospitality.

Research for this book encompassed multiple stints of fieldwork over the years, which were made possible by the financial support of four different centers and projects: the Center for Indigenous and Intercultural Research (CIIR; ANID/FONDAP/1522A003), Anillos Cultura y Crisis Climática (ATE230065), the Instituto Milenio para la Investigación en Violencia y Democracia VioDemos (ANID/Millennium Science Initiative Program/ ICS2019_025), and the Fondecyt Project "After Harm: Interdisciplinary Explorations of Reparation in Chile" (1230912). Fieldwork involved collaborations with wonderful colleagues to whom I am grateful for the time spent together and the thinking we shared: Martín Fonck, Julian Moraga, Daniela Jacob, and Paolo Perasso. Further inspiration came from other collaborations in the running of the aforementioned projects, in particular the documentary

Cañi, directed by Josefina Buschmann, and a dissertation by Marisol Verdugo and Matías González. Initial phases of fieldwork benefited from the guidance of colleagues at the Villarrica campus of the Pontificia Universidad Católica de Chile (Francisca de la Maza, Gonzalo Salazar, and Gonzalo Valdivieso).

In writing and editing this book, I was lucky enough to count on the kind and caring support of numerous colleagues. I want to thank Sophie Haines, Magnus Course, Stine Krøijer, Joe Feldman, Mattias Rassmussen, Cristóbal Bonelli, Fabian Flores, Daniel Renfrew, Elliott Oakley, and Marcelo González for commenting on early drafts from this book and materials related to it. I am grateful to Fernando Pairican for letting me learn so much about Mapuche political history from him while writing this book. Laura Ogden and Marco Mendoza endured longer readings of my work, and I have no words to express my gratitude to them. I am also grateful to Alison Stent, Mikaela Bell, Azul Puig, Caleb Yunis, and Liam Davies for their invaluable help in the editing phase. Owen Gurrey was an incredibly generous and attentive guide in the later stages of the book process—thank you!

Some of the ideas discussed in this book were inspired by conservations with other researchers. I thank Florencia Trentini, Mara Dicenta, and Francisco Araos, among other colleagues already mentioned in these acknowledgments, for the opportunity to think with them about the role of conservation frontiers in Latin America, in the context of the *In Focus* issue "Patagonian Conservation Frontiers," published by the *Journal of Latin American and Caribbean Anthropology* in 2023. Further inspiration comes from conversations with Natalia Orrego, Josefina Arriagada, Daniela Collao, Nancy Donald, and Gonzalo Aguirre, all of them carrying out amazing research on environment, infrastructure, and Indigeneity in Chile as part of their PhD projects.

Some materials discussed in chapters 1, 2, and 5 appeared in two articles: "Emerging Landscapes of Private Conservation: Enclosure and Mediation in Southern Chilean Protected Areas," published by *Geoforum* in 2018, and "Can Natives Be Settlers? Emptiness, Settlement, and Indigeneity on the Settler Colonial Frontier in Chile," published by *Anthropology Theory* in 2021. I thank the editorial teams from the two journals for their advice. From the beginning to the end, it has been an absolute pleasure working with the editorial team at University of Arizona Press, in particular Allyson Carter, Alana Enriquez, and Amanda Krause, and I feel grateful to them as well as to the marvelous editorial board of the series Critical Green Engagements for trusting me with this book project.

Like many others, I experience writing as an indissociable process of enriching discovery, frustration, impasse, and joy. I am quite reserved, and I am aware that all these feelings were often unnoticedly transmitted to loved ones. I also know that their love was always behind me throughout this process. For this and much more, I am indebted to my parents, Maria Antonietta and Giuseppe; my brother, Pierpaolo; and my wife, Bernardita, who unfailingly supported me (and *me ha soportado*) at every turn of this long process. The book is dedicated to my son, "baby Lorenzo." Now a ten-month-old child learning to crawl, in a few years I hope he will come to learn about and love our world, despite all the harm my and previous generations have caused. Whenever I look at him, I feel that there is hope for the future.

Notes

Introduction

1. Agamben distinguishes two variants of the "anthropological machine," one ancient and the other modern. In the ancient version, the nonhuman is produced by the humanization of the animal, a category that has been customarily extended to those considered animals in human forms, such as foreigners or non-Christians in certain Western traditions. The modern version of the anthropological machine animalizes humans by establishing a unique animal nature shared by all humans. In doing so, it sets a divide between humans with human life and those dehumanized to the point that their life can only be animal (2004, 37).

2. Another emblematic example of animal personhood in European history comes from court cases against animals, such as rats, accused of causing pestilence and crop destruction (Phillips 2015, 21–22).

3. One of the most recognizable cases of anti-humanism is Foucault's reappraisal of the human subject as a historical construct articulated around taken-for-granted ideals of individual rationality and freedom from social constraints (see Braidotti 2013, 23).

4. An example of system theory comes from biologists and philosophers Maturana and Varela (1984), who focus on human engagements with nonhuman life as constituting cognition, rather than an object of human epistemic operations (Wolfe 2010, xii). Haraway's commentary on the figure of the cyborg as a defining image of humanity in the twentieth century (1991) is one of the most well-known examples of the transhumanist imaginary.

5. First highlighted by Levi-Strauss (1995), a recurrent cosmogonic theme across Indigenous South America is the process of differentiation through which different entities were created. In several Amerindian myths, humanity is the original

condition of both animals and humans. Only later were they divided into different types of being through the emergence of specific physicalities shaping each
group's ability to think and act (Viveiros de Castro 1998, 472).

6. As a counterpoint to structural representations of human society and thought
    exemplified by the figure of the tree, the rhizome is the image of the world as
    if it were constituted of immanent relations across different ontological fields.
    These can be mapped—but never predicted—by relying on general structural
    principles.

7. According to the latest 2017 national census (INE 2017), the populations of
    Villarrica, Pucón, and Currarehue amount, respectively, to 55,478, 28,923, and
    7,489 habitants. Currarehue clearly differs from the other two municipalities, as
    can be seen in its demographic and economic indicators. According to the larg-
    est economic survey in Chile, CASEN (Encuesta de Caracterización Socioeco-
    nómica Nacional), in 2017 the percentage of the population experiencing mul-
    tidimensional poverty corresponded to 25.4 percent in Pucón and 25.3 percent
    in Villarrica but 38.4 percent in Currarehue (see CASEN 2017). In Currarehue,
    roughly 66 percent of the population self-identifies as Mapuche and 70 percent
    live in rural areas—in contrast with an approximate 27 percent of the population
    being Indigenous and 35 percent living rurally for the other two municipalities,
    Villarrica and Pucón. The difference is due to Carrarehue's smaller size and to
    a major historical presence of settlers from Europe and other regions of Chile
    in Villarrica and Pucón, whose territories are flatter and thus more suited to
    agriculture than the more mountainous Currarehue.

8. The three municipalities belong to the region of Araucanía, also known as the
    "ninth region." With 28.5 percent of the population classified as living under
    multidimensional poverty, Araucanía is one of the poorest regions of the coun-
    try. This situation can be explained by a long history of economic stagnation
    associated with low degrees of agricultural productivity and high rates of land
    concentration.

9. In Spanish, the masculine gender is conventionally applied to plural terms. In
    Chile, gender-neutral conventions in Spanish, mostly based on the use of -x or
    -e, are increasingly common in daily usage as a consequence of the long crit-
    ical linguistic work by feminist and LGBTIQA+ organizations. In rural areas,
    however, gender-neutral conventions are rare and did not appear in any of my
    interviews or conversations. While I am aware that the use of Spanish terms in
    this book is gender biased, I opted not to alter the standard masculine conven-
    tion used by my interviewees and interlocutors.

10. As reported in the latest national census of 2017, 1,745,147 Chilean citizens
    identify as Mapuche, a figure corresponding to 9.9 percent of the national pop-
    ulation. Roughly a third of the Mapuche population lives in the capital, Santiago
    (INE 2017). Indigenous Communities located around the towns of Pucón, Vil-
    larrica, and Currarehue rarely exceed 200 inhabitants. As in most Indigenous
    Communities in Mapuche areas, they consist of individually owned plots of land

with dispersed homesteads. The average area of these properties is remarkably lower than that of those owned by non-Indigenous residents.

11. As part of my intention to make research for this book more easily accessible to the general public, I was involved in the making of a documentary about different social representations of forests among residents of Pichares, a hamlet not far from the town of Pucón. The documentary, *Cañi*, directed by Josefina Buschmann, is available freely on various video-sharing platforms. I explain the focus and methodology of the local history book *Magti* in chapter 2.

12. Names appearing in this book are pseudonyms, a convention indicated by the Research Ethics Review Committee at my university. I am aware that anonymization might undervalue individual contributions to this book; I hope to do justice to the many people who have made this book possible in my acknowledgments.

13. Fieldwork has been carried out in Spanish. Mapuche individuals fluent in the Mapudungun language are today a minority in the localities where I carried out fieldwork. In conversations in Spanish, however, key Indigenous concepts are likely to be employed. Spanish nouns have a lexical gender. Mapudungun is a traditionally spoken language. Several Mapuche terms have at least three different written versions as presented by the three most commonly used alphabet systems: *Unificado, Raguileo*, and *Azümchefe*. The term *Mapudungun* can also be found in its variant *Mapuzugun* and, in southern territories historically inhabited by Huilliche communities, *Chedungun*. In this book, I follow definitions and written conventions presented in Maria Catrileo's dictionary *Diccionario lingüístico-etnográfico de la lengua Mapuche*.

Chapter 1

1. Some regions with more desert-like conditions responded more clearly to colonial expectations of emptiness. This was the case of the Patagonian steppe, which nineteenth-century explorers described as "an absolutely empty expanse upon which man can build everything from nothing" (Nouzeilles 1999, 420).

2. Literature on *mestizaje* is vast and heterogenous, being treated as both a national ideology across Latin America and a historical process. For more on this topic in Latin America, please see Cornejo Polar (1994) and Wade (2005). About *mestizaje* in Chile, see Morandé (1984) and Montecino (1991).

3. In debates about coloniality in Latin America, *blanqueamiento* typically refers to the "ideology and practice of 'whitening' or becoming more 'Europeanized'" (Radcliffe and Westwood 1996, ix).

4. The invasion of Mapuche territories occurred simultaneously on the other side of the Andes, where the Argentinean army launched a campaign that would go down in official history as the "Conquest of the Desert" (see Briones y Delrio 2007). Through guerilla warfare strategies, in particular raids known as *malones*, Mapuche resistance on both sides of the Andes delayed the invasions for several decades, though the militaries in both countries had planned them as rapid actions.

5. This is the case of APRA (Asociación para la Paz y la Reconciliación en La Araucanía, "The Association for Peace and Reconciliation in Araucanía"). Founded in
   2019, APRA acquired notoriety in August 2020 when groups of armed militants
   associated with it violently expelled Mapuche activists from public offices in
   six towns around the Araucanía region, which they had occupied in support of
   demands by Mapuche prisoners holding a hunger strike. Evictions were accompanied by racist chants and the burning of statues representing Mapuche symbols and historical figures in town squares (see Urrejola 2019).

6. This testimony can be found in *Coilaco Alto: un silencio verde en la geografía*,
   a historical book authored by a local organization in Coilaco and published in
   2011 in collaboration with the Villarrica campus of the Pontificia Universidad
   Católica de Chile (Grupo de Pequeños Productores e Innovadores Campesinos
   de Coilaco Alto 2012).

7. For settlers' public land claims in Argentina, see Rasmussen 2021 and Picone
   2025.

8. To this day, despite a decline in rural population, ranchers continue to cross the
   Argentina-Chile border as part of their husbandry strategies (Freddi 2022).

9. *Diosito* is a diminutive term meant as a form of affection, according to the large
   use of diminutives in Chilean Spanish, especially in rural areas. Among elder
   residents, araucaria trees are often referred to as "pines" since this species, just
   like pine trees (*pinos*), used to be lumbered for commercial purposes before
   prohibitions were enforced in the 1990s.

10. In resource frontiers designated for timber extraction, forest management has
    become one of the key technologies used by modern statecraft in its efforts to
    achieve "control and legibility of nature" (Mathews 2011, 19). Legibility also
    extends to the economic life of frontier populations, who experience forest man-
    agement through contradictory lenses: as a technical tool for managing natural
    resources, as a source of subsidies and technologies that can be used instrumen-
    tally, and as a policing force addressing concerns over both intentional and unin-
    tentional acts of illegal logging. For more on this topic see Di Giminiani 2016.

11. Wildfires are common throughout southern Chile during the summer (see
    Tironi and Manriquez 2019). The most destructive and recent event of this type
    took place in 2023, causing several deaths and huge economic losses across
    several south-central regions.

12. For more on conflicts over hydroelectric energy in Mapuche areas, see Kelly
    2019.

Chapter 2

1. Millalén defines *lof* as a socio-political and territorial organization composed by
   a set of nuclear families with affective and kinship ties structured along patrilin-
   eal descent (2006, 38).

2. A *Comunidad Indígena* is a residential and administrative unit composed of individually owned plots of land. It is represented by a locally elected board in interactions with state authorities. This board, however, has no legal standing in relation to issues involving community members, such as property transactions. This unit was introduced in 1993 through Indigenous Law 19,253 and replaced the older term *reducción*, which is still colloquially used in some rural areas.

3. In the 1950s, when relations of *reducción* members with the state became increasingly individualized, the cacique began to lose representative authority and finally disappeared, being replaced in the 1990s with the newly instituted boards of *Comunidades Indígenas* (Di Giminiani 2018, 118).

4. *Magti* is the Mapudungun term indicating the endogenous tree *Maytenus boaria*, commonly known in Spanish as *maitén* throughout the Southern Cone. The locality of Maite likely received its name for its high concentration of this tree. Most Mapuche families living in and around Maite belong to the Indigenous Community Juan Huaquifil, named after the founding cacique. The gathering of oral and photographic material for this book was made possible by the work of two colleagues, Martin Fonck and Paolo Perasso. For more on the experience of this collaboration, inevitably fraught with controversies over individual participation and collective representation among community members and researchers, see Perasso et al. 2018, 250.

5. Some Mapuche travelers used to be identified with a specific denomination, *nampulkafe*, literally "the one who travels abroad" (Bello 2011, 215).

6. During the first half of the twentieth century, an evident preference for intra-ethnic marriages contributed to the continuity of Mapuche kinship networks (Foerster 2018, 239). More common exceptions were the cases of non-Indigenous women, known as *chiñuras*, marrying Mapuche men and relocating to their husbands' property in line with the customary preference for patrilocality. Outmigration, assimilatory pressures, and increased participation in inter-ethnic educational and work contexts are historical factors explaining the present-day higher incidence of inter-ethnic marriages (see Valenzuela and Unzueta 2015).

7. Conflicts over land ownership among reservation members were the main justification for a prolonged process of land formalization aimed at instituting private ownership within *reducciones*. Land formalization accelerated in the 1980s as a consequence of the Pinochet dictatorship's introduction of a bill in 1979 (Decree Law 2,568) prescribing the division of all *reducciones* (see Caniuqueo 2013; González 1986; Mallon 2005). While some reservation members looked positively at the assignation of private titles within formerly communal land, others were vocal against the cyclical attempts of policymakers to enforce the dissolution of the status of reservation land, thus making Indigenous properties available to the real estate market in the name of economic freedom. Today,

properties within a *Comunidad Indígena* can only be transacted among individuals holding a state Indigenous affiliation certificate (*Certificado de Calidad Indígena*), and thus cannot be mortgaged (Di Giminiani 2018, 134).

8.   For more on the role of fugitivity in anti-colonial discourses and critical interventions, see Roberts 2015.

9.   The flag *wenufoye*, literally "the canelo tree of the sky," was designed in the 1990s by the largest Mapuche organization of the time, *Aukiñ Wallmapu Ngulam* or *Consejo de Todas las Tierras* ("Council of All Lands"). A ritualistic drum known as a *kultrun* is represented in the middle of the flag. Since then, the *wenufoye* has been adopted as the main symbol of identification with the Mapuche people across the country. It has also been formally used by Chilean institutions in Mapuche areas or on the occasions of Mapuche ceremonies, even though some activists see this use as an instance of appropriation. Other Mapuche flags, mostly associated with regional groups, are also in use.

10. The variant *mawiza* can also be found in several orthographic systems. Another Mapudungun term for "hill" is *wingkul* (Catrileo 1998, 98) or *winkul*.

11. *Ngillatun* derives from the verb *nguillan*, "to ask for" and "to elevate" (Alonqueo 1979, 23). *Ngillatun* are aimed at the fulfilment of a vast array of appeals, including the positive resolution of land claims (Di Giminiani 2018, 169). The recipient of these appeals is the main deity Chao Ngenchen, occasionally referred to as Chao Dios in some areas of southern Chile. This entity has been described by many of my interlocutors as equivalent to the Christian god, except that it is approached through Mapuche customs (*a la mapuche*). *Ngillatun* are large events taking place in a ceremonial field known as *ngillatuwe* and marked by the presence of a *rewe* in its middle, which in most areas of southern Chile consists of a step-notched tree trunk of laurel (*triwe*) adorned with branches of *maki* (*Aristotelia chilensis*) and canelo (*Drimys winteri*). Ritual specialists, such as *ngenpin* and *machi* shamans, are typically in charge of the organization, which includes collective dances such as *purrum*, and incantations known as *llellipun*. *Ngillatun* are characterized by strict etiquette, concerning for instance greetings among organizers and guests and prohibition of eating meat and drinking alcohol before the large final meal marking the end of the ritual. For more on this ritual, see Alonqueo 1979, Catrileo 2014, Foerster 1993, and Ñanculef 2016.

12. The agential nature of mountains in Andean contexts has been depicted in numerous works: see de la Cadena 2015; Pazzarelli 2019; Salas 2019.

13. For more on master spirits in Indigenous South America, see Fausto 1999.

14. Across many Indigenous groups of South America, the value of autonomy—not to be confused with individualism—is a central feature of ethical reflections on more-than-human relationality (González Gálvez et al. 2019, 4).

15. Social relations of exchange are regarded as an essential trait of Mapuche ethics and customary sociability, threatened by the effects of assimilation. Relations of this sort include mutual visits and gift-making, as in the case of *trafkintu*, a lifelong friendship tie sanctioned by past exchange of goods (Course 2011, 37).

16. To avoid mischievous acts by ngen, protection can also be sought from other master spirits. This is the case of ngen associated with particularly large rocks located along a road or a trail. Around Coilaco Valley, I heard about a big rock that locals simply referred to as "the saint," *El Santo*. Residents and travelers used to leave a coin to appeal for protection during a trip through the forests. For similar cases, see Bonelli and Gonzalez 2018, 446 and Melin et al. 2020, 85.

17. *Kupalme* is commonly found as a variant for the term *küpal*.

18. For more on Mapuche notions of health and healing practices, see Bacigalupo 2007, Bacigalupo 2016, and Kristensen 2019.

Chapter 3

1. Given the widespread nature of illegal environmental activities in frontier areas, the history of environmentalism in Latin America has been tragically marked by the killings of numerous activists. The most well-known case is the homicide of the rubber tapper and union leader Chico Mendes in Brazil in 1988 (Gudynas 1992, 109).

2. As reported on the organization's website, one of the most emblematic actions undertaken by CODEFF included a public campaign against the logging of the Patagonian cypress (*Fitzroya cupressoides*), known in Spanish as *alerce*, located mostly in the southern region of Los Lagos. Thanks to this campaign, the Patagonian cypress was declared a national monument, and a logging ban has been enforced since 1976.

3. Established in 1985, Canelo de Nos is the most renowned NGO in Chile specializing in alternative development and popular education since the late stages of Pinochet's dictatorship.

4. One of the largest nationwide movements of the last three decades was *Patagonia sin Represa* ("Patagonia Without Dams"), which emerged in 2007 to successfully repel the contentious plan for the construction of the hydroelectric project Hidroaysén in Patagonia.

5. One of the main targets of forest activism is the reform or even erasure of Decree Law 701. Established in 1974 with the goal of incentivizing transnational timber production, it is based on the importation of fast-growing species such as *Eucalyptus globulus* and Monterrey pine trees (*Pinus radiata*).

6. Adriana Hoffmann, who died in 2022, was one of the most influential figures in the environmental movement in Chile and Latin America. Besides her scientific contribution to national botany, she participated in multiple environmental organizations, including the Lahuen Foundation, which was responsible for the creation of the first private protected area in Chile, the Cañi Sanctuary, which we will hear more about in chapter 5. In 2000, she was appointed by President Ricardo Lagos as director of the "National Commission for the Environment" (*Comisión Nacional del Medio Ambiente*), the precursor of the Ministry of the Environment established in 2007. She resigned in 2007 due to a lack of support

by government authorities in pushing forward environmental reforms (Aravena 2022).

7. The main objective of AIFBN is "to promote sustainable forest development with a focus on the native forest and the equal distribution of this resource to the entire society" (see https://bosquenativo.cl/).

8. The category of *cuico* is flexible and can apply to a wide range of subjects, including places and people. It includes potentially anyone with professional jobs and upper middle-class salaries and lifestyles.

9. The Mapudungun *trafkintu* refers to a customary Mapuche practice in which the goods exchanged should ideally be hardly comparable and of different values. The exchange lacks commercial calculation and is meant to sanction lifelong friendships (see Di Giminiani 2018, 132).

10. Along with the Andean condor, a southern Andean deer is represented within the coat of arms of Chile.

11. In Chile, as prescribed by Law 19.300 of 1994, scientists employed by private companies can partake in environmental impact assessments (Barandarian 2018, 23).

Chapter 4

1. For more on the mission and history of the Chilean Union of Ornithologists, see https://aveschile.cl/ (last accessed January 15, 2024). A network with similar purposes is the *Red de Observadores de Aves y Vida Silvestre de Chile* ("Network of Observers of the Birds and Forest Life of Chile"); see https://www.redobserva dores.cl/.

2. eBird was developed as a crowdsourcing platform by the Cornell Lab of Ornithology at Cornell University. As an example of citizen science, this platform allows users to upload information from avian censuses as well as to use learning resources on avian recognition and behavior, including species profiles. For more information, please refer to their website, https://ebird.org/home.

3. The piper is crucial for the research projects described in this chapter and yet hard to find on the market. Some of the researchers I met actually built their first piper by connecting a camera probe to a swimming pool broom. Eventually, they purchased a tool specifically designed for ecological research from a laboratory in Canada.

4. A scientific report co-authored by some of my interlocutors illustrated a rare case of predation by the native chimango hawk (*Chimango caracara*) against the nest of another predatory bird, the rufous-legged owl (*Strix rufipes*). The report presented the hypothesis that this rare occurrence might have originated in the relocation of the rufous-legged owl from more pristine, higher sections of the mountains to a lower and more degraded section of the forest, one of the ideal habitats for the chimango hawk along with agricultural areas (Ibarra et al. 2017c).

5. In their article, Tomás Ibarra and Kathy Martin state that forest policy in Chile "protects young but encourages the harvest of large-decaying trees. Also, stands with a dense understory are commonly considered wasteful and indicative of 'unhealthy and dirty forest conditions' by landowners and forest managers in Chile" (2015, 425).

6. One of the earliest and most influential works in ethno-ornithology in Chile is the 2003 volume *Multi-Ethnic Bird Guide of the Austral Temperate Forests of South America*, edited by biologist and philosopher Ricardo Rozzi (Rozzi et al. 2003), for whom ecological knowledge among Indigenous Mapuche and Yahgan people can be a source of inspiration when articulating senses of kinship with birds and feelings of belonging to more-than-human communities among humans (see Taylor 2010, 172).

Chapter 5

1. The Malleco Reserve was indeed the first in Latin America. The Forest Law of 1925 prescribed the establishment of a centralized national park management system (Klubock 2014, 101).

2. A renowned private protected area dedicated to tourism is Reserva Biológica Huilo-Huilo, which hosts an upscale hotel and other facilities. Located roughly one hundred kilometers from the town of Pucón, this park is located in what once was the operational premises of a state-owned forestry company, Complejo Forestal y Maderero Panguipulli, active in the 1970s and later privatized and sold to forest entrepreneurs during Pinochet's dictatorship (Huiliñir-Curío et al. 2019).

3. *Pewenche* is a regional category of identity within the more encompassing category of Mapuche. Such a self-identification is particularly strong in Andean areas near the Biobío River, the historic border of Wallmapu, the Mapuche homeland. Another example of regional self-identity is *Lafkenche*, roughly translatable as "people of the sea." Not all Mapuche people in southern Chile ascribe to a regional identity (Di Giminiani 2018, 67).

4. *Piñones* resemble large pine nuts. They can be boiled in water, similarly to chestnuts, or ground and made into flour for the preparation of breads and cakes. Other non-timber products informally gathered in southern Andean valleys are mushrooms, such as the corral mushroom known as *change* (*Ramaria flava*), and *digüeñe* (*Cyttaria espinosae*), a parasite species growing on *Nothofagus* trees. Within national parks, araucaria nut collection is generally tolerated but remains illegal, with the exception of agreements with local Mapuche communities. Controversies occasionally arise between locals and gatherers from more distant urban centers, who are treated by the former as illegitimate competitors. For more on *piñones* and other non-timber forest products, see Barreau et al. 2016.

5. As indicated in the website of Ferias Araucanía, one of the largest cattle auctions in southern Chile, located in the city of Temuco, prices in October 2022 ranged

from CLP\$1,500,000 to slightly over CLP\$3,000,000, according to the type of cows in question. A legal minimum salary in Chile is CLP\$400,000 (roughly US\$410 at the time of writing).

6. I thank Martín Fonck, one of my fellow researchers while doing fieldwork around Cañi Sanctuary, for sharing this anecdote.

Chapter 6

1. Classification of state protected areas was introduced in 1967 through Decree Law 531. This decree was based on the 1940 multilateral agreement, the Washington Convention on Nature Protection and Wildlife Preservation in the Western Hemisphere, which was signed by most countries in the Americas. For more information on the updated list of state protected areas in Chile, please refer to the CONAF webpage (https://www.conaf.cl/parques-nacionales/parques-de-chile/).

2. The most recent case of eviction from a protected area happened in Chiloé National Park, a protected area located in the southern island of Chiloé. The establishment of this national park in 1982 over state-owned land occupied for decades by Mapuche communities meant the relocation of several households, which was partially remedied through a land ownership agreement in the following decade (Aylwin 2011).

3. The main reason for the emergence of Ad Mapu was the reversal of Decree Law 2,568, which had been approved in 1979. It its initial version, this decree lifted all restrictions concerning the commercialization of community land, a prospect that would have likely led to the massive sale and dismantlement of Mapuche collective land titles (Richards 2013, 119).

4. In October 2021, a land takeover was reported by national media. Roughly a dozen individuals built a shelter and occupied the park administration cabin within the Malleco National Reserve, located in the proximity of the town of Collipulli (Zamorano 2021).

5. The most well-known case of land transfers within protected areas concerns the Quinquén Community, located in a high section of the Andes near the town of Lonquimay. In 1972, a group of Mapuche families moved into the state-owned forest reserve, recently instituted following the acquisition of a large estate by the state as part of the Allende government's agrarian reforms (Bengoa 2000, 51–52; Cuadra 2011, 95). The area corresponded to an araucaria forest customarily used for nut harvesting and grazing by local Mapuche landholders. Soon after the military coup, the state reserve was transferred back to the owners of the estate before the agrarian reform. Commercial logging of araucaria trees resumed, while Mapuche families were evicted (Klubock 2014, 249). In 1991, mobilizations by members of the Quinquén Community, relying on alliances with environmental NGOs, were pivotal to the purchase of the property by the state and the later establishment of a protected area where commercial logging was prohibited. In 2007, after several years of negotiations involving both

CONADI and CONAF, the ownership of the forest reserve was transferred to the Quinquén Community through an arrangement that included a mixture of individual and collective property and the enforcement of a forest management plan overseen by CONAF officers (Cuadra 2011, 97–99).

6. A few residents from Maite were active members of *Aukiñ Wallmapu Ngulam*, also known in Spanish as *Consejo de Todas las Tierras* ("Council of All Lands"), founded in 1991 and for a long time the largest of all Mapuche associations (Mallon 2005, 181; Pairican 2014, 91).

7. Updated versions of the management plans in 2013 and 2018 are available as public documents.

8. During the 1930s, under the advice of a group of Santiago-based natural historians, the Chilean parliament introduced a series of legal reforms, such as Law 4,363 of 1931, which limited logging in protected areas and introduced subsidies for reforestation in properties destined for commercial forestry (Camus 2006, 172).

9. As of 2005, 38 percent of land reforested through the 701 Decree Law belonged to smallholders owning less than 100 hectares, while the rest was assigned to medium- and large-scale landowners (Agraria 2005).

10. The official mission of CONAF is to "contribute to the sustainable management of native forests, xerophytic formations, and timber plantations through actions of industrial promotion, monitoring of forest legislation, protection of vegetation resources, and conservation of biodiversity for the benefit of society." Mission statement retrieved from www.conaf.cl.

11. Most officers with a degree in forest engineering graduated from the forestry school of the Universidad Austral de Chile, one of the most prestigious places for forestry science in the country and known for its early adoption of more sustainable models of forestry in its curriculum. During the 1990s, forestry scientists from this department became outspoken critics of transnational timber companies responsible for the dissemination of cash crop plantations in southern Chile (Camus 2006, 317–318; Klubock 2014, 272–273). Some officers, inspired by more community-based and ecological approaches to commercial forestry, are also actively involved in the Association of Forest Engineers for the Native Forest (Agrupación de Ingenieros Forestales por el Bosque Nativo—AIFBN), the largest grassroots organization specialized in sustainable forestry in the country.

12. CONAF officers specializing in forest management have recently been involved in the implementation of a new subsidy scheme designed to prompt reforestation with native species as prescribed by the 2008 "Law on Native Forest Recovery and Forestry Development" (*Ley Sobre Recuperación del Bosque Nativo y Fomento Forestal, no. 20.283*). While the native forest law brought unprecedented state assistance to landowners and organizations interested in protection, its implementation has arguably had little impact on small-scale agroforestry. In the aftermath of the introduction of the legislation, only 3 percent of landowners' applications to reforestation programs specifically designed for

native forest protection were successful, while smallholders were almost entirely excluded from these programs (Neira and Rivas 2013). Around the Andean valleys of southern Chile, small landholders continue to depend on state subsidization, mostly designed around the principles of industrial forestry development (*fomento forestal*) and implemented through extension programs.

13. Growth of protected land accelerated swiftly in 2018 when the Pumalín parks and other protected areas owned by the Tompkins Foundation were transferred to the Chilean state (Montes 2019).

14. Rangers were employed informally by municipal and regional governments as guards for forest reserves until 1914, when the first ranger, Manuel Alvarado, was integrated as park ranger in the Ministerio de Tierras y Colonización, the ministry in charge of the land distribution and colonization process in southern Chile and Patagonia (Camus and Lazo 2014, 60).

15. Research has shown that Mapuche electoral preferences align with regional trends, exhibiting significant differences between rural and urban areas. As a result, any connection between the Mapuche population and right-wing support is weak. Over the past three decades, there has been a noticeable trend toward favoring Mapuche candidates for local government positions, particularly for the role of mayor (see Cayul and Corvalán 2024).

16. From the time Chile achieved independence in 1810 until the military annexation of Mapuche territories, the *parlamentos* gradually devolved into mere announcements from Chilean authorities regarding the concession or repression of Mapuche rights. The last *parlamento* took place in Tapihue in 1825, resulting in a treaty that recognized Mapuche sovereignty (Herr 2019, 75). However, this treaty was later disavowed by Chilean authorities when the army invaded Mapuche lands a few decades later.

Epilogue

1. On October 26, 2019, after the announcement of thirty pesos' (four U.S. cents') increase in public transport fares in the capital, Santiago, secondary students launched ticket evasion protests in and around metro stations. The increase was small, but it was only the latest of several introduced over the previous few months. Ticket evasions were met with police force, and videos of *carabineros* (police) shooting tear gas around the metro station and even pushing students off metro stairs began to circulate online, galvanizing support for the protests. Clashes between protesters and police escalated quickly, leading to the closure of the metro system and paving the way for riots and looting that would continue for a few days. Protests routinely took place every Friday in the city center. President Piñera decided to take a hardline approach to the protests, including the imposition of a curfew, and insinuated the existence of a global left-wing conspiracy with the following words: "We are at war against a powerful enemy, who is willing to use violence without any limits." Police repression was particularly

harsh, with a dramatic number of irreversible eye mutilations due to the use of rubber bullets—besides at least thirty deaths—linked to the clashes. According to international human rights organizations, Chile experienced its most severe case of human rights infringement since Pinochet's dictatorship (see Office of the United Nations High Commissioner for Human Rights 2019).

2.   In 2020, a referendum was held with the option of maintaining the 1980 constitution or replacing it with a constitution written by electoral representatives. The new constitution option won with over 78 percent of the vote, and a few months later, the election of the members of the constitutional convention saw the rise of independent leftist candidates and members of social movements as a central force in the drafting process. Environmental issues occupied a central place in the new draft (see Luque-Lora 2002). Another referendum was held in 2022, this time to approve or refuse the new constitutional draft. A series of scandals and the failed inclusion of centrist and right-wing constitutional members in the drafting of articles were the main reasons for the new constitution's rejection. Meanwhile, as a reaction against 2019 protests and the new constitutional process and following the rise in criminality after the COVID-19 pandemic, a relatively new populist right-wing party, Partido Republicano, erupted in Chilean politics. This was despite the presidential victory of left-wing former student activist and parliamentary member Gabriel Boric, at only 36 years of age. In 2023, a new constitutional convention, this time with fewer members (50 instead of 154) and limited participation of independent candidates and Indigenous representatives, was formed. Partido Republicano became the dominant party. Paradoxically, a party who strenuously defended the Pinochet-era constitution was in charge of leading the process for drafting a new constitution, this time with an overt conservative agenda. The new draft was again discarded when, in December 2023, a new referendum saw its rejection option win 56 percent of the vote. After four years and two failed attempts, the 1980 constitution is still the basis of the Chilean political system.

3.   On March 3, 2020, the Ministry of Health confirmed the first case of the SARS-CoV-2 virus in the country. After initial comforting messages about the lack of a real threat and the strength of its health system in Chile, Piñera's government was soon forced to take drastic measures to reduce contagion, including long periods of lockdown. Unemployment, particularly in the informal economy, skyrocketed, and concerns over food provision became a reality, epitomized by the return of soup kitchens (*ollas communes*) organized by local grassroots organizations, which had been particularly popular during the economic crisis of the early 1980s. That said, 2021 was a more hopeful year. New subsidies were introduced, workers had the opportunity of withdrawing part of their pension funds, and a successful vaccination campaign led to a visible reduction in the mortality rate of the virus.

4.   On July 22, 2022, the widely read newspaper *La Tercera* reported worrisome news about the status of the largest body of water in the proximity of Santiago

with the following headline, "The end of the Aculeo Lagoon?" (Montes 2022). Winter in 2024 brought more rain than the previous few years and with it the hope that the lake would be partly restored.

5. On March 20, 2024, the International Union of Geological Sciences (IUGS) announced its decision against declaring the Anthropocene to be a geological epoch. See the official announcement: https://www.iugs.org/_files/ugd/f1fc07_40d1a7ed58de458c9f8f24de5e739663.pdf?index=true, last accessed January 10, 2025.

6. For more on the social impact of species reintroduction in Chile, see Root-Bernstein and Guerrero-Gatica 2024.

References

Abram, Simone, and Marianne E. Lien. 2011. "Performing Nature at World's Ends." *Ethnos* 76 (1): 3–18.

Agamben, Giorgio. 2004. *The Open: Man and Animal.* Stanford University Press.

Agraria. 2005. *Evaluación de impacto. Programa bonificación forestal DL 701.* CONAF.

Agrawal, Arun. 2005. *Environmentality: Technologies of Government and the Making of Subjects.* Duke University Press.

Agrawal, Arun, and Clark Gibson. 1999. "Enchantment and Disenchantment: The Role of Community in Natural Resource Conservation." *World Development* 27 (4): 629–649.

Albanese, Catherine L. 1991. *Nature Religion in America: From the Algonkian Indians to the New Age.* University of Chicago Press.

Aldunate, Carlos. 2001. *El factor ecológico: las mil caras del pensamiento verde.* LOM Ediciones.

Alonqueo, Martín. 1979. *Instituciones religiosas del pueblo mapuche.* Editorial Nueva Universidad.

Altamirano, Tomás A., José Tomás Ibarra, Kathy Martin, and Cristian Bonacic. 2017. "The Conservation Value of Tree Decay Processes as a Key Driver Structuring Tree Cavity Nest Webs in South American Temperate Rainforests." *Biodiversity and Conservation* 26 (10): 2453–72.

Altieri, Miguel A. 2018. *Agroecology: The Science of Sustainable Agriculture.* Westview Press.

Altrudi, Soledad. 2022. "Between Care and Control: The Patagonian Cougar's Tale." *Green Letters* 26 (1): 28–43.

Alvarado Lincopi, Claudio. 2021. *Mapurbekistán, ciudad, cuerpo y racismo. Diáspora mapuche en Santiago, siglo XX.* Pehuén Editores.

Antileo, Enrique. 2020. *Aquí estamos todavía. Anticolonialismo y emancipación en los pensamientos políticos mapuche y aymara Chile Bolivia 1990–2006*. Pehuén Editores.

Antonelli, Michele, Davide Donelli, Lucrezia Carlone, Valentina Maggini, Fabio Firenzuoli, and Emanuela Bedeschi. 2022. "Effects of Forest Bathing (Shinrin-Yoku) on Individual Well-Being: An Umbrella Review." *International Journal of Environmental Health Research* 32 (8): 1842–1867.

Appel, Ariel, and Nurit Bird-David. 2023. "'More-Than-'Bird': Cultivating More-Than-Categorical Attentiveness Among Israeli Practitioners of Bird Language." *American Ethnologist* 50: 609–621.

Araos, Francisco, Emilia Catalán, David Nuñez, et al. 2023. "Cuidando la Patagonia Azul: prácticas y estrategias de los pueblos originarios para curar las zonas marinas del sur de Chile." *The Journal of Latin American and Caribbean Anthropology* 28 (4): 286–297.

Aravena, Francisco. 2022. El Café Diario: el legado de Adriana Hoffmann en la causa medioambiental. *La Tercera*, March 22. https://www.latercera.com/pod cast/noticia/el-cafe-diario-el-legado-de-adriana-hoffmann-en-la-causamedio ambiental/5QSAFMT2KFHNTKTDUVVGYTUOAQ/.

Archambault, Julie. 2016. "Taking Love Seriously in Human-Plant Relations in Mozambique: Toward an Anthropology of Affective Encounters." *Cultural Anthropology* 31 (2): 244–71.

Argyrou, Vassos. 2005. *The Logic of Environmentalism: Anthropology, Ecology and Postcoloniality*. Berghahn Books.

Armus, Teo. 2019. "'We Are at War': 8 Dead in Chile's Violent Protests over Social Inequality." *Washington Post*, October 21. https://www.washingtonpost.com/nation /2019/10/21/chile-protests-santiago-dead-state-emergency/.

Arsel, Mursel, and Bram Büscher. 2012. "Nature™ Inc.: Changes and Continuities in Neoliberal Conservation and Market-Based Environmental Policy." *Development and Change* 43 (1): 53–78.

Atterton, Peter, and Tamra Wright, eds. 2019. *Face to Face with Animals: Levinas and the Animal Question*. Suny Press.

Aylwin, José. 2011. "Conservación en territorios indígenas: marcos jurídicos y experiencias nacionales y comparadas y directrices internacionales." In *Los desafíos de la conservación en los territorios indígenas en Chile*, edited by José Aylwin and Ximena Cuadra, 9–91. Observatorio de Derechos de los Pueblos Indígenas.

Babidge, Sally. 2016. "Contested value and an ethics of resources: Water, mining and indigenous people in the Atacama Desert, Chile." *The Australian Journal of Anthropology* 27(1): 84–103.

Bacigalupo, Ana Mariella. 2007. *Shamans of the Foye Tree: Gender, Power, and Healing Among Chilean Mapuche*. University of Texas Press.

Bacigalupo, Ana Mariella. 2016. *Thunder Shaman: Making History with Mapuche Spirits in Chile and Patagonia*. University of Texas Press.

Badmington, Neil, ed. 2000. *Posthumanism*. Bloomsbury Publishing.

Bakker, Karen. 2010. "The Limits of 'Neoliberal Natures': Debating Green Neoliberalism." *Progress in Human Geography* 34 (6): 715–735.

Ballestero, Andrea. 2019. *A future history of water.* Duke University Press.

Barad, Karen. 2007. *Meeting the Universe Halfway: Quantum Physics and the Entanglement of Matter and Meaning.* Duke University Press.

Barandiarán, Javiera. 2018. *Science and Environment in Chile: The Politics of Expert Advice in a Neoliberal Democracy.* MIT Press.

Barla, Josef. 2019. *The Techno-Apparatus of Bodily Production: A New Materialist Theory of Technology and the Body.* Transcript Verlag.

Barreau, Antonia, José Tomás Ibarra, Felice S. Wyndham, Alejandro Rojas, and Robert A. Kozak. 2016. "How Can We Teach Our Children If We Cannot Access the Forest? Generational Change in Mapuche Knowledge of Wild Edible Plants in Andean Temperate Ecosystems of Chile." *Journal of Ethnobiology* 36 (2): 412–32.

Barrena, José, Machiel Lamers, Simon Bush, and Gustavo Blanco. 2019. "Governing Nature-Based Tourism Mobility in National Park Torres del Paine, Chilean Southern Patagonia." *Mobilities* 14 (6): 745–761.

Bauer, Kelly. 2021. *Negotiating Autonomy: Mapuche Territorial Demands and Chilean Land Policy.* University of Pittsburgh Press.

Beer, Clare M. 2022. Bankrolling Biodiversity: The Politics of Philanthropic Conservation Finance in Chile. *Environment and Planning E: Nature and Space* 6 (2). https://doi.org/10.1177/25148486221108171.

Bello, Alvaro. 2011. *Nampülkafe. El viaje de los mapuches de la Araucanía a las pampas argentinas. Territorio, política y cultura en los siglos XIX y XX.* Ediciones Universidad Católica de Temuco.

Bengoa, José. 2000. *Historia del pueblo mapuche: siglo XIX y XX.* LOM Ediciones.

Bengoa, José. 2007. *El tratado de Quilín: documentos adicionales a la historia de los antiguos mapuches del sur.* Editorial Catalonia.

Bengoa, José. 2014. *Mapuche, colonos y el estado nacional.* Editorial Catalonia.

Bennett, Jane. 2001. *The Enchantment of Modern Life: Attachments, Crossings, and Ethics.* Princeton University Press.

Bennett, Jane. 2010. *Vibrant Matter: A Political Ecology of Things.* Duke University Press.

Berglund, Eeva K. 1998. *Knowing Nature, Knowing Science: An Ethnography of Environmental Activism.* White Horse Press.

Berglund, Eeva, and David Anderson. 2003. "Introduction: Towards an Ethnography of Ecological Underprivilege." In *Ethnographies of Conservation: Environmentalism and the Distribution of Privilege,* edited by Eeva Berglund and David Anderson, 1–15. Berghahn Books.

Berlant, Lauren. 2011. *Cruel Optimism.* Duke University Press.

Birkhead, Tim R., and Sebastianus van Balen. 2008. "Bird-Keeping and the Development of Ornithological Science." *Archives of Natural History* 35 (2): 281–305.

Blair, James. 2017. "Settler Indigeneity and the Eradication of the Non-Native: Self-Determination and Biosecurity in the Falkland Islands (Malvinas)." *Journal of the Royal Anthropological Institute* 23 (3): 580–602.

Blaser, Mario. 2010. *Storytelling Globalization from the Chaco and Beyond.* Duke University Press.

Blaser, Mario, and Marisol de la Cadena. 2017. "The Uncommons: An Introduction." *Anthropologica* 59 (2): 185–193.

Bloch, John P. 1998. *New Spirituality, Self, and Belonging: How New Agers and Neo-Pagans Talk About Themselves.* Greenwood Publishing Group.

Boccara, Guillaume. 2007. *Los vencedores: historia del pueblo mapuche en la época colonial.* Línea Editorial IIAM.

Bonelli, Cristóbal. 2015. "Eating One's Worlds: On Foods, Metabolic Writing and Ethnographic Humor." *Subjectivity* 8 (3): 181–200.

Bonelli, Cristóbal. 2017. "Aguas equívocas en el sur de Chile." In *A contra-corriente: agua y conflicto en Latinoamérica,* edited by Cristóbal Bonelli and Giselle Vila, 119–136. Editorial Abya Yala.

Bourdieu, Pierre. 1977. *Outline of a Theory of Practice.* Cambridge University Press.

Boyer, Christopher. 2015. *Political Landscapes: Forests, Conservation, and Community in Mexico.* Duke University Press.

Braidotti, Rosi. 2013. *The Posthuman.* Polity Press.

Briones, Claudia, and Walter Delrio. 2007. "'La Conquista del Desierto' desde perspectivas hegemónicas y subalternas." *Runa* 27: 23–48.

Brockington, Dan. 2002. *Fortress Conservation: The Preservation of the Mkomazi Game Reserve, Tanzania.* Indiana University Press.

Brockington, Dan, and Rosaleen Duffy. 2010. "Capitalism and Conservation: The Production and Reproduction of Biodiversity Conservation." *Antipode* 42 (3): 469–484.

Brosius, J. Peter, Anna Tsing, and Charles Zerner. 1998. "Representing Communities: Histories and Politics of Community-Based Natural Resource Management." *Society and Natural Resources* 11 (2): 157–68.

Buchadas, Ana, Siyu Qin, Patrick Meyfroidt, and Tobias Kuemmerle. 2022. "Conservation Frontiers: Understanding the Geographic Expansion of Conservation." *Journal of Land Use Science* 17 (1): 12–25.

Buffum, Bill, Georg Gratzer, and Yeshi Tenzin. 2009. "Forest Grazing and Natural Regeneration in a Late Successional Broadleaved Community Forest in Bhutan." *Mountain Research and Development* 29 (1): 30–35.

Bunch, Mary. 2014. "Posthuman Ethics and the Becoming Animal of Emmanuel Levinas." *Culture, Theory and Critique* 55 (1): 34–50.

Büscher, Bram, and Veronica Davidov. 2016. "Environmentally Induced Displacements in the Ecotourism–Extraction Nexus." *Area* 48 (2): 161–67.

Büscher, Bram, and Robert Fletcher. 2020. *The Conservation Revolution: Radical Ideas for Saving Nature Beyond the Anthropocene.* Verso Books.

Buschmann, Josefina, director. 2018. *Cañi.* Film; online video. Posted December 27, 2018, by Centro de Estudios Interculturales e Indígenas. YouTube, 17:29. https://www.youtube.com/watch?v=4BbkDJN6XFI.

Bustos, Beatriz. 2022. "Rethinking Rural Citizenship in Commodity Regions: Lessons from the Los Lagos Region, Chile." *Geographical Review* 112 (5): 707–724.

Butler, Judith. 1990. *Gender Trouble: Feminism and the Subversion of Identity*. Routledge.

de la Cadena, Marisol. 2015. *Earth Beings: Ecologies of Practice Across Andean Worlds*. Duke University Press.

de la Cadena, Marisol, and Mario Blaser. 2018 (eds.). *A World of Many Worlds*. Duke University Press.

Calbucura, Jorge. 1996. "El proceso legal de abolición de la propiedad colectiva: el caso mapuche." In *Fronteras, etnias, culturas: América Latina siglos XVI-XX*, edited by Chiara Vangelista. Ediciones Abya Yala.

Campbell, Jeremy M. 2014. "Speculative Accumulation: Property-Making in the Brazilian Amazon." *The Journal of Latin American and Caribbean Anthropology* 19(2): 237–259.

Campbell, Jeremy M. 2015. *Conjuring Property: Speculation and Environmental Futures in the Brazilian Amazon*. University of Washington Press.

Camus, Pablo. 2006. *Ambiente, Bosques y Gestión Forestal en Chile, 1541–2005*. LOM Ediciones.

Camus, Pablo, and Ernst Hajek. 1998. *Historia ambiental de Chile*. Pontificia Universidad Católica de Chile.

Camus, Pablo, and Ángel Lazo. 2014. *Guardaparques, su historia y vivencias en la contribución a la conservación del Sistema Nacional de Áreas Silvestres Protegidas del Estado (1914–2014)*. Corporación Nacional Forestal.

Camus, Pablo, and María Eugenia Solari. 2008. "La invención de la selva austral: bosques y tierras despejadas en la cuenca del río Valdivia (siglos XVI–XIX)." *Revista de Geografía Norte Grande* 40: 5–22.

Candea, Matei. 2008. "Fire and Identity as Matters of Concern in Corsica." *Anthropological Theory* 8 (2): 201–216.

Candea, Matei. 2010. "'I fell in love with Carlos the meerkat': Engagement and Detachment in Human–Animal Relations." *American Ethnologist* 37 (2): 241–258.

Candea, Matei. 2013. "Habituating Meerkats and Redescribing Animal Behaviour Science." *Theory, Culture & Society* 30 (7–8): 105–28.

Candea, Matei. 2019. *Comparison in Anthropology: The Impossible Method*. Cambridge University Press.

Caniuqueo, Sergio. 2006. "Siglo XX en el Gulumapu: de la fragmentación del Wallmapu a la Unidad Nacional Mapuche. 1880 a 1978." In *¡ ... Escucha, winka ... ! Cuatro ensayos de historia nacional mapuche y un epílogo sobre el futuro*, edited by Pablo Marimán, Sergio Caniuqueo, José Millalén, and Rodrigo Levil, 129–217. LOM Ediciones.

Caniuqueo, Sergio. 2013. Dictadura y pueblo mapuche 1973 a 1978. Reconfiguración del colonialismo chileno. *Revista de Historia Social y de las Mentalidades* 17 (1): 89–132.

Carrier, James G., and Donald Macleod. 2005. "Bursting the Bubble: The Socio-Cultural Context of Ecotourism." *Journal of the Royal Anthropological Institute* 11 (2): 315–334.

Casagrande, Olivia. 2021. "Towards a Tuwün Wariache? Place-Making and Creative Acts of Traversing in the Mapuche City." *Journal of the Royal Anthropological Institute* 27 (4): 949–975.

CASEN 2017. *Resultados Encuesta Casen 2017*. Santiago: Ministerio de Desarrollo Social y Familia, Gobierno de Chile.

Casey, Edward. 1996. "How to Get from Space to Place in a Fairly Short Stretch of Time: Phenomenological Prolegomena." In *Senses of Place*, edited by Steven Feld and Keith Basso, 13–52. School of American Research Press.

Casey, Edward. 2001. "Between Geography and Philosophy: What Does It Mean to Be in the Place-World?" *Annals of the Association of American Geographers* 91 (4): 683–93.

Catrileo, María Ester. 1998. *Diccionario lingüístico-etnográfico de la lengua mapuche*. Editorial Andrés Bello.

Catrileo, María Ester. 2014. "El ngillatun como sistema conceptual mapuche." *Estudios Filológicos* 53: 27–38.

Cárcamo-Huechante, Luis. 2006. "Milton Friedman: Knowledge, Public Culture, and Market Economy in the Chile of Pinochet." *Public Culture* 18 (2): 413–435.

Caruso, Emily. 2014. "State Governmentality or Indigenous Sovereignty? Protected Area Comanagement in the Ashaninka Communal Reserve in Peru." In *Indigenous Peoples, National Parks, and Protected Areas: A New Paradigm Linking Conservation, Culture, and Right*, edited by Stan Steven, 150–171. University of Arizona Press.

Cayul, Pedro, and Alejandro Corvalán. 2024. "Indigenous Representation and Participation: The Case of the Chilean Mapuche." *Electoral Studies* 90 (102818): 1–12.

Cepek, Michael. 2011. "Foucault in the Forest: Questioning Environmentality in Amazonia." *American Ethnologist* 38 (3): 501–515.

Chakrabarty, Dipesh. 2021. *The Climate of History in a Planetary Age*. University of Chicago Press.

Chernilo, Daniel. 2017. *Debating Humanity: Towards a Philosophical Sociology*. Cambridge University Press.

Cherstich, Igor, Martin Holbraad, and Nico Tassi. 2020. *Anthropologies of Revolution: Forging Time, People, and Worlds*. University of California Press.

Chihuailaf, Elicura. 1999. *Recado confidencial a los chilenos*. LOM Ediciones.

Ciccariello-Maher, George. 2006. "The Internal Limits of the European Gaze: Intellectuals and the Colonial Difference." *Radical Philosophy Review* 9 (2): 139–165.

CONAF. 2008. *Plan de manejo Reserva Nacional Villarrica-Hualalafquén*. Ministerio de Agricultura, Gobierno de Chile.

Conklin, Beth A., and Laura R. Graham. 1995. "The Shifting Middle Ground: Amazonian Indians and Eco-Politics." *American Anthropologist* 97 (4): 695–710.

Connolly, William E. 2017. *Facing the Planetary: Entangled Humanism and the Politics of Swarming*. Duke University Press.

Coole, Diana, and Samantha Frost. 2010. "Introducing the New Materialisms." In *New Materialisms: Ontology, Agency and Politics*, edited by Diana Coole and Samantha Frost, 1–43. Duke University Press.

Cooperativa. 2019. "Talas ilegales han arrasado 10 mil hectáreas de bosque nativo chileno en seis años." Cooperativa, October 8, 2019. Accessed August 1, 2020. https://www.cooperativa.cl/noticias/pais/regiones/talas-ilegales-han-arrasado-10-mil-hectareas-de-bosque-nativo-chileno-en/2019-10-08/113448.html.

Cordero, Rodrigo. 2016. *Crisis and Critique: On the Fragile Foundations of Social Life*. Routledge.

Cornejo Polar, Antonio. 1994. "Mestizaje, transculturación, heterogeneidad." *Revista de Crítica Literaria Latinoamericana* 20 (40): 368–71.

Correa, Martín, Raúl Molina, and Nancy Yáñez. 2005. *La reforma agraria y la tierra mapuche: Chile 1962–1975*. LOM Ediciones.

Cosgrove, Denis. 1984. *Social Formation and Symbolic Landscape*. Croom Helm.

Coulthard, Glen S. 2007. "Subjects of Empire: Indigenous Peoples and the 'Politics of Recognition' in Colonial Contexts." *Contemporary Political Theory* 6: 437–460.

Coulthard, Glen S. 2014. *Red Skin, White Masks: Rejecting the Colonial Politics of Recognition*. Minnesota University Press.

Course, Magnus. 2010. "Of Words and Fog Linguistic Relativity and Amerindian Ontology." *Anthropological Theory* 10 (3): 247–63.

Course, Magnus. 2011. *Becoming Mapuche: Person and Ritual in Indigenous Chile*. University of Illinois Press.

Course, Magnus. 2013. "The Clown Within: Becoming White and Mapuche Ritual Clowns." *Comparative Studies in Society and History* 55 (4): 771–99.

Course, Magnus. 2021. "The Woman Who Shed Her Skin: Towards a Humble Anthropocentrism in the Outer Hebrides." In *Environmental Alterities*, edited by Cristobal Bonelli and Antonia Walford, 45–70. Mattering Press.

Cresswell, Tim. 2004. *Place: A Short Introduction*. Blackwell Publishing.

Critchley, Simon. 2014. *Ethics of Deconstruction: Derrida and Levinas*. Edinburgh University Press.

Cronon, William. 1996. "The Trouble with Wilderness: Or, Getting Back to the Wrong Nature." *Environmental History* 1 (1): 7–28.

Crosby, Alfred. 2004. *Ecological Imperialism: The Biological Expansion of Europe, 900–1900*. Cambridge University Press.

Crow, Joanna. 2013. *The Mapuche in Modern Chile: A Cultural History*. University Press of Florida.

Cuadra, Ximena. 2011. "El proceso de conformación del territorio indígena de conservación de Quinquén: una experiencia para el cuidado, manejo y protección de los bienes comunes de Comunidades Mapuche." In *Los desafíos de la conservación en los territorios indígenas en Chile*, edited by José Aylwin and Ximena Cuadra, 93–128. Observatorio de Derechos de los Pueblos Indígenas.

Cunsolo, Ashlee, and Neville R. Ellis. 2018. "Ecological Grief as a Mental Health Response to Climate Change-Related Loss." *Nature Climate Change* 8 (4): 275–281.

Curilaf, Luis Alberto. 2015. *Kurarewe en el boquete de Trankura: territorio, migraciones y tráfico comercial*. Cóndor Blanco Ediciones.

Curtin, Deane. 2002. "Ecological Citizenship." In *Handbook of Citizenship Studies*, edited by Engin F. Isin and Bryan S. Turner, 293–304. Sage Publishing.

Das, Madhumita, and Bani Chatterjee. 2015. "Ecotourism: A Panacea or a Predicament?" *Tourism Management Perspectives* 14: 3–16.

Das, Veena. 2012. "Ordinary Ethics." In *A Companion to Moral Anthropology*, edited by Didier Fassin, 133–149. John Wiley & Sons.

Dauvergne, Peter. 2016. *Environmentalism of the Rich*. MIT Press.

Delaney, David. 2010. *Race, Place, and the Law, 1836–1948*. University of Texas Press.

Deleuze, Gilles. 1990. *Expressionism in Philosophy: Spinoza*. MIT Press.

Deleuze, Gilles, and Felix Guattari. 1987. *A Thousand Plateaus: Capitalism and Schizophrenia*. University of Minnessota Press.

Deleuze, Gilles, and Felix Guattari. 1994. *What Is Philosophy?* Columbia University Press.

Descola, Philippe. 2013. *Beyond Nature and Culture*. University of Chicago Press.

Despret, Vinciane. 2004. "The Body We Care For: Figures of Anthropo-zoo-genesis." *Body & Society* 10 (2–3): 111–34.

Despret, Vinciane. 2022. *Living as a Bird*. Polity Press.

Diaz, Paula. 2021. "El florecimiento de la quila: del anuncio de 'calamidades' a una oportunidad para la restauración ecológica." *Ladera Sur*, February 15. https://laderasur.com/articulo/el-florecimiento-de-la-quila-del-anuncio-de-calamidades-a-una-oportunidad-para-la-restauracion-ecologica/.

Dicenta, Mara, and Ana Cecilia Gerrard. 2023. "Ecotourism, Infrastructures, and the Drama of Sovereignty on a Border Island." *The Journal of Latin American and Caribbean Anthropology* 28 (4): 298–309.

Di Giminiani, Piergiorgio. 2016. "How to Manage a Forest: Environmental Governance in Neoliberal Chile." *Anthropological Quarterly* 89 (3): 723–751.

Di Giminiani, Piergiorgio. 2018. *Sentient Lands: Indigeneity, Property, and Political Imagination in Neoliberal Chile*. University of Arizona Press.

Di Giminiani, Piergiorgio, and Marcelo González Gálvez. 2018. "Who Owns the Water? The Relation as Unfinished Objectivation in the Mapuche Lived World." *Anthropological Forum* 28 (3): 199–216.

Di Giminiani, Piergiorgio, and Sophie Haines, 2020. "Introduction: Translating Environments." *Ethnos* 85 (1): 1–16.

Di Giminiani, Piergiorgio, and Elliott Oakley. 2023. "The Making of a Conservation Frontier: Nation-Building, Green Productivism and Environmentalism in Patagonia." *The Journal of Latin American and Caribbean Anthropology* 28 (4): 266–275.

Di Giminiani, Piergiorgio, Miguel Pérez, and Costanza Quezada. 2020. "Nueva normalidad, vieja precariedad: la crisis pandémica en Santiago de Chile." *City & Society* 32 (2): 1–10.

Dobson, Andrew. 2007. "Environmental Citizenship: Towards Sustainable Development." *Sustainable Development* 15 (5): 276–285.

Dominy, Michèle D. 1995. "White Settler Assertions of Native Status." *American Ethnologist* 22 (2): 358–74.

Dominy, Michèle D. 2001. *Calling the Station Home: Place and Identity in New Zealand's High Country*. Rowman & Littlefield.

Duarte, Luiz. 2021. "The Vitality of Vitalism in Contemporary Anthropology: Longing for an Ever Green Tree of Life." *Anthropological Theory* 21 (2): 131–153.

Dudley, Nigel, and Sue Stolton. 1999. *Conversion of Paper Parks to Effective Management: Developing a Target. Report to the WWF*. World Bank Alliance from the IUCN/WWF Forest Innovation Project.

Dunlap, Thomas R. 1993. "Australian Nature, European Culture: Anglo Settlers in Australia." *Environmental History Review* 17 (1): 25–48.

Durán, Manuel A. 2013. "Heroísmo, violencia y libertad en los discursos sobre la masculinidad tradicional en Chile." *Liminales: Escritos sobre Psicología y Sociedad* 2 (3): 13–41.

Elkins, Caroline, and Susan Pedersen, eds. 2005. *Settler Colonialism in the Twentieth Century: Projects, Practices, Legacies*. Routledge.

Erickson, Bruce. 2011. "Recreational Activism: Politics, Nature, and the Rise of Neoliberalism." *Leisure Studies* 30 (4): 477–94.

Escalona, M., and Jonathan Barton. 2024. "'Wallmapu-Araucanía in Flames! An Historical Political Ecology of Fire in the Domination of Southern Chile." *Journal of Historical Geography* 86 (27–38).

Escobar, Arturo. 2017. *Designs for the Pluriverse: Radical Interdependence, Autonomy, and the Making of Worlds*. Duke University Press.

Esposito, Roberto. 2020. *Pensiero istituente: tre paradigmi di ontologia politica*. Piccola Biblioteca Einaudi.

Fairhead, James, Melissa Leach, and Ian Scoones. 2012. "Green Grabbing: A New Appropriation of Nature?" *Journal of Peasant Studies* 39 (2): 237–261.

Falzon, Mark-Anthony. 2020. *Birds of Passage: Hunting and Conservation in Malta*. Berghan Books.

Fanon, Frantz. 1965. *A Dying Colonialism*. Translated by Haakon Chevalier. Grove Press.

Fausto, Carlos. 1999. "Of Enemies and Pets: Warfare and Shamanism in Amazonia." *American Ethnologist* 26 (4): 933–56.

Feld, Steven, and Keith H. Basso, eds. 1996. *Senses of Place*. School of American Research Press.

Ferguson, James. 2010. "The Uses of Neoliberalism." *Antipode* 41: 166–184.

Fernández-Armesto, Felipe. 2005. *So You Think You're Human? A Brief History of Humankind*. University of Oxford Press.

Fisher, Berenice, and Joan C. Tronto. 1990. "Toward a Feminist Theory of Caring." In *Circles of Care: Work and Identity in Women's Lives*, edited by Emily Abel and Margaret Nelson, 35–62. State University of New York Press.

Fletcher, Robert. 2014. *Romancing the Wild: Cultural Dimensions of Ecotourism.* Duke University Press.

Foerster, Rolf. 1993. *Introducción a la religiosidad mapuche.* Editorial Universitaria.

Foerster, Rolf. 2018. *¿Pactos de sumisión o actos de rebelión? Una aproximación histórica y antropológica a los mapuches de la costa de Arauco, Chile.* Pehuén Editores.

Foerster, Rolf, and Sonia Montecino. 1988. *Organizaciones, líderes y contiendas mapuches: 1900–1970.* Ediciones Centros Estudios de la Mujer.

Foucault, Michel. 1982. "The Subject and Power." *Critical Inquiry* 8 (4): 777–795.

Foucault, Michel. 2002. *The Archaeology of Knowledge.* Routledge.

Foucault, Michel. 2008. *The Birth of Biopolitics: Lectures at the Collège de France, 1978–1979.* Palgrave Macmillan.

Freddi, Andrea. 2002. "'En la pampa todos somos gauchos . . .' Etnografía del arreo en la frontera de la Norpatagonia." *CUHSO* 32 (1): 419–446.

Gaard, Greta. 2017. *Critical Ecofeminism.* Lexington Books.

Gago, Verónica. 2017. *Neoliberalism from Below: Popular Pragmatics and Baroque Economies.* Duke University Press.

Garcia, Rocío M., and Mattias B. Rasmussen. 2024. "Settling Environmental Citizenship: The Presentation of Self in Conservation Encounters." *The Journal of Latin American and Caribbean Anthropology* 29 (1): 17–26.

Garretón, Manuel Antonio. 1994. "Transición incompleta y régimen consolidado. Las paradojas de la democratización chilena." *Revista de Ciencia Política* 1: 45–65.

Gatt, Caroline. 2018. *An Ethnography of Global Environmentalism: Becoming Friends of the Earth.* Routledge.

Gell, Alfred. 1992. "The Technology of Enchantment and the Enchantment of Technology." In *Anthropology, Art and Aesthetics*, edited by Jeremy Coote and Anthony Shelton, 40–63. Clarendon Press.

Gershon, Ilana. 2011. "Neoliberal Agency." *Current Anthropology* 52 (4): 537–555.

Gieryn, Thomas F. 1999. *Cultural Boundaries of Science: Credibility on the Line.* University of Chicago Press.

Ginn, Franklin. 2015. "When Horses Won't Eat: Apocalypse and the Anthropocene." *Annals of the Association of American Geographers* 105 (2): 351–59.

Glaskin, Katie. 2018. "Other-Than-Humans and the Remaking of the Social." *Journal of the Royal Anthropological Institute* 24 (2): 313–29.

Goebel, Michael. 2017. "Settler Colonialism in Postcolonial Latin America." In *The Routledge Handbook of the History of Settler Colonialism*, edited by Edward Cavanagh and Lorenzo Veracini, 139–52. Routledge.

Goldman, Mara. 2020. *Narrating Nature: Wildlife Conservation and Maasai Ways of Knowing.* University of Arizona Press.

Goldman, Marcio. 2013. *How Democracy Works: An Ethnographic Theory of Politics.* Sean Kingston Publishing.

González, Héctor. 1986. "Propiedad comunitaria o individual. Las leyes indígenas y el pueblo mapuche." *Nütram* 2 (3): 7–13.

González Gálvez, Marcelo. 2015. "The Truth of Experience and its Communication: Reflections on Mapuche Epistemology." *Anthropological Theory* 15 (2): 141–57.

González Gálvez, Marcelo. 2016. *Los mapuches y sus otros: persona, alteridad y sociedad en el sur de Chile.* Editorial Universitaria.

González Gálvez, Marcelo, Piergiorgio Di Giminiani, and Giovanna Bacchiddu. 2019. "Theorizing Relations in Indigenous South America: Dependence on Otherness and the Ethics of Autonomy." *Social Analysis* 63 (2): 1–23.

Gott, Richard. 2007. "Latin America as a White Settler Society." *Bulletin of Latin American Research* 26 (2): 269–89.

Gow, Peter. 1991. *Of Mixed Blood: Kinship and History in Peruvian Amazonia.* Oxford University Press.

Grandia, Liza. 2012. *Enclosed: Conservation, Cattle, and Commerce among the Q'eqchi'Maya Lowlanders.* University of Washington Press.

Gray, Carlos. 2015. *Los archivos de la memoria: la historia no contada de Pucón.* RIL Editores.

Grebe, María Ester. 1986. "Algunos paralelismos en los sistemas de creencia mapuche: los espíritus del agua y la montaña." *CUHSO* 3: 143–54.

Greco, Monica. 2005. "On the Vitality of Vitalism." *Theory, Culture & Society* 22 (1): 15–27.

Gressier, Catie. 2015. *At Home in the Okavango: White Batswana Narratives of Emplacement and Belonging.* Berghahn Books.

Grupo de Pequeños Productores e Innovadores Campesinos de Coilaco Alto. 2011. *Coilaco Alto: un silencio verde en la geografía.* Pontificia Universidad Católica de Chile, Sede Regional Villarrica.

Gudynas, Eduardo. 1992. "Los múltiples verdes del ambientalismo latinoamericano." *Nueva Sociedad* 122: 104–15.

Hage, Ghassan. 2015. *Alter-Politics: Critical Anthropology and the Radical Imagination.* Melbourne University Publishing.

Hale, Charles R., and Rosamel Millaman. 2005. "Cultural Agency and Political Struggle in the Era of the 'Indio Permitido.'" In *Cultural Agency in the Americas*, edited by Doris Sommer, 281–304. Duke University Press.

Han, Clara. 2012. *Life in Debt: Times of Care and Violence in Neoliberal Chile.* University of California Press.

Harambour, Alberto. 2019. *Soberanías fronterizas: estados y capital en la colonización de Patagonia (Argentina y Chile, 1830–1922).* Ediciones Universidad Austral de Chile.

Haraway, Donna. 1988. "Situated Knowledges: The Science Question in Feminism and the Privilege of Partial Perspective." *Feminist Studies* 14 (3): 575–99.

Haraway, Donna. 1991. *Simians, Cyborgs, and Women: The Reinvention of Nature.* Routledge.

Haraway, Donna. 2008. *When Species Meet.* University of Minnesota Press.

Harrison, Robert P. 1992. *Forests: The Shadow of Civilization.* University of Chicago Press.

Harvey, David. 2007. *A Brief History of Neoliberalism.* Oxford University Press.

Harvey, Penny, Christian Krohn-Hansen, and Knut G. Nustad. 2019. "Introduction." In *Anthropos and the Material*, edited by Penny Harvey, Christian Krohn-Hansen, and Knut G. Nustad, 1–31. Duke University Press.

Head, Lesley. 2016. *Hope and Grief in the Anthropocene: Re-conceptualising Human-Nature Relations.* Routledge.

Heatherington, Tracey. 2010. *Wild Sardinia: Indigeneity and the Global Dreamtimes of Environmentalism.* University of Washington Press.

Helmreich, Stefan. 2009. *Alien Ocean: Anthropological Voyages in Microbial Seas.* University of California Press.

Herbrechter, Stefan. 2013. *Posthumanism: A Critical Analysis.* Bloomsbury.

Herr, Pilar M. 2019. *Contested Nation: The Mapuche, Bandits, and State Formation in Nineteenth-Century Chile.* University of New Mexico Press.

Hidalgo, Rodrigo, and Hugo Zunino. 2012. "Negocio inmobiliario y migración por estilos de vida en la Araucanía lacustre: la transformación del espacio habitado en Villarrica y Pucón." *Revista AUS* 11: 10–13.

High, Casey, and Elliott Oakley 2020. "Conserving and Extracting Nature: Environmental Politics and Livelihoods in the New 'Middle Grounds' of Amazonia." *The Journal of Latin American and Caribbean Anthropology* 25 (2): 236–247.

Hirsch, Eric. 1995. "Landscape: Between Place and Space." In *The Anthropology of Landscape: Perspectives on Place and Space*, edited by Eric Hirsch and Michael O'Hanlon. Oxford University Press.

Hofflinger, Álvaro, and Héctor Nahuelpan. 2018. "Formación ciudadana, racismo y colonialismo de asentamiento: el caso mapuche." In *Educación y juventudes. Investigaciones y debates para el Chile del futuro*, edited by Cristóbal Villalobos, María Jesús Morel, and Ernesto Treviño, 79–110. Ediciones UC.

Holbraad, Martin. 2020. "The Shapes of Relations: Anthropology as Conceptual Morphology." *Philosophy of the Social Sciences* 50 (6): 495–522.

Holbraad, Martin, and Morten Axel Pedersen. 2017. *The Ontological Turn: An Anthropological Exposition.* Cambridge University Press.

Holmes, George. 2015. "Markets, Nature, Neoliberalism, and Conservation Through Private Protected Areas in Southern Chile." *Environment and Planning A* 47 (4): 850–66.

Huiliñir-Curío, Viviana. 2018. "De senderos a paisajes: paisajes de las movilidades de una comunidad mapuche en los Andes del sur de Chile." *Chungará* 50 (3): 487–99.

Huiliñir-Curío, Viviana, Hugo Zunino, and Luis Fernando De Matheus e Silva. 2019. "Exclusión y desigualdad en localidades próximas a la Reserva Ecológica Privada

Huilo-Huilo en el sur de Chile." *ACME: An International E-Journal for Critical Geographies* 18 (2): 335–63.

Hutton, Jon, William M. Adams, and James C. Murombedzi. 2005. "Back to the Barriers? Changing Narratives in Biodiversity Conservation." *Forum for Development Studies* 32 (2): 341–370.

Ibarra, José Tomás, and Kathy Martin. 2015. "Biotic Homogenization: Loss of Avian Functional Richness and Habitat Specialists in Disturbed Andean Temperate Forests." *Biological Conservation* 192 (2015): 418–427.

Ibarra, José Tomás, and José Cristóbal Pizarro. 2016. "Hacia una etno-ornitología interdisciplinaria, intercultural e intergeneracional para la conservación biocultural." *Revista Chilena de Ornitología* 2 (1): 1–6.

Ibarra, José Tomás, and Lorena Guzmán. 2016. "Las aves del bosque chileno cooperan entre sí reciclando sus nidos." *El Mercurio*, June 17. https://repositorio.uc.cl/handle/11534/66761.

Ibarra, José Tomás, Nicolás Gálvez, Tomás A. Altamirano, et al. 2017a. "Seasonal Dynamics of Avian Guilds Inside and Outside Core Protected Areas in an Andean Biosphere Reserve of Southern Chile." *Bird Study* 64 (3): 410–20.

Ibarra, José Tomás, Michaela Martin, Kristina L. Cockle, and Kathy Martin. 2017b. "Maintaining Ecosystem Resilience: Functional Responses of Tree Cavity Nesters to Logging in Temperate Forests of the Americas." *Scientific Reports* 7 (4467): 1–9.

Ibarra, José Tomás, Tomás A. Altamirano, Alejandra Vermehren, F. Hernán Vargas, and Kathy Martin. 2017c. "Observations of a Tree-Cavity Nest of the Rufous-Legged Owl and Predation of an Owl Nestling by a Chimango Caracara in Andean Temperate Forests." *Journal of Raptor Research* 51 (1): 85–88.

Ibarra, José Tomás, Julián Caviedes, Antonia Barreau, et al. 2022. "Escuchando a los abuelos: transdisciplina, aves y gente para cultivar la memoria biocultural." *Revista Latinoamericana de Ciencias Sociales, Niñez y Juventud* 20 (3): 1–22.

Igoe, Jim. 2017. *The Nature of Spectacle: On Images, Money, and Conserving Capitalism*. University of Arizona Press.

Igoe, Jim, and Dan Brockington. 2007. "Neoliberal Conservation: A Brief Introduction." *Conservation and Society* 5 (4): 432–449.

INE. 2017. *Resultados Definitivos Censo 2015*. Instituto Nacional de Estadísticas, Gobierno de Chile.

Ingold, Tim. 2000. *The Perception of the Environment: Essays on Livelihood, Dwelling and Skill*. Routledge.

Ingold, Tim. 2001. "From the Transmission of Representations to the Education of Attention." In *The Debated Mind: Evolutionary Psychology Versus Ethnography*, edited by Harvey Whitehouse. Berg Publishers.

İpek, Yasemin. 2022. "Entrepreneurial Activism: Ethical Politics and Class-Based Imaginations of Change in Lebanon." *American Ethnologist* 50 (3): 474–490.

Isla, Ana. 2005. "Conservation as Enclosure: An Ecofeminist Perspective on Sustainable Development and Biopiracy in Costa Rica." *Capitalism Nature Socialism* 16 (3): 49–61.

Janoschka, Michael, and Heiko Haas, eds. 2013. *Contested Spatialities, Lifestyle Migration and Residential Tourism*. Routledge.

Jensen, Casper Bruun, and Atsuro Morita. 2015. "Infrastructures as Ontological Experiments." *Engaging Science, Technology, and Society* 1: 81–87.

Jørgensen, Dolly. 2015. "Rethinking Rewilding." *Geoforum* 65: 482–488.

Keller, Peter. 2001. "El Cañi Forest Sanctuary: A New Model for Chile." *Institute of Current World Affairs Letters* February 2001: 1–7. http://www.icwa.org/wp-content/uploads/2015/10/PK-12.pdf.

Kelly, Alice B. 2011. "Conservation Practice as Primitive Accumulation." *Journal of Peasant Studies* 38 (4): 683–701.

Kelly, Sarah. 2019. "Megawatts Mask Impacts: Small Hydropower and Knowledge Politics in the Puelwillimapu, Southern Chile." *Energy Research and Social Science* 54: 224–35.

Kipnis, Andrew. 2015. "Agency Between Humanism and Posthumanism: Latour and His Opponents." *HAU: Journal of Ethnographic Theory* 5 (2): 43–58.

Kirksey, Eben. 2015. *Emergent Ecologies*. Duke University Press.

Klubock, Thomas Miller. 2014. *La Frontera: Forests and Ecological Conflict in Chile's Frontier Territory*. Duke University Press.

Knight, Tony. 2017. "Pyrenean Rewilding and Ontological Landscapes: A Future(s) Dwelt-in Ethnographic Approach." In *Anthropologies and Futures: Researching Emerging and Uncertain Worlds*, edited by Juan Francisca Salazar, Sarah Pink, Andrew Irving, and Johannes Sjöberg. Bloomsbury Publishing.

Knorr-Cetina, Karin. 1999. *Epistemic Cultures: How the Sciences Make Knowledge*. Harvard University Press.

Kohn, Eduardo. 2012. "Proposal 1: Anthropology Beyond the Human." *Cambridge Anthropology* 30 (2): 136–141.

Kohn, Eduardo. 2013. *How Forests Think: Toward an Anthropology Beyond the Human*. University of California Press.

Kohn, Eduardo. 2022. "Forest Forms and Ethical Life." *Environmental Humanities* 14 (2): 401–418.

Kolers, Avery. 2009. *Land, Conflict, and Justice: A Political Theory of Territory*. Cambridge University Press.

Kopenawa, Davi, and Bruce Albert. 2019. *The Falling Sky: Words of a Yanomami Shaman*. The Belknap Press of Harvard University Press.

Kristensen, Dorthe Brogård. 2019. *Patients, Doctors and Healers: Medical Worlds Among the Mapuche in Southern Chile*. Palgrave Macmillan.

Krøijer, Stine. 2020. "Civilization as the Undesired World: Radical Environmentalism and the Uses of Dystopia in Times of Climate Crisis." *Social Analysis* 64 (3): 48–67.

Krøijer, Stine, and Cecilie Rubow. 2022. "Introduction: Enchanted Ecologies and Ethics of Care." *Environmental Humanities* 14 (2): 375–384.

Kumar, Malreddy P. 2011. "(An) Other Way of Being Human: 'Indigenous' Alternative(s) to Postcolonial Humanism." *Third World Quarterly* 32 (9): 1557–1572.

Lara, Antonio, Alexia Wolodarsky-Franke, Juan Carlos Aravena, Marco Cortés, Shawn Fraver, and Fernando Silla. 2003. "Fire Regimes and Forest Dynamics in the Lake Region of South-Central Chile." In *Fire and Climatic Change in Temperate Ecosystems of the Western Americas*, edited by Thomas Veblen, William Baker, Gloria Montenegro, and Thomas Swetnam. Springer Publishing.

Latour, Bruno. 1999. *Pandora's Hope: Essays on the Reality of Science Studies*. Harvard University Press.

Latour, Bruno. 2004. *Politics of Nature How to Bring the Sciences into Democracy*. Harvard University Press.

Latour, Bruno. 2005. *Reassembling the Social: An Introduction to Actor-Network-Theory*. Oxford University Press.

Latour, Bruno. 2014. "Anthropology at the Time of the Anthropocene: A Personal View of What Is to Be Studied." Distinguished lecture delivered at the American Anthropological Association annual meeting, Washington, D.C., December 2014.

Law, John. 2015. "What's Wrong with a One-World World?" *Distinktion: Scandinavian Journal of Social Theory* 16 (1): 126–139.

Law, John, and Michael Lynch. 1988. "Lists, Field Guides, and the Descriptive Organization of Seeing: Birdwatching as an Exemplary Observational Activity." *Human Studies* 11: 271–303.

Lazo, Iván, and Enrique Silva. 1993. "Diagnóstico de la ornitología en Chile y recopilación de la literatura científica publicada desde 1970 a 1992." *Revista Chilena de Historia Natural* 66: 103–18.

Lee, Jo. 2007. "Experiencing Landscape: Orkney Hill Land and Farming." *Journal of Rural Studies* 23 (1): 88–100.

Levinas, Emmanuel. 1979. *Totality and Infinity: An Essay on Exteriority*. Martinus Nijhoff Publishers.

Levi-Strauss, Claude. 1995. *The Story of Lynx*. University of Chicago Press.

Lewis, Courtney. 2019. *Sovereign Entrepreneurs: Cherokee Small-Business Owners and the Making of Economic Sovereignty*. University of North Carolina Press.

Llewelyn, John. 2012. *The Rigor of a Certain Inhumanity: Toward a Wider Suffrage*. Indiana University Press.

Loncon, Elisa, Alvaro Gainza, Natalia Hirmas, and Diego Mellado. 2022. *Colonialismo cultural y ontología indígena en comunidades pewenche de Alto Biobío*. LOM Ediciones.

Lorimer, Jamie. 2015. *Wildlife in the Anthropocene: Conservation After Nature*. University of Minnesota Press.

Lorimer, Jamie, Chris Sandom, Paul Jepson, Chris Doughty, Maan Barua, and Keith J. Kirby. 2015. "Rewilding: Science, Practice, and Politics." *Annual Review of Environment and Resources* 40: 39–62.

Luque-Lora, Rogelio. 2022. "Chile's Social Uprising and Constituent Process: Toward a More-Than-Human Understanding." *Interface: A Journal on Social Movements* 13 (2): 323–352.

Luna, Juan Pablo, ed. 2021. *La chusma inconsciente: la crisis de un país atendido por sus propios dueños*. Editorial Catalonia.

MacDonald, Helen. 2002. "'What Makes You a Scientist Is the Way You Look at Things': Ornithology and the Observer 1930–1955." *Studies in History and Philosophy of Science* 33 (1): 53–77.

Mallon, Florencia. 2005. *Courage Tastes of Blood: The Mapuche Community of Nicolás Ailío and the Chilean State, 1906–2001*. Duke University Press.

Manning, Erin, and Brian Massumi. 2014. *Thought in the Act: Passages in the Ecology of Experience*. University of Minnesota Press.

Marchant, Carla, and Fernand Rojas. 2015. "Transformaciones locales y nuevas funcionalidades económicas vinculadas a las migraciones por amenidad en la Patagonia Chilena." *Journal of Alpine Research* 103 (3): 1–19.

Marimán, José. 2012. *Autodeterminación: ideas políticas mapuche en el albor del siglo XXI*. LOM Ediciones.

Marimán, Pablo, ed. 2002. *Parlamento y territorio mapuche*. Escaparate Ediciones.

Marimán, Pablo. 2006. "Los Mapuche antes de la conquista militar chileno-argentina." In *¡ . . . Escucha, winka . . . ! Cuatro ensayos de historia nacional mapuche y un epílogo sobre el futuro*, edited by Pablo Marimán, Sergio Caniuqueo, José Millalén, and Rodrigo Levil. LOM Ediciones.

Martínez-Alier, Joan. 2002. *The Environmentalism of the Poor: A Study of Ecological Conflicts and Valuation*. Edward Elgar Publishing.

Martínez-Alier, Joan, Michiel Baud, and Héctor Sejenovich. 2016. "Origins and Perspectives of Latin American Environmentalism." In *Environmental Governance in Latin America*, edited by Fabio De Castro, Barbara Hogenboom, and Michiel Baud. Palgrave Macmillan.

Martínez-Reyes, José. 2016. *Moral Ecology of a Forest: The Nature Industry and Maya Post-Conservation*. University of Arizona Press.

Masco, Joseph. 2017. "The Crisis in Crisis." *Current Anthropology* 58 (S15): S65–S76.

Massumi, Brian. 2002. *Parables for the Virtual: Movement, Affect, Sensation*. Duke University Press.

Mathews, Andrew. 2011. *Instituting Nature: Authority, Expertise, and Power in Mexican Forests*. MIT Press.

Mathews, Andrew. 2022. *Trees Are Shape Shifters: How Cultivation, Climate Change, and Disaster Create Landscapes*. Yale University Press.

Maturana, Humberto, and Francisco Varela. 1984. *El árbol del conocimiento: las bases biológicas del entendimiento humano*. Grupo Editorial Lumen.

Mazzarella, William. 2004. "Culture, Globalization, Mediation." *Annual Review of Anthropology* 1: 345–367.

Mbembe, Achille. 2019. *Necropolitics*. Duke University Press.

McAllister, Carlota. 2020. "No One Can Hold It Back: The Theopolitics of Water and Life in Chilean Patagonia Without Dams." *Social Analysis* 64 (4): 121–139.

McIntosh, Janet. 2016. *Unsettled: Denial and Belonging Among White Kenyans*. University of California Press.

Melin, Miguel, Pablo Mansilla, and Manuela Royo. 2019. *Cartografíacultural del Wallmapu: elementos para descolonizar el mapa en territorio mapuche*. LOM Ediciones.

Mendoza, Marcos. 2018. *The Patagonian Sublime: The Green Economy and Post-Neoliberal Politics*. Rutgers University Press.

Merleau-Ponty, Maurice. 1962. *Phenomenology of Perception*. London.

Meza, Laura. 2009. "Mapuche Struggles for Land and the Role of Private Protected Areas in Chile." *Journal of Latin American Geography* 8 (1): 149–63.

Millalén, José. 2006. "La sociedad mapuche prehispánica: kimün, arqueología y etnohistoria." In *¡ . . . Escucha, winka . . . ! Cuatro ensayos de historia nacional mapuche y un epílogo sobre el futuro*, edited by Pablo Marimán, Sergio Caniuqueo, José Millalén, and Rodrigo Levil. LOM Ediciones.

Millaleo, Salvador. 2021. *Por una via chilena a la plurinacionalidad: intervenciones de una década (2010–2020)*. Editorial Catalonia.

Milton, Kay. 2002. *Loving Nature: Towards an Ecology of Emotion*. Routledge.

Mitchell, William J. T. 2002. *Landscape and Power*. University of Chicago Press.

Mol, Annemarie. 2002. *The Body Multiple: Ontology in Medical Practice*. Duke University Press.

Mol, Annemarie, Ingunn Moser, and Jeannette Pols, eds. 2010. *Care in Practice: On Tinkering in Clinics, Homes, and Farms*. Kerber Verlag.

Monbiot, George. 2014. *Feral: Rewilding the Land, the Sea, and Human Life*. University of Chicago Press.

Montecino, Sonia. 1991. *Madres y huachos: alegorías del mestizaje chileno*. Editorial Catalonia.

Montes, Carlo. 2022. "¿El fin de la laguna de Aculeo? Últimas lluvias tienen cero impacto en su caudal." *La Tercera*, July 22.

Montes, Rocío. 2019. "Chile recibe de los Tompkins la mayor donación de tierras privadas de la historia." *El País*, April 30. https://elpais.com/internacional/2019/04/29/america/1556563652_462137.html.

Moore, Amelia. 2019. *Destination Anthropocene: Science and Tourism in the Bahamas*. University of California Press.

Moore, Jason W. 2015. *Capitalism in the Web of Life: Ecology and the Accumulation of Capital*. Verso Books.

Morandé, Pedro. 1984. *Cultura y modernización en América Latina: ensayo sociológico acerca de la crisis del desarrollismo y de su superación*. Universidad Católica de Chile.

Morgensen, Scott. 2012. "Theorising Gender, Sexuality and Settler Colonialism: An Introduction." *Settler Colonial Studies* 2 (2): 2–22.

Murray, Marjorie, Sofia Bowen, Nicole Segura, and Marisol Verdugo. 2015. "Apprehending Volition in Early Socialization: Raising 'Little Persons' Among Rural Mapuche Families." *Ethos* 43 (4): 376–401.

Nadasdy, Paul. 2005. "Transcending the Debate over the Ecologically Noble Indian: Indigenous Peoples and Environmentalism." *Ethnohistory* 52 (2): 291–331.

Næss, Arne. 1989. *Ecology, Community and Lifestyle: Outline of an Ecosophy.* Cambridge University Press.

Nájera, Andrea, and Javier Simonetti. 2010. "Enhancing Avifauna in Commercial Plantations." *Conservation Biology* 24 (1): 319–24.

Ñanculef, Juan. 2016. *Tayiñ mapuche kimün epistemología mapuche, sabiduría y conocimientos.* Cátedra Indígena, Universidad de Chile.

Narotzky, Susana, and Niko Besnier. 2014. "Crisis, Value, and Hope: Rethinking the Economy." *Current Anthropology* 55 (S9): S4-S16.

Neira, Eduardo, and Esteban Rivas. 2013. "Evaluación del fondo de conservación, recuperación y manejo sustentable del bosque nativo (Ley N°20.283)." *Revista Bosque Nativo,* 52: 26–28.

Nouzeilles, Gabriela. 1999. "Patagonia as Borderland: Nature, Culture, and the Idea of the State." *Journal of Latin American Cultural Studies* 8 (1): 35–48.

Núñez, Andrés, Enrique Aliste, and Álvaro Bello. 2014. "El discurso del desarrollo en Patagonia-Aysén: la conservación y la protección de la naturaleza como dispositivos de una renovada colonización. Chile, siglos XX-XXI." *Scripta Nova* 493 (46): 1–13.

Oakley, Elliott. 2020. "Demarcated Pens and Dependent Pets: Conservation Livelihoods in an Indigenous Amazonian Protected Area." *The Journal of Latin American and Caribbean Anthropology* 25 (2): 248–65.

Offen, Karl H. 2003. "The Territorial Turn: Making Black Territories in Pacific Colombia." *Journal of Latin American Geography* 2 (1): 43–73.

Office of the United Nations High Commissioner for Human Rights. 2019. *Report of the Mission to Chile from 30 October to 22 November 2019.* United Nations.

Ogden, Laura A. 2011. *Swamplife: People, Gators, and Mangroves Entangled in the Everglades.* University of Minnesota Press.

Ogden, Laura A. 2021. *Loss and Wonder at the World's End.* Duke University Press.

Ojeda, Diana. 2012. "Green Pretexts: Ecotourism, Neoliberal Conservation and Land-Grabbing in Tayrona National Natural Park, Colombia." *Journal of Peasant Studies* 39 (2): 357–75.

Olwig, Kenneth. 2005. "Representation and Alienation in the Political Land-Scape." *Cultural Geographies* 12 (1): 19–40.

Otero, Luis. 2006. *La huella del fuego: historia de los bosques nativos, poblamiento y cambios en el paisaje del sur de Chile.* Pehuén Editores.

Pairican, Fernando. 2014. *Malón: la rebelión del movimiento mapuche. 1990–2013.* Pehuén Editores.

Pairican, Fernando. 2020. *Toqui: guerra y tradición en el siglo XIX.* Pehuén Editores.

Paley, Julia. 2001. *Marketing Democracy: Power and Social Movements in Post-Dictatorship Chile.* University of California Press.

Palsson, Gisli. 2016. *Nature, Culture and Society: Anthropological Perspectives on Life.* Cambridge University Press.

Papadopoulos, Dimitris, María Puig de la Bellacasa, and Maddalena Tacchetti. 2023. "Introduction: No Justice, No Ecological Peace: The Groundings of Ecological

Reparation." In *Ecological Reparation: Repair, Remediation and Resurgence in Social and Environmental Conflict*, edited by Dimitris Papadopoulos, María Puig de la Bellacasa, and Maddalena Tacchetti. Bristol University Press.

Park, Yun-Joo, and Patricia Richards. 2007. "Negotiating Neoliberal Multiculturalism: Mapuche Workers in the Chilean State." *Social Forces* 85 (3): 1319–39.

Pasternak, Shiri. 2017. *Grounded Authority: The Algonquins of Barriere Lake Against the State*. University of Minnesota Press.

Pauchard, Aníbal, and Pablo Villarroel. 2002. "Protected Areas in Chile: History, Current Status, and Challenges." *Natural Areas Journal* 22 (4): 318–30.

Pazzarelli, Francisco. 2019. "Looks Like Viscera: Folds, Wraps, and Relations in the Southern Andes." *Social Analysis* 63 (2): 45–65.

Pedersen, Morten Axel. 2020. "Anthropological Epochés: Phenomenology and the Ontological Turn." *Philosophy of the Social Sciences* 50 (6): 610–646.

Peluso, Nancy Lee, and Christian Lund. "New Frontiers of Land Control: Introduction." *Journal of Peasant Studies* 38 (4): 667–681.

Perasso, Paolo, Constanza Christian, and Daniela Carvajal. 2018. "Aprendiendo a hacer conservación-participativa: contribuciones de la antropología social." *Revista Austral de Ciencias Sociales* 35: 239–60.

Phillips, Anne. 2015. *The Politics of the Human*. Cambridge University Press.

Picone, Maria de los Angeles. 2025. *Landscaping Patagonia: Spatial History and Nation-Making in Chile and Argentina*. The University of North Carolina Press.

Pike, Sarah M. 2017. *For the Wild: Ritual and Commitment in Radical Eco-Activism*. University of California Press.

Pinto, Jorge. 2003. *La formación del estado y la nación, y el pueblo mapuche. De la inclusión a la exclusión*. Dibam, Servicio Nacional del Patrimonio Cultural, Gobierno de Chile.

Pizarro, Juan Cristóbal, and Brendon Larson. 2017. "Feathered Roots and Migratory Routes: Immigrants and Birds in the Anthropocene." *Nature and Culture* 12 (3): 189–218.

Postero, Nancy, and Nicole Fabricant. 2019. "Indigenous Sovereignty and the New Developmentalism in Plurinational Bolivia." *Anthropological Theory* 19 (1): 95–119.

Povinelli, Elizabeth A. 2002. *The Cunning of Recognition: Indigenous Alterities and the Making of Australian Multiculturalism*. Duke University Press.

Prieto, Manuel, and Carl Bauer. 2012. "Hydroelectric Power Generation in Chile: An Institutional Critique of the Neutrality of Market Mechanisms." *Water International* 37 (2): 131–46.

Puig de la Bellacasa, María. 2012. "'Nothing Comes without Its World': Thinking with Care." *Sociological Review* 60 (2): 197–216.

Puig de la Bellacasa, María. 2017. *Matters of Care: Speculative Ethics in More than Human Worlds*. University of Minnesota Press.

Pyne, Stephen J. 1997. "Frontiers of Fire." In *Ecology and Empire: Environmental History of Settler Societies*, edited by Tom Griffiths and Libby Robin. University of Washington Press.

Quidel, José. 2016. "El quiebre ontológico a partir del contacto mapuche hispano." *Chungará* 48 (4): 713–19.

Quidel, José. 2020. *La noción mapuche de che (persona)*. Unpublished PhD dissertation. Universidad Estadual de Campinas.

Quijano, Anibal. 2000. "Colonialidad del poder, eurocentrismo y América Latina." In *Colonialidad del Saber, Eurocentrismo y Ciencias Sociales*, edited by Edgardo Lander. CLACSO-UNESCO.

Quilaqueo, Daniel, and Segundo Quintriqueo. 2010. "Saberes educativos mapuches: un análisis desde la perspectiva de los kimches." *Polis* 9 (26): 337–60.

Quintriqueo, Segundo, and Héctor Torres. 2013. "Construcción de conocimiento mapuche y su relación con el conocimiento escolar." *Estudios Pedagógicos* 39 (1): 199–216.

Quiroz, Daniel. 1985. "La colonia 'Nueva Transvaal' de Gorbea: documentos y noticias (1901–1903)." *Boletín del Museo Regional de la Araucanía de Temuco* 2: 11–23.

Radcliffe, Sarah, and Andrew Webb. 2015. "Subaltern Bureaucrats and Postcolonial Rule: Indigenous Professional Registers of Engagement with the Chilean State." *Comparative Studies in Society and History* 57 (1): 248–73.

Radcliffe, Sarah, and Sallie Westwood. 1996. *Remaking the Nation: Place, Identity and Politics in Latin America*. London.

Rasmussen, Mattias. 2019. "Rewriting Conservation Landscapes: Protected Areas and Glacial Retreat in the High Andes." *Regional Environmental Change* 19 (5): 1371–1385.

Rasmussen, Mattias. 2021. "Institutionalizing Precarity: Settler Identities, National Parks and the Containment of Political Spaces in Patagonia." *Geoforum* 119: 289–297.

Rasmussen, Mattias, and Christian Lund. 2018. "Reconfiguring Frontier Spaces: The Territorialization of Resource Control." *World Development* 101: 388–399.

Rauch, Marcos, Emilia Catalán, Guido Aguilera, Ivonne Valenzuela, Sandro Maldonado, and Paula Martínez. 2018. "Gestión intercultural para la conservación en Áreas Silvestres Protegidas del Estado: aprendizajes y desafíos." *Revista Austral de Ciencias Sociales* 35: 183–204.

Renfrew, Daniel. 2018. *Life Without Lead: Contamination, Crisis, and Hope in Uruguay*. University of California Press.

Reuque Paillalef, Rosa Isolde. 2002. *When a Flower Is Reborn: The Life and Times of a Mapuche Feminist*. Duke University Press.

Reyes, Carlos. 2022. "Encuesta CEP: un 70% de los mapuche está en contra de que se establezca un 'estado independiente' y el 59% no justifica el uso de la fuerza para reclamar tierras." *La Tercera*, August 3. https://www.latercera.com/politica/noticia/encuesta-cep-un-70-de-los-mapuche-esta-en-contra-de-que-se-establezca-un-estado-independiente-y-el-59-no-justifica-el-uso-de-la-fuerza-para-reclamar-tierras/SSJRFYLSVZG5RLRMIZXPELENG4/.

Richards, Patricia. 2013. *Race and the Chilean Miracle: Neoliberalism, Democracy, and Indigenous Rights*. University of Pittsburgh Press.

Rival, Laura. 1993. "The Growth of Family Trees: Understanding Huaorani Perceptions of the Forest." *Man* 28 (4): 635–52.

Roberts, Neil. 2015. *Freedom as Marronage*. University of Chicago Press.

Rojas, Alejandro. 1994. "The Environmental Movement and the Environmentally
Concerned Scientific Community in Chile." *Revista Europea de Estudios Lati-
noamericanos y del Caribe/European Review of Latin American and Caribbean
Studies* 56: 93–118.

Romero Toledo, Hugo. 2014. "Ecología política y represas: elementos para el análisis
del Proyecto HidroAysén en la Patagonia chilena." *Revista de Geografía Norte
Grande* 57: 161–175.

Root-Bernstein, Meredith, and Matías Guerrero-Gatica. 2024. "Building Alliances
and Consensus Around Social-Ecological Rewilding in Chile." *Frontiers in Conservation Science* 5: 1–13.

Rose, Nikolas. 2006. "Governing 'Advanced' Liberal Democracies." In *The Anthropology of the State: A Reader*, edited by Aradhana Sharma and Akhil Gupta. Blackwell
Publishing.

Rossello, Diego. 2017. "All in the (Human) Family? Species Aristocratism in the Return
of Human Dignity." *Political Theory* 45 (6): 749–771.

Rozzi, Ricardo, Francisca Massardo, Christopher Anderson, et al. 2003. *Multi-Ethnic
Bird Guide of the Austral Temperate Forests of South America*, translated by Christopher Anderson. Fantástico Sur-Universidad de Magallanes.

Salas, Guillermo. 2019. *Lugares parientes: comida, cohabitación y mundos andinos*.
Fondo Editorial de la PUCP.

Schiebinger, Londa, and Claudia Swan, eds. 2007. *Colonial Botany: Science, Commerce, and Politics in the Early Modern World*. University of Pennsylvania Press.

Schild, Verónica. 2007. "Empowering Consumer Citizens or Governing Poor Female
Subjects? The Institutionalization of 'Self-Development' in the Chilean Social Policy Field." *Journal of Consumer Culture* 7 (2): 179–203.

Schlosberg, David, and Elizabeth Bomberg. 2008. "Perspectives on American Environmentalism." *Environmental Politics* 17 (2): 187–199.

Seigworth, Gregory J., and Melissa Gregg. 2010. "An Inventory of Shimmers." In *The
Affect Theory Reader*, edited by Melissa Gregg and Gregory J. Seigworth. Duke
University Press.

Sepulveda, Bastien, and Silvain Guyot. 2016. "Escaping the Border, Debordering
the Nature: Protected Areas, Participatory Management, and Environmental
Security in Northern Patagonia (i.e. Chile and Argentina)." *Globalizations* 13
(6): 767–86.

Sheild Johansson, Miranda. 2019. "'The Mountain Ate His Heart': Agricultural Labor
and Animate Land in a Protestant Andean Community." *The Journal of Latin
American and Caribbean Anthropology* 24 (2): 573–590.

Silva, Eduardo. 1997. "The Politics of Sustainable Development: Native Forest Policy
in Chile, Venezuela, Costa Rica and Mexico." *Journal of Latin American Studies*
29 (2): 457–493.

Simonetti, Cristián. 2019. "Weathering Climate: Telescoping Change." *Journal of the Royal Anthropological Institute* 25 (2): 241–64.

Simpson, Audra. 2014. *Mohawk, Interruptus: Political Life Across the Borders of Settler States.* Duke University Press.

Skewes, Juan Carlos, Debbie Guerra, Susana Rebolledo, and Lorenzo Palma. 2020. "La regeneración de los bosques: paisaje, prácticas y ontologías en el sur de Chile." *Estudios Atacameños* 65: 385–405.

Soper, Kate. 1990. "Feminism, Humanism and Postmodernism." *Radical Philosophy* 55 (1): 11–17.

Soto, Daniela, Marcelo González, and Piergiorgio Di Giminiani. 2023. "Innovation as Translation in Indigenous Entrepreneurship: Lessons from Mapuche Entrepreneurs in Chile." *Canadian Journal of Development Studies* 44 (3): 454–473.

de Steiguer, J. Edward. 2006. *The Origins of Modern Environmental Thought.* University of Arizona Press.

Stengers, Isabelle. 2005. "The Cosmopolitical Proposal." In *Making Things Public: Atmospheres of Democracy,* edited by Bruno Latour and Peter Weibel. MIT Press.

Stevens, Stan. 2014. "Indigenous Peoples, Biocultural Diversity, and Protected Areas." In *Indigenous Peoples, National Parks, and Protected Areas: A New Paradigm Linking Conservation, Culture, and Rights,* edited by Stan Steven. University of Arizona Press.

Strathern, Marilyn. 1988. *The Gender of the Gift: Problems with Women and Problems with Society in Melanesia.* University of California Press.

Strathern, Marilyn. 2004 [1991]. *Partial Connections, Updated Edition.* Altamira Press.

Strathern, Marilyn. 2020. *Relations: An Anthropological Account.* Duke University Press.

Suzuki, Yuka. 2017. *The Nature of Whiteness: Race, Animals, and Nation in Zimbabwe.* University of Washington Press.

Swanson, Heather Anne, Marianne E. Lien, and Gro B. Ween. 2018. "Introduction: Naming the Beast, Exploring the Otherwise." In *Domestication Gone Wild: Politics and Practices of Multispecies Relations,* edited by Marianne Elisabeth Lien, Heather Anne Swanson, and Gro B. Ween. Duke University Press.

Táíwò, Olúfẹ́mi O. 2022. *Reconsidering Reparations.* Oxford University Press.

Taylor, Bron Raymond. 2010. *Dark Green Religion: Nature Spirituality and the Planetary Future.* University of California Press.

Tecklin, David, Carl Bauer, and Manuel Prieto. 2011. "Making Environmental Law for the Market: The Emergence, Character, and Implications of Chile's Environmental Regime." *Environmental Politics* 20 (6): 879–98.

Tecklin, David, and Claudia Sepúlveda. 2014. "The Diverse Properties of Private Land Conservation in Chile: Growth and Barriers to Private Protected Areas in a Market-Friendly Context." *Conservation and Society* 12 (2): 203–17.

Tidemann, Sonia C., and Andrew Gosler, eds. 2012. *Ethno-Ornithology: Birds, Indigenous Peoples, Culture and Society.* Earthscan Research Editions.

Tilley, Christopher. 1994. *A Phenomenology of Landscape: Places, Paths, and Monuments*. Berg Publishers.

Tironi, Manuel, and Tania Manríquez. 2019. "Lateral Knowledge: Shifting Expertise for Disaster Management in Chile." *Disasters* 43 (2): 372–389.

Trentini, Florencia. 2023. "Between Conservation and Care: Ontological Mixtures and Juxtapositions in Protected Areas of Patagonia, Argentina." *The Journal of Latin American and Caribbean Anthropology* 28 (4): 276–85.

Tsing, Anna. 2015. *The Mushroom at the End of the World: On the Possibility of Life in Capitalist Ruins*. Princeton University Press.

Ulianova, Olga, and Fernando Estenssoro. 2012. "El ambientalismo chileno: la emergencia y la inserción internacional." *Si Somos Americanos. Revista de Estudios Transfronterizos* 12 (1): 183–214.

Undurraga, Tomas, and Gonzalo Aguirre. 2023. "'Now They Tell Me to Preserve It': Changing Environmental Imaginaries in Southern Chile." *Geoforum* 141: 1037–48.

Urrejola, José. 2019. "Chile: destrucción de monumentos como protesta contra la historia oficial." *DW Actualidad*, November 11. https://www.dw.com/es/chile-destrucci%C3%B3n-de-monumentos-como-protesta-contra-la-historia-oficial/a-51202577.

Urry, John, and Jonas Larsen. 2011. *The Tourist Gaze 3.0*. Sage Publishing.

Valenzuela, Eduardo, and María Belén Unzueta. 2015. "Parental Transmission of Ethnic Identification in Mixed Couples in Latin America: The Mapuche Case." *Ethnic and Racial Studies* 38 (12): 2090–107.

Venkatesan, Soumhya, James Laidlaw, Hylland Eriksen, Jonathan Mair, and Martin Keir. 2015. "Debate: 'The Concept of Neoliberalism Has Become an Obstacle to the Anthropological Understanding of the Twenty-First Century.'" *Journal of the Royal Anthropological Institute* 21 (4): 911–923.

Veracini, Lorenzo. 2010. *Settler Colonialism: A Theoretical Overview*. Palgrave Macmillan.

Viroli, Maurizio. 1992. *From Politics to Reason of State: The Acquisition and Transformation of the Language of Politics, 1250–1600*. Cambridge University Press.

Viveiros de Castro, Eduardo. 1998. "Cosmological Deixis and Amerindian Perspectivism." *Journal of the Royal Anthropological Institute* 4 (3): 469–88.

Viveiros de Castro, Eduardo. 2011. "Zeno and the Art of Anthropology: Of Lies, Beliefs, Paradoxes, and Other Truths." *Common Knowledge* 17 (1): 128–45.

Viveiros de Castro, Eduardo. 2014. *Cannibal Metaphysics*. University of Minnesota Press.

Viveiros de Castro, Eduardo. 2019. "On Models and Examples: Engineers and Bricoleurs in the Anthropocene." *Current Anthropology* 60 (S20): S296–S308.

Wade, Peter. 2005. "Rethinking Mestizaje: Ideology and Lived Experience." *Journal of Latin American Studies* 37 (2): 239–57.

Wakild, Emily. 2017. "Protecting Patagonia: Science, Conservation and the Pre-History of the Nature State on a South American Frontier, 1903–1934." In *The Nature State: Rethinking the History of Conservation*, edited by Wilko Hardenberg, Matthew Kelly, Claudia Leal, and Emily Wakild, 53–70. Routledge.

Walford, Antonia. 2017. "Raw Data: Making Relations Matter." *Social Analysis* 61 (2): 65–80.

Walters, Michael. 2003. *A Concise History of Ornithology*. Croom Helm.

Waterton, Emma. 2013. "Landscape and Non-Representational Theories." In *The Routledge Companion to Landscape Studies*, edited by Peter Howard, Ian Thompson, Emma Waterton, and Mick Atha, 84–93. Routledge.

West, Paige. 2005. "Translation, Value, and Space: Theorizing an Ethnographic and Engaged Environmental Anthropology." *American Anthropologist* 107 (4): 632–42.

West, Paige. 2006. *Conservation Is Our Government Now: The Politics of Ecology in Papua New Guinea*. Duke University Press.

West, Paige, and James G. Carrier. 2004. "Ecotourism and Authenticity: Getting Away from It All?" *Current Anthropology* 45 (4): 483–498.

West, Paige, Jim Igoe, and Dan Brockington. 2006. "Parks and Peoples: The Social Impact of Protected Areas." *Annual Review of Anthropology* 35: 251–277.

Whitehouse, Andrew. 2015. "Listening to Birds in the Anthropocene: The Anxious Semiotics of Sound in a Human-Dominated World." *Environmental Humanities* 6 (1): 53–71.

Wolfe, Cary. 2010. *What Is Posthumanism?* University of Minnesota Press.

Wolfe, Patrick. 1999. *Settler Colonialism and the Transformation of Anthropology: The Politics and Poetics of an Ethnographic Event*. Cassell.

Wolfe, Patrick. 2013. "Recuperating Binarism: A Heretical Introduction." *Settler Colonial Studies* 3: 257–79.

Woodhouse, Keith Makoto. 2018. *The Ecocentrists: A History of Radical Environmentalism*. Columbia University Press.

Woods, Kevin M. 2019. "Green Territoriality: Conservation as State Territorialization in a Resource Frontier." *Human Ecology* 47: 217–232.

Yusoff, Kathryn. 2013. "Insensible Worlds: Postrelational Ethics, Indeterminacy and the (K)nots of Relating." *Environment and Planning D: Society and Space* 31 (2): 208–226.

Zamorano, Carlos. 2021. "Conaf ofició a la Fiscalía de Collipulli por ocupación en Reserva Forestal Malleco." *La Tercera*, October 7. https://www.latercera.com/nacional/noticia/conaf-oficio-a-la-fiscalia-de-collipulli-por-ocupacion-en-reserva-forestal-malleco/T7DTIFSHQNDXPPLQCWVLNTIJLM/.

Zavala, José Manuel. 2005. "Aproximación antropológica a los parlamentos hispano-mapuches del siglo XVIII." *Austerra* 1 (2): 49–59.

Zunino, Hugo, and Viviana Huiliñir-Curío. 2016. "La construcción de lugares alternos en la Cordillera de los Andes del sur de Chile: utopía y disrupción de la modernidad." *XIV Coloquio Internacional de Geocrítica: Las Utopías y la Construcción de la Sociedad del Futuro*. https://www.ub.edu/geocrit/xiv-coloquio/Zunino Huilinir.pdf.

Index

abandonment, prospects of, 53–57
abandono. See abandonment, prospects of
actually existing alterhumanisms: boundaries and transformations, 18–2; four
alterhumanisms, 23–27
Ad Mapu, 197
affect, term, 21–22
afinar el oído, 131
Agamben, Giorgio, 8, 14, 241n1
Agrawal, Arun, 154, 193
agricultural technicians (*agrónomos*), 205
AIFBN. *See* Association of Forest Engineers
for the Native Wood
Albert, Federico, 97
Allende, Salvador, 157–58
alterhumanism, 148–49; actually existing
alterhumanisms, 18–27; becoming
ecological citizens, 191–21; becoming
environmentalists, 163–90; boundaries
and transformations, 18–27; definition
of, 9–14; ecologist alterhumanism, 121–
49; experience of ecocentrism, 91–120;
experiencing ethics in, 13–14; lessons of
posthumanism, 14–18; meaning of "alter,"

10; overview, 3–8; resettlement histories,
59–90
alterity: first meaning of, 10–11; second
meaning of, 11–13; third meaning of, 13
Alto Biobío, reserve, 195
American kestrel (*Falco sparverius*), 122
analytic bordering zones, 6
Ancient Forest International Foundation, 171
Andean deer (*Hippocamelus bisulcus*), 108
animal personhood, 241n2
animism, 16, 82
animosity, existence of, 54–55
Anthropocene, 77, 226–31
anthropocentrism, thinking beyond, 14–15
anthropogenic disturbance, 141, 144, 147
anthropological machine, 241n1
anti-Indigenous sentiment, presence of,
54–55
APRA. *See* Asociación para la Paz y la Reconciliación en La Araucanía
Araucaria araucana. See araucaria
araucaria (*Araucaria araucana*), 163
Araucaria nuts, 173–74, 200
Argyrou, Vassos, 117

arrival (*llegada*), transformative event of, 103–5
aseraderos (sawmills), 33
ashy-headed goose (*Chloephaga polioceph-ala*), 129
Asociación para la Paz y la Reconciliación en La Araucanía (APRA), 244
assimilation, explaining roots of, 68–69
Association of Forest Engineers for the Native Wood (AIFBN), 100
Aukiñ Wallmapu Ngulam, 246n9
austral parakeet (*Enicognathus ferrugineus*), 122
autonomy, achieving, 218–19
avian ecology, perceiving: birdwatching, 126–30; emplacement, 130–35; human disturbance, 143–49; overview, 121–26; relating data, 135–43
avian guilds, 129–30, 134–35, 138, 140
awinkarse, 68–69, 76
Aylwin, Patricio, 98, 159–60

bajo pueblo. See low people
Barad, Karen, 125, 148
becoming human: domestication of frontier forests, 31–58; ecologist alterhumanism, 121–49; experience of ecocentrism, 91–120; overview, 3–8; resettlement histories, 59–90; through nonhuman others, 13
becoming human through and with nonhu-man others, 7, 22, 63, 81, 88, 93, 119, 124, 147, 156, 167, 180, 219
becoming human through others, 34
becoming human with others, 13–14, 34
beliefs, characterizing cosmological possibil-ities as, 74–75
Bellacasa, Puig de la, 84
belonging, feelings of, 53–57
Bennett, Jane, 50, 94, 116
biennial araucaria nut collection (*piñoneo*), 173–74
"big ones" (*los grandes*), 55–56

Biobío River, 36–37
Biodiversity and Protected Areas Service, 217
birders, becoming, 126–27
birds, perceiving: birdwatching, 126–30; emplacement in avian ecology, 130–36; human disturbance, 143–49; overview, 121–26; relating data, 135–43
birdwatching: dismissing as legitimate prac-tice, 126; incorporation into ecological research, 129; knowledge pertaining to, 128; necessity of, 129–30; origins of interest in, 127–28; pleasure of, 128–29; rise of ornithology in Chile, 126–27; and selective gazing, 126–27
black rhinoceros (*Diceros bicornis*), 108
bosque. See wood, category
bosque limpio. See clean wood
bosque nativo, category, 141–42
boundaries and transformations, 18; "awareness of different voices," 19–20; categorization and distinction of forests, 22; debate around ontological pluralism, 20; *human* as universal category, 19; representing alterhuman-isms, 20–21. *See also* actually existing alterhumanisms
boundary work, 126. *See also* birdwatching
Bourdieu, Pierre, 96
bracketing, 74
Brockington, Dan, 168
Buddhism, 109
Buschmann, Josefina, 9
Butler, Judith, 217

Campbell, Jeremy M., 43
Campephilus magellanicus. See Magellanic woodpecker
campesinos, category, 32, 41, 55, 166, 178
Candea, Matei, 51, 132
Cañi (documenary), 91
Cañi Mountain, 104, 136, 147, 163, 171, 176, 178, 182, 186

Cañi Sanctuary, 26, 104, 121, 188, 247n6; beginnings of, 171; enclosures and paths, 176, 179–83; goals of, 173; mediating tensions, 185–86; overview, 163–64, 171; as paragon of participatory conservation, 172–73; perspective on forest grazing, 174–76; training programs of, 184
care, concept, 84–86
care, distinction between conservation and, 213–16
CASEN. *See* Encuesta de Caracterización Socioeconómica Nacional
Castro, Eduardo Viveiros de, 16, 74, 82
cattle, owning, 174–75
cattle ranchers, 25, 43, 66, 167, 192, 202–3, 209; dangers of uncontrolled understory growth for, 85–86; as economic actors, 83–84; enclosures and paths for, 176–78; mitigation of, 181; and path designs, 182–83; paving way for nongovernmental conservation, 174–76; resistance to conservation, 185, 187–88
Center for Environmental Research and Planning (CIPMA), 97
Chakrabarty, Dipesh, 77, 229
Chao Ngenchen, deity, 81
che, 60, 73, 79, 82–83
Chicago boys, 159
Chihuailaf, Elicura, 79
Chile: brief history of protected areas in, 167–71; Cañi nature reserve in, 91–92; colonizer-colonized dichotomy defining, 59–63; compatibility with Indigenous belonging, 68; crises in, 223–27; ecotourism in, 112–16; emplacement in avian ecology in, 130–36; environmentalism in, 96–100; environmentalist circles in, 105–6; forest bathing in, 106; forest policy in, 249n6; Indigenous-settler relations in remote Andes valleys, 38–39; neoliberalism in, 157–61; nongovernmental conservation in, 163–90; paving way for nongovernmental conservation in, 171–

76; reimagining conservation commons at frontier in, 210–16; rise of ornithology in, 126–27; scientific forestry in, 205; settler colonialism in, 35–41; two-tier social system in, 38. *See* alterhumanism in
Chilean Andes, stories in landscape of, 4–5
Chilean Union of Ornithologists (*Unión de Ornitólogos de Chile*), 127
chilenización, 40, 196
Chimango caracara. See chimango hawk
chimango hawk (*Chimango caracara*), 248n4
Chloephaga poliocephala. See ashy-headed goose
Christianity, conversion to, 68
chucao (*Scelorchilus rubecula*), 122
Chusquea quila. See quila
CIPMA. *See* Center for Environmental Research and Planning
circulating references, 138–39
cleaning the fields, term. *See* fire, finding ideal partner in
clean wood (*bosque limpio*): action of keeping, 174; aesthetic and moral valorizations of, 180; and definition of *landscape*, 179; and forest management, 48; as object of praise, 47–48
Club de la Naturaleza, 214
Coalition of Parties for Democracy (*Concertación de Partidos por la Democracia*y), 98, 159–60, 197
CODEFF. *See* Committee for the Defense of the Flora and Fauna of Chile
Coilaco, Chile, 26, 57, 61, 175; agricultural labor in, 84; animosity between settlers and Mapuche neighbors, 54–55; colonies and Mapuche residents around, 54; and forest domestication, 47–51; land redistribution process in, 39–40; process of settlement in, 32–33; respecting forests, 70–78; and wood preservation, 45–46
Coilaco Alto: un silencio verde en la geografía, 244

Coilaco Valley, 33, 45–47, 50–51, 57, 60, 71;
    aesthetic judgments of forest landscapes
    in, 48–49
collaboration, potential for, 145–48
collectivity, term, 22
colonial encroachment, characterizing, 64
colonización por poblamiento. See settler
    colonialism
colonized groups, 10, 64
colonizers, 10–11, 43, 61, 67
colonos indígenas. See Indigenous settlers
colonos nacionales, 32, 38–39, 168. *See also*
    national settlers
colonos. See settlers
Comisión Radicadora de Indígenas, 64
Committee for the Defense of the Flora and
    Fauna of Chile (CODEFF), 97
commodification, wilderness experiences,
    115–16
commons, reimagining: attitudes toward
    Indigenous politics, 211; critical reinter-
    pretations of conservation values, 213;
    cultural assimilation process, 210–11;
    implementing care, 213–16; interactions
    between farming communities and state,
    211–12; reiterating universalistic princi-
    ples of environmentalism, 212
community-based conservation. *See* nongov-
    ernmental conservation
Complejo Forestal y Maderero Panguipulli,
    249n1
comunidades ecológicas. See ecological
    communities
Comunidad Indígena ("Indigenous Commu-
    nity"), 60, 245n2
CONADI. *See* Consejo Nacional de Desar-
    rollo Indígena
CONAF. *See* Corporación Nacional Forestal
*Concertación de Partidos por la Democ-
    racia. See* Coalition of Parties for
    Democracy
concesiones de colonización, 38
Conquest of the Desert, 243n4

Consejo Ambiental Pucón ("Environmental
    Council of Pucón"), 101
Consejo de Todas las Tierras, 246n9
Consejo Nacional de Desarrollo Indígena
    (CONADI), 198
consejos consultivos, 199
conservation: agreements on, 199–204;
    becoming ecological citizens, 191–21;
    characterizing power of, 155–56; coping
    with refusal of, 183–88; discourses and
    practices of, 154–55; dispossession
    through, 166; examining power of,
    156–57; and instituting thought, 155–56;
    as major force in shaping of contem-
    porary world, 153–54; power relations
    in, 154; reimagining commons, 210–16;
    transforming thinking of nature and
    wilderness, 153–54
conservation frontiers: becoming ecological
    citizens, 191–21; ecologist alterhuman-
    ism, 121–49; overview, 3–8; shaping
    wilderness spaces, 5–6
conservation landscapes, 180–81, 183. *See
    also* wilderness enclosures
Conservation Land Trust, 100
conservation science, message of: addressing
    social and political challenges, 143–44;
    engagement with public institutions, 145;
    evidence-based recommendations, 144–
    45; potential for collaboration, 145–48
coping (with refusal of conservation):
    context-specific strategies, 183–84;
    empathic attitudes, 184; fence main-
    tenance, 186–87; lacking ecological
    concerns, 184–85; recognizing privileged
    status and skills, 185–86; transformative
    mediations, 187–88
Cordero, Rodrigo, 228
Corporación Nacional Forestal (CONAF),
    26, 48, 144, 168, 191–92, 204, 214;
    national parks and land disputes in
    Wallampu, 199–203; state logics in par-
    ticipator conservation, 204–6, 209

corridas de cerco, 64–65

Cosgrove, Denis, 179

cosmological notions, rewriting, 109–11

Coulthard, Glen S., 218

Course, Magnus, 12

COVID-19 pandemic, 224–25, 231, 253n2

cows, grazing habits of, 174–75. *See also* cattle ranchers

crisis: and Anthropocene, 228–31; critical reflection following, 228; first crisis, 224; and futures of rewilding, 231–36; living with, 227–31; overview of, 223–27; resembling state of *impasse*, 228; second crisis, 224–5; term, 227–28; third crisis, 225

Crutzen, Paul, 226

cultural revitalization, 85–88

Currarehue (municipal area), 25–26, 54, 83, 92, 99, 101, 121, 242n7

Das, Veena, 14

data, relating, 135; characterization of humans, 141–43; first conclusion, 139; good data, 137–38; interdependence, 140–41; plotting, 136; sample establishment, 138; scientific accuracy, 137; second conclusion, 139–40; stabilization, 138–39; successful gathering of data on forest structure, 137; third conclusions, 140

decaying trees, importance of, 139–40. *See also* data, relating

Decree Law 701 (*Decreto Ley no. 701*), 159

Decreto Ley no. 701. See Decree Law 701

Defenders of the Chilean Wood, 99

delegitimization, humanities, 10–11

Deleuze, Gilles, 16, 21, 138

Descola, Philippe, 14–15, 82

Despret, Vinciane, 129, 140

de Steiguer, J. Edward, 117

detachment, tension between engagement and, 132–33

dialogue, term, 216–18

Diceros bicornis. See black rhinoceros

diosito, term, 244n9

dispossession, 34, 43, 58, 93, 171, 177, 201, 204, 210; alterhumaniusm rooted in, 62–63; common arguments in debates about, 166–67; creating instances of, 183; defining, 63–64; latency and continuity of, 64; potential for, 188; power relations in conservation emerging from, 154; and private protected areas, 165–66; triggered by wilderness enclosures, 178; of ways of *becoming human through and with nonhuman others*, 156

disturbance, term, 124. *See also* human disturbance

domestication. *See* frontier forests, domestication of

Dunlap, Thomas R., 33

durmientes. See railroad sleepers

eBird, 248n2

ecocentrism, experience of: being transformed by wilderness, 100–111; environmentalism in Chile, 96–100; overview, 91–96; political economy of enchantment, 112–16; question of true humanity, 116–20

ecofemenism, critical reflections of, 118

ecological citizens: conservation agreements, 199–204; limits of Indigenous sovereignty, 216–20; national parks and land disputes, 195–99; overview, 191–94, 220–21; reimagining conservation commons, 210–16; state logics in participatory conservation, 204–10

ecological communities (*comunidades ecológicas*), 112

ecological crisis, 223–27

ecologist alterhumanism: birdwatching, 126–30; emplace in avian ecology, 130–36; human disturbance, 143–49; overview, 121–26; relating data, 135–43 ecotourism, 172; commodification of wilderness experiences, 115–16; empowerment and, 115; "leave no trace" principle, 181–82; mass tourism and, 113–14; success of, 115

El Niño-Southern Oscillation, 225

emplacement, 63, 78, 81; in avian ecology, 130–36; as basis and analytical accomplishment, 134–35; bird identification, 131; centrality of, 135; importance of place in science, 133–34; man interference with wildlife behavior, 131–32; methodologies of, 130–31; tension between detachment and engagement, 132–33; term, 124–26. *See also* human disturbance

empowerment, ecotourism and, 114

enchantment: centrality of, 108–9; commodification of wilderness experiences remains, 115–16; defining, 94–96; learning to be transformed by wilderness, 100–111; political economy of, 112–16; and question of true humanity, 116–19; realization of, 107–8; rewriting cosmological notions, 109–11; unfolding of, 111

enclosures. *See* wilderness enclosures

Encuesta de Caracterización Socioeconómica Nacional (CASEN), 242

engagement, tension between detachment and, 132–33

ENGOs: establishment of new private and public protected areas, 114–15; responding to specific local and environmental threats, 101–2

ENGOs. *See* environmental non-governmental organizations

Enicognathus ferrugineus. See austral parakeet

Environmental Council of Pucón. See *Consejo Ambiental Pucón*

environmental ethic, reclaiming, 86–88

environmentalism, enchantment/human authenticity in: being transformed by wilderness, 100–111; Chilean environmentalism, 96–100; definitions, 92–93; environmentalist alterhumanism, 93–94; overview, 91–96, 119–20; political economy of enchantment, 112–16; precarious ecocentrism, 116–19; question of true humanity, 116–19

environmentalist alterhumanism, 119; radical potential of, 93–94

environmentalists: affecting relations among humans, 106–7; becoming, 163–67; core motivation of, 119; demarcation of, 101; ecocentrism as essential in forming, 116–19; forest as "locus of truth and meaning", 105–6; meditative activities of, 105–6; and realization of enchantment, 107–9; reiterative experiences of, 103; rewriting cosmological notions, 109–11; transformative event of arrival, 103–5; unequal collectivity of, 102–3; unfolding of enchantment for, 111

environmental non-governmental organizations (ENGOs), 91–92, 98–99; conflicts and divisions within, 110–11; and private protected areas, 167–71

Esposito, Roberto, 155

Estación Silencio. See Sielnt Station

estallido social. See social explosion

ethno-ornithology, 146–47

eucalyptus (*Eucalyptus globulus*), 159

Eucalyptus globulus. See eucalyptus

extension officers (*extensionistas*), 205

Fabricant, Nicole, 219

Facebook, 102

Falco sparverius. See American kestrel

Fanon, Frantz, 11

farming: communities, 26, 143, 212; landscapes, 166–67, 179, 187; populations, 25, 104, 112, 156–57, 165, 170, 175, 188, 200

farming landscape, defining, 179. *See also* wilderness enclosures

fences, maintaining, 186–87
fences and fines approach, 168
Ferias Araucanía, 249n5
fire: finding ideal partner in, 41–43; local
    views on controlled use of, 50–51. *See
    also* frontier forests, domestication of
Fisher, Berenice, 84
Fitzroya cupressoides. See Patagonian
    cypress
Fletcher, Robert, 113
Foreman, David, 232
forest, category, 43–45
forest bathing, 106
forest engagement, 70, 75, 77, 81, 106–7
Forest Law of 1925, 249n1
Forestry Institute of Chile (*Instituto Forestal
    de Chile*), 205
forests: aesthetic judgments of landscapes
    of, 48–49; categorization and distinction
    of, 22; characterizing cosmological pos-
    sibilities as beliefs, 74–75; as commons,
    204–10; as dangerous places, 71–72;
    and *kolüm* phenomenon, 75; as "locus
    of truth and meaning", 105–6; presence
    of *newen*, 71–73; presence of *ngen* in,
    73–74; reiterating false, romanticized
    image, 70–71; respecting, 70–78; shaping
    human perception, 77; shared practices
    and attitudes toward, 70–71; vitality of,
    71. *See also* conservation; frontier forests,
    domestication of
fortress conservation, 168
Foucault, Michel, 161, 194
Four Volcano Viewpoint. *See* Cañi Mountain
frontier, defining, 5–6
frontier forests, domestication of: aesthetic
    judgments of forest landscapes, 48–59;
    brief history of settler colonialism,
    35–41; category articulation, 43–45;
    eventfulness of settler colonialism, 43;
    existence of wood, 45–47; existence of
    woods, 41–47; fire as ideal partner, 41–
    43; forest management, 48; human labor,

47–53; limited trust in human abilities,
    50; marginal domestications, 49–50; and
    other forms of domestication, 49; over-
    view, 31–35, 57–58; potential dangers of
    human interference, 50–51; wilderness
    regrowth, 46–47
Frontier (*la Frontera*), 5. *See also* frontier,
    defining
Fundación Lahuen. See Lahuen Foundation
fundos. See local agricultural estates

Gaia Reiki, 106
Global North, 97
Global South, 96, 235
good data, defining, 137–38
green grabbing, 100, 165–66
green productivism, 112–16
Grupo de Guías Cañi, 172
Guattari, Felix, 16, 138
guilds. *See* avian guilds
Guyot, Silvain, 195–96

habitus, 185
hacer patria, project, 35, 40–41
Haraway, Donna, 17, 133
Hare Khrishna, 109
Helmreich, Stefan, 123, 143
hikers, mitigation of, 181
Hippocamelus bisulcus. See Andean deer
Hoffmann, Adriana, 99, 247n6
Holbraad, Martin, 20
Huaiquifil, Juan, 65–67
Hualalafquén National Reserve, 191–92, 214
human, remaking: becoming ecological
    citizens, 191–21; nongovernmental con-
    servation, 163–90; overview, 153–61
human activities, studying impact of. *See*
    data, relating
human disturbance: birdwatching, 126–30;
    emplacement in avian ecology, 130–35;
    overview, 121–26
human-environmental relations, generaliz-
    able accounts of, 123

humanity: configuration of, 7, 89, 94, 120, 230; defining alterhumanism, 9–14; definition as universal condition, 10; definition of, 8, 10, 14, 57, 126, 227; delegitimization of, 10–11; meanings of, 19, 89, 154, 161; paradigmatic definition of, 8; understandings, 12, 92–93, 96, 167, 189; working as "anthropological machine," 14

human labor: aesthetic judgments of forest landscapes, 48–49; belief in human capacity, 47; forest management, 48; limited trust in, 50; marginal domestications, 49–50; other forms of domestication, 49; potential dangers of, 50–51; selective logging, 47–48; and vitality, 51–53; wood and, 43–45

Husserl, Edmund, 75

hydroelectric plants (*centrales de paso*), 101–2

ILO. *See* Indigenous and Tribal Peoples Convention

Indigenous and Tribal Peoples Convention (ILO), 199

"Indigenous Community." *See Comunidad Indígena*

Indigenous Law 19,235, 198

Indigenous ownership, 192

Indigenous people, 35, 37, 42, 55, 59, 64, 71, 202, 207, 217, 219; limits of Indigenous sovereignty, 216–20. *See also* Indigenous settlers

Indigenous settlers: becoming settlers but remaining Mapuche, 63–70; conclusions on, 88–90; emergence of figure of, 62; forest engagements, 70–78; overview, 59–63; symbolism of, 65–66; taking responsibility for nonhuman life, 83–90; talking about place, 78–83

Instagram, 102

Instituto de Ecología Política, 98

interdependence, birds and, 140–41

interminable humanism, 82

International Union of Geological Sciences (IUGS), 226

intimate nationhood: brief history of settler colonialism, 35–41; and existence of woods, 41–47; feelings of belonging, 53–57; human labor and, 47–53; overview, 31–35, 57–58; and prospects of abandonment, 53–57

intra-actions, term, 148

IUGS. *See* International Union of Geological Sciences

Jørgensen, Dolly, 233

Juzgados de Indios, 198

Kimün, 74

Klubock, Thomas Miller, 40

Kohn, Eduardo, 11, 77

Kumar, Malreddy P., 10–11

küpal, 79, 247n17

labor, nonhuman vitality and, 12–13. *See also* human labor

la cordillera, 32, 73

Lahuen Foundation, 171

land, disputes of, 195–99

land distribution, 35, 203, 252n14; secondary objective of, 64

land ownership, conflicts over, 209, 245n7, 250n2

landscape, analytics of, 178–81. *See also* wilderness enclosures

land takeover (*toma*), 200–201. *See also* rights and obligations, defining

lanzamientos, 40

Latour, Bruno, 16, 44, 118, 126, 138–39, 229

Lavín, Joaquín, 157–58

"Law of Colonization" (*Ley de Colonización y Terrenos Baldíos*), 37–38

Law of Conservation Right, 169

Law of Restoration of Native Woods and Forest Promotion, 169

"leave no trace," principle, 181–82
lenga (*Nothofagus pumilio*), 163
Levinas, Emmanuel, 13
Levi-Strauss, Claude, 69, 241n5
limpiar los campos (cleaning the fields). *See* fire, finding ideal partner in
Llanquihue (reserve), 42, 195
local agricultural estates (*fundos*), 65
local and scientific knowledge, dialogue between, 145–48
local knowledge, valorization of, 145–48
lof (Mapuche residential communities), 59
logging, avian life affected by, 140. *See also* data, relating
lonko, 64, 66, 245n2
loss, defining, 105
low people (*bajo pueblo*), 65

Magellanic woodpecker (*Campephilus magellanicus*), 122–23, 182
Maichín River, 191
Maite (village), 80, 209, 214–15; defining rights and obligations, 199–204; descriptions of agricultural labor, 84; locality of, 245n4; overview, 59–61; remaining Mapuche in, 65–69; respecting forests, 70–73; ritualized petitions for permission, 81; uncontrolled understory, 85–86; workshops in, 87
making homeland. *See hacer patria*, expression
Malleco National Reserve, 168, 195, 249n1, 250n4
Mapuche alterhumanism, 23, 63, 77, 78, 83, 89
Mapuche conflict, term, 197–98
Mapuche people, 22, 55, 148, 209, 211, 246n9; activism of, 68, 86, 196, 216–18, 244n5; becoming settlers but remaining, 63–70; being Mapuche as form of belonging, 67–68; communities, 60, 62, 70, 146, 149, 197, 201, 208, 210, 212, 214, 217, 249n4; emplacement

as central dimension of personhood, 78–79; forest engagements, 70–78; granting collective endowment titles to, 64–65; and historical faith in dialogue, 216–20; Indigenous settlers and, 59–63; landholders, 5–6, 8, 25, 39, 58, 70, 84, 86–89, 110, 147, 192, 198, 203–4, 209; national parks and land disputes in Wallmapu, 195–99; quintessential customary food for, 173; reclaiming environmental ethic, 86–88; recruiting displaced individuals, 66–67; reimagining conservation commons at frontier, 210–16; relationship with state concerning management, 196–97; relations with *paisanos*, 54; rural residents, 38, 55, 65, 67, 86, 196, 211; social relations of exchange, 246n15; and state logics, 204–10; taking responsibility of nonhuman life, 83–90; transformation of, 42; and Villarrica-Hualalafquén National Reserve, 199–204
marginal domestications, 49–50
Martínez-Alier, Joan, 96
mass tourism, ecotourism and, 113–14
material acts, 181
Maturana, Humberto, 241n4
Maytenus boaria, 245n4
Mbembe, Achille, 11
McIntosh, Janet, 54
meditative activities, 105–6
Mendoza, Marcos, 113–14
Merleau-Ponty, Maurice, 179
mestizaje, resonance with, 35–36
Mirador Melidekiñ. See Cañi Mountain
Mis Abuelos Me Lo Contaron. See My Grandparents Told Me
Monbiot, George, 232
Monterrey pine trees (*Pinus radiata*), 50, 159, 247n5
mountain lions (*Puma concolor puma*), 44
My Grandparents Told Me (*Mis Abuelos Me Lo Contaron*), 146

Næss, Arne, 96
Ñanculef, Juan, 72
National Commission for the Environment, 247n6
national heritage, characterizing protected areas as, 207–8
national parks, 5, 25, 170, 174, 192; agreements regarding, 199; araucaria nut collection, 249n4; classification of, 207–8; establishing, 97, 100, 168; and land disputes, 195–96
national settlers, 32, 39–40
native forests (*bosques nativos*), 33, 44, 84, 99, 104, 130, 141–42
naturalism, 14–15, 94; constitution of, 117–18
nature, drive for mastery over, 10–11
nature, saving: becoming ecological citizens, 191–21; nongovernmental conservation, 163–90; overview, 153–61
neoliberalism, consequences of, 157–61
nests, use of, 139. *See also* data, relating
Network of Free Seeds. See *Red de Semilla Libre*
New Age, 107, 109
newen: ethical implications of knowledge of, 75–76; presence of, 71–73
ngen, 82, 87; avoiding mischievous acts by, 247n16; ethical implications of knowledge of, 75–76; in Mapuche cosmology, 110; in oral accounts, 81; presence of, 73–74
ngillatun, term, 72, 246n11
nongovernmental conservation: brief history of protected areas, 167–71; mediations on, 183–88; overview, 163–67, 188–90; paving way for, 171–76; wilderness enclosures in, 176–83
nonhuman autonomy, question of: characterizing cosmological possibilities as beliefs, 74–75; following value of respect, 75–77; *kolüm* phenomenon, 75; possibility of objectification, 77–78; presence of *newen*, 71–73; presenting forests as dangerous places, 71–72; reiterating

false, romanticized images, 70–71; shared practices and attitudes toward forestry, 70–71
nonhuman life, taking responsibility for: agricultural labor, 83–84; care as concept, 84–86; reclaiming environmental ethic, 86–88
nonhuman others, 7–8, 22–23, 153, 156; and alterhumanism, 9–13; and avian ecology, 124, 142–43, 147–48; becoming environmentalists, 167, 180; and domestication of frontier forests, 52–53; and ecological citizens, 213, 219, 227; and experience of ecocentrism, 93, 117, 119; and Indigenous settlers, 75, 81, 88; ontological differentiation from, 63
nonhumans, paradigmatic role of, 12
non-timber activities, banning, 171–76
Nothofagus obliqua. See Patagonian oak
Nothofagus pumilio. See *lenga*
nuts, collecting, 173–74

Ogden, Laura, 105
ontological epoche, 75
ontological pluralism, debate around, 20
ontologies, characterizing, 16
ornithology, rise of, 126–27

Pacification of Araucanía, 5
paisanos, term, 54
pampa. See forest, category
paper park, 199–200
parcelas. See residential plots
park rangers (*guardaparques*), 206
parlamentos, 36–37
Parque Nacional Patagonia, 100
Parque Nacional Pumalín Douglas Tompkins, 100
participatory conservation: conservation agreements, 199–204; limits of Indigenous sovereignty, 216–20; national parks and land disputes, 195–99; overview, 191–94, 220–21; reimagining conserva-

tion commons, 210–16; state logics in, 204–10

Patagonian cypress (*Fitzroya cupressoides*), 247n2, 248n2

Patagonian oak (*Nothofagus obliqua*), 45, 48

Patagonia Without Dams, 247n4

paternalism, defining, 52–53

paths, designs of, 182–83. *See also* wilderness enclosures

paths. *See* wilderness enclosures

Pedersen, Susan, 20, 75

Pewenche, term, 173–74, 249n3

Phillips, Anne, 10

Pichares, Chile, 163–64

Pichi Juan, figure, 41–42

Piñera, Sebastián, 159–60, 224

Pinochet, Augusto, 5, 97, 159, 197

piñones, food staple, 173–74

Pinus radiata. See Monterrey pine trees

piper, term, 122

place, talking about: capability for social relationships, 82–83; emplacement as central dimension of personhood, 78–79; evoking different feelings and actions, 78–79; genealogical and geographic connections, 79–80; interminable humanism, 82; resources resisting full domestication, 80–81; view of settlement as engagement with place, 81–82

place of origin. *See tuwün*

plasma, defining, 44. *See also* forest, category

plotting, data and, 136

plurinationality, identifying, 218–19

political crisis, 223–27

Pontificia Universidad Católica de Chile, 121

Postero, Nancy, 219

posthumanism, lessons of, 14–18

posthuman theory, 16–18

precarious ecocentrism, 116–19

protected areas, brief history of, 167–71

protected areas, defining rights and obligation toward: action-oriented argument,

203–4; ancestral rights, 201–3; context, 199–201; historical argument of past occupancy and dispossession, 201–3

proxies, birds serving as, 130. *See also* birdwatching

Pucón, Chile, 25, 26, 31–32, 44, 57; and avian ecology, 121, 145–46; economy of enchantment in, 112, 114–15, 119; and ecotourism, 92; environmentalism in, 99, 101, 103–4, 106–7, 110; fame of, 31–32; history of colonization in, 39; Indigenous mobilizations around, 54; land redistribution process in, 39–40; and nongovernmental conservation, 163–64, 171–72; successful ecotourism boom in, 26; taking responsibility for nonhuman life in, 83

Pucón in Transition, 101

Pumalín Park, 169

Pyne, Stephen J., 42043

Quidel, José, 79

Quijano, Anibal, 35

quila (*Chusquea quila*), 223–23

Quinquén Community, 250n5

racial discrimination, existence of, 54–55

radicación, 64; process of, 65

railroad sleepers (*durmientes*), 45

Rasmussen, Mattias, 180

reason of the conservation state, logic, 194, 208–10, 215–16

Red de Semilla Libre (Network of Free Seeds), 102

reducción, 37; establishment of, 64; land grabbing affecting, 65

regrowth, 46–47, 52

relating, action, 20–22

resettlement, histories of: becoming settlers but remaining Mapuche, 63–70; conclusions, 88–90; forest engagements, 70–78; overview, 59–63; taking responsibility for nonhuman life, 83–90; talking about place, 78–83

residential plots (*parcelas*), 112
respect: ethical significance of, 76–77; following value of, 75–76; and ritualized permissions, 76
reverence, respect and, 76–77
rewilding: and Anthropocene crisis, 234–36; belief grounding, 231–32; as experimental process, 232; futures of, 231–36; problematic implications of, 232–33; reparation an, 234–; standing in face of, 49; term, 46–47, 105; transcending wilderness enclosures, 233–34
rights and obligations, defining: action-oriented argument, 203–4; ancestral rights, 201–3; context, 199–201; historical argument of past occupancy and dispossession, 201–3
Rosales, Vicente Pérez, 42
rufous-legged owl (*Strix rufipes*), 248

samples, establishing, 138. *See also* data relating
sanitary crisis, 223–27
Santuario el Cañi. See Cañi Sanctuary
SARS-CoV-2, 224–25
sawmills, 33, 45, 205
Scelorchilus rubecula. See chucao
scientific forestry, 204–5
seed exchange celebration, 102
selective gaze, 126–27
selective logging, 47–48, 144, 206
selva. See forest, category
Sepulveda, Claudia, 195–96
settler colonialism: centering dispossession, 63–70; defining, 63–64; eventfulness of, 43; existence of woods, 41–47; intersections, 36; meaning of, 35–36; resonance with *mestizaje*, 35–36; tracing origins of, 36–41
settlers: brief history of settler colonialism, 35–41; feelings of belonging, 53–57; finding ideal partner in fire, 41–43; human labor and, 47–53; intimate nationhood

of, 31–35; Mapuche people becoming, 63–70; marginal domestications and, 49–50; overview, 57–58; and prospect of abandonment, 53–57
settlers' alterhumanism, 34, 52, 57–58, 167, 189
shinrin-yoku, 106
Silent Station, 182
Sistema Nacional de Áreas Silvestres Protegidas del Estado (SNASPE), 168, 195
smallholders, 32, 46, 55, 175, 251n9, 252n12
"small ones" (*los pequeños*), 56–57
SNASPE. *See* Sistema Nacional de Áreas Silvestres Protegidas del Estado
"social climbers" (*arribistas*), 68
social explosion (*estallido social*), 224
Soulé, Michael, 232
southern frontier, brief history of protected areas in, 167–71
sovereignty, term, 218–19
spirituality, environmentalism and, 109–11
stabilization, data and, 138–39
state logics (in participatory conservation): CONAF objectives, 205–6; limiting Indigenous aspirations, 208; national heritage, 207–8; policing local populations, 207; reason of the conservation state, 208–10; scientific forestry, 204–5; value of protected forests: 206–7
state-owned land (*terrenos fiscales*), 37, 59
state power, 192–94, 208, 212, 219
Stengers, Isabelle, 134–35
Strathern, Marilyn, 21
Strix rufipes. See rufous-legged owl
styles of development, debate on, 98–99
subjectivization, 24, 165, 167, 189–90, 193–94, 212, 216, 220; process, 154–57
system theory, 15

Temuco (city), 32
Tercera, La, 253n4
terrenos fiscales. See state-owned land
territorialization, 134–35

thinking through the middle, 134–35
thought, instituting, 155–56
Tilley, Christopher, 179
timber plantations (*plantaciones*), 33, 70, 99, 104, 251n10
Títulos de Merced, 64, 66
toma. See land takeover
Tompkins, Douglas, 100, 169
Tompkins Conservation Foundation, 100
trafkintu, term, 102
Tragedy of the Chilean Wood, The, 99–100
trails, designs of, 182–83. *See also* wilderness enclosures
trees, linking birds to. *See* data, relating
triadic relationships. *See* data, relating
Tronto, Joan C., 84
true humanity, question of, 116–19
tuwün (place of origin), 62–63, 79–80, 201–2

uncommoning, term, 215–16
Unión de Ornitólogos de Chile. See Chilean Union of Ornithologists
Universidad Austral de Chile, 251n11

values (commercial and ethical), creation of, 114–15
Varela, Francisco, 241n4
Villarrica, Chile, 25–26, 31, 60, 114, 145–46, 164, 172, 195, 199
Villarrica-Hualalafquén National Reserve, 195, 199–201
Villarrica Lake, 31
Villarrica National Park, 172
vitality, human labor and, 51–53
Vivar, Jerónimo de, 223

walks (through protected areas), 182–83
Wallmapu, 36, 216–17, 223; national parks and land disputes in, 195–99
Washington Convention on Nature Protection, 250n1
welfare support (*asistencialismo*), 185
Whitehouse, Andrew, 134
wild boars (*Sus scrofa*), 44
wilderness, learning to be transformed by: environmentalist dispositions and tastes, 100–101; forest as "locus of truth and meaning", 105–6; meditative activities, 105–6; realization of enchantment, 107–9; regrowth of wilderness, 46–47; reiterative experiences, 103; relations among humans, 106–7; rewriting cosmological notions, 109–11; seed exchange celebration, 102; specific local and environmental threats, 101–2; transformative event of arrival, 103–5; unequal collectivity of environmentalists, 102–3
wilderness enclosures: disapproval of, 176–77; dispossession triggered by, 177–78; and landscape notion, 178–81; and "leave no trace" principle, 181–82; mitigation of cattle ranchers and hikers, 181; trail designs, 182–83
Wildlife Preservation in the Western Hemisphere, 250n1
wood: category, 43–45; and commercial forestry, 45; exemplifying value of hard wood, 46–47; existence of, 46; preserving for future, 45–46

Yusoff, Kathryn, 148

About the Author

Piergiorgio Di Giminiani is an associate professor of anthropology at the Pontificia Universidad Católica de Chile. He is the author of *Sentient Lands: Indigeneity, Property, and Political Imagination in Neoliberal Chile* and co-editor of *Theorizing Relations in Indigenous South America* and *The Futures of Reparation in Latin America: Imagination, Translation, and Belonging.*